South Downs Library Copy

THE CHALLENGE OF CORINTHIANS

The Challenge of
of
Corinthians

MICHAEL ASHTON

THE CHRISTADELPHIAN

404 SHAFTMOOR LANE
HALL GREEN
BIRMINGHAM B28 8SZ
2006

First Published 2006

ISBN 085189 169 1

Printed and bound in England by:

THE CROMWELL PRESS
Trowbridge
Wiltshire
BA14 0XB

PREFACE

IN the Apostle Paul's two letters to Corinth can be found advice for many modern situations that affect believers in the Lord Jesus Christ. First century Corinth, with its rampant worldliness is the direct counterpart of twenty-first century western society. The liberty of the Corinthians who lived in those far-off days was of the same stamp as that which is valued by modern society – the freedom to choose, the freedom to indulge in self-gratification, the freedom to express individuality. The effect of the teachings of the gospel upon this worldly and self-centred society was bound to create tensions, and the apostle's measured and sound advice, based often on the Old Testament scriptures, was designed to help individuals from many different backgrounds draw together to serve their new Master.

As well as providing advice for individuals about how to live godly lives within a godless society, the two letters are full of biblical wisdom to apply to many ecclesial situations. Breaking of bread meetings were being disrupted; worldly methods were being used to deal with spiritual problems; rather than brethren and sisters combining their efforts to produce unity, the ecclesia was being pulled apart. At each turn, the apostle drew his readers back to God's word and the example of the Lord Jesus; he encouraged them to apply these in their personal lives, and when they met together.

In the midst of a society where human achievement was elevated, the message of these two letters was designed to impress this one great truth: "no flesh should glory in God's presence". May the readers of this book learn the same lesson.

Birmingham, 2006   MICHAEL ASHTON

CONTENTS

1

THE GOSPEL REACHES ACHAIA

PAUL's two letters to the group of Christian believers in Corinth are challenging for different reasons. The first letter raises issues that are strikingly relevant for today's disciples, such as the part women can play in formal worship, problems about sex and marriage, and about how to retain a separation to God while living in a world given over to fleshly pleasures and debauchery. It also covers matters affecting not just individuals but the community of believers, such as problems of partisanship and schism, failure to discern the importance of submitting to the ecclesial body of Christ, and relationships with false religious worship.

The second letter presents different problems. Here the challenge lies more in the nature of the apostle's approach to the situation in the Corinthian ecclesia, his apparent boasting, and the complex language of the letter. The tone of the two letters is so different, it is necessary to ask what occurred between the writing of the first and the writing of the second, and why the apostle is able to speak with authority in the first, yet needs to justify his apostolic call in the second.

The objective of this study is twofold. First we must look at the background to the letters, to see why the apostle was writing, and the circumstances of the first readers. Secondly we want to look at the issues he tackled, both as they applied to first century Corinth and how they affect us today.

From Athens to Corinth

Paul first entered Corinth on his own after leaving Athens, and must have noticed immediately the great difference between these two Greek cities. Athens was a centre of learning and culture in the ancient world, a magnet for intellectuals and a university city; Corinth was a bustling, cosmopolitan, commercial seaport. Although only forty-five miles apart, in human terms they were at opposite ends of the spectrum, and they presented very different challenges.

In his early life, Paul would have been at home in Athens. He met Greek intellectuals there who showed an interest, but only a passing one, in his message. They were men who had a passion "to tell or to hear some new thing" (Acts 17:21)*. The passion in Corinth was differently directed. While Athene (called Minerva by the Romans) the goddess of wisdom, medicine and the arts was the goddess of the Athenians, Aphrodite (or Venus) the goddess of love was worshipped at Corinth. Her shrine on the prominent hill, the Acrocorinth, dominated all other temples (such as the temple of Apollo in the lower city), and according to the

Ruins of Corinth looking south towards the Acrocorinth from the northern road to Lechaion

* All Bible quotations from NKJV, unless otherwise stated

Greek historian Strabo (63 BC – AD 24) a thousand beautiful women officiated in the city as public prostitutes before Venus's altar. Associated with these activities was all manner of crime and corruption, making the character of Corinth distinctly and radically different from Athens. Just entering the city would be a challenge to Paul. It was the Sodom of the New Testament world.

But Corinth is not to be contrasted only with Athens. Before Paul preached in Athens he suffered at the hands of his fellow-countrymen in Thessalonica and Berea. He wrote about his experiences to the Corinthians, and said: "Jews request a sign, and Greeks seek after wisdom; but we preach Christ crucified" (1 Corinthians 1:22,23). He therefore left behind him in Athens "the wisdom of this world", and in Thessalonica a group of Jews clamouring for signs. In Corinth he "determined not to know anything among you except Jesus Christ and Him crucified" (2:2).

Who would have thought that in such a crime-ridden, degraded and immoral centre as Corinth, the Lord could say to Paul, "I am with you, and no one will attack you to hurt you; for I have many people in this city" (Acts 18:10)? Corinth was renowned for its vice and corruption. To call someone "a Corinthian" was to mark him or her out at best as a vain follower of worldly fashion, and at worst as a person of the lowest and most corrupt morals. The term "a Corinthian girl" referred to a prostitute. Yet the apostle took the Truth to Corinth and its inhabitants, and was assured by Jesus that many would respond to the gospel call.

If we today complain about the poor response to our preaching, we ought to consider carefully the differences between so-called 'cultured' Athens, where there were insufficient converts for Paul even to establish an ecclesia, and the gutters of Corinth where the word of God was welcomed and embraced, causing men and women to turn their lives around completely to become servants of the Lord Jesus Christ. "The base things of the world and the things which are despised God has chosen ... to bring to nothing the things that are, that no flesh should glory in His presence" (1 Corinthians 1:28,29).

3

THE CHALLENGE OF CORINTHIANS

*Map showing Corinth & Athens with expanded detail below showing
the sea ports of Lechaion and Cenchrea*

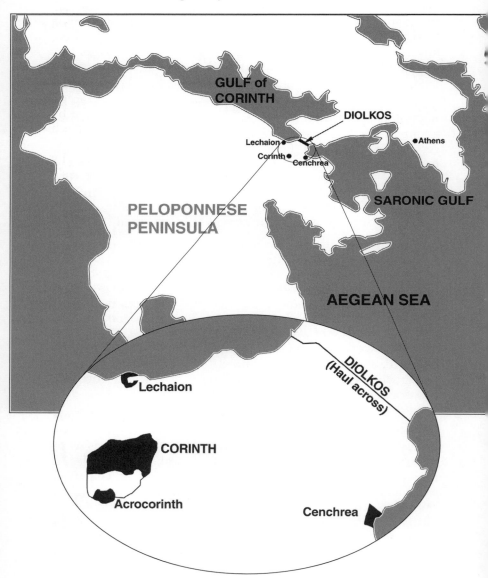

Corinth's Geographical Setting

Corinth is situated on a narrow isthmus of land connecting the Peloponnesian peninsula to the mainland of Greece. This narrow neck of land is only four miles wide, and traders in ancient times, instead of transporting goods around the hazardous southern coastline of the Peloponnese, took them this short distance by land between two sheltered gulfs running north-west and south-east respectively from the city of Corinth (see maps facing). Cargo and sometimes the ships themselves were hauled by

carts through *"The Diolkos"* (literally 'haul across'), a paved route about 6 kilometres long that connected the Corinthian and Saronic gulfs before the so-called

Corinth Canal was dug in the late nineteenth century AD. The isthmus was called "the bridge of the sea" by Pindar, and Corinth itself was called "the city of the two seas" by Horace and Ovid.

Through its being situated on this important trade route, the city was open to influences from all manner of foreign parts. Goods from Italy and western nations landed at the port of Lechaion, and goods from the

Aegean islands, Asia Minor and eastern nations landed at Cenchrea. Every form of luxury and practice entered its markets.

Athenians may well have looked down their patrician noses at Corinth, believing it to be a moral and intellectual sewer, but as the commercial centre of the province of Achaia, Corinth was also the seat of the Roman proconsul, who when Paul first visited the city was Gallio (Acts 18:12). Corinth had been captured and destroyed by the Romans in 146/7 BC, but colonised again a hundred years later by order of Julius Caesar. The Romans divided Greece into two provinces, Macedonia and Achaia. As the provincial capital of Achaia, Corinth was a leading city in the Roman empire. It was the administrative centre of Achaia, and thus the city through which not only trade but also travellers passed.

This created a further distinction between Corinth and Athens. The latter was the epitome of Greek culture, but Corinth was essentially a Roman city whose geographical position and imperial status would allow teachings introduced there to spread quickly throughout the empire.

A further factor made Corinth highly suitable for Paul's purposes, and this reveals how the spread of the gospel was providentially assisted. The Roman emperor at the time was Claudius, and by a decree in AD 50 he had banished all Jews from Rome (Acts 18:2). Some of these made their way to Corinth, swelling the numbers of Jews in the city when the apostle first arrived. According to Suetonius (the biographer of the Caesars), their banishment from Rome was because of disturbances concerning Chrestus (or Christus). This may either have been political uprisings by Jewish Christians, or more probably disputes arising from Jewish expectations about the Messiah.

Aquila and Priscilla

Among the Jews who fled Rome at that time were a married couple, Aquila and Priscilla, with whom the Apostle Paul lodged. Aquila was originally from Pontus, a province of Asia Minor that had political connections with Judea, and – through the marriage of its king Polemo to Agrippa's sister

Bernice – with the later history of the apostle. It is impossible to say with certainty whether Aquila and Priscilla learned the gospel before arriving in Corinth, or if they were converted by the apostle. We know that Jews from Pontus heard Peter's speech on the day of Pentecost (Acts 2:9), and it is possible that Aquila and Priscilla were in his audience. Equally, they may have met Christian teachings in Pontus or in Rome before they fled to Corinth.

From the information in the book of Acts, they travelled widely, and lived at various times in Corinth, Ephesus and Rome. Groups of believers met regularly in their homes in these different cities. All these factors suggest they had considerable wealth. Paul was able to stay with them in Corinth and ply his trade, for they too were tentmakers. The apostle was fiercely independent so that he would not be chargeable to any one (2 Corinthians 11:9; 1 Thessalonians 2:9; 2 Thessalonians 3:8).

From the account in Acts 18:3, it seems that Paul found lodgings with Aquila and Priscilla first of all because they were of the same trade, and not because they shared the same faith in Jesus. This would suggest that they were ignorant of the gospel when they originally arrived in Corinth. But that situation soon changed, and this husband and wife team became as successful in their subsequent preaching as they apparently were in their commercial undertakings.

Preaching in the Synagogue

No doubt accompanied by Aquila and Priscilla, Paul "reasoned in the synagogue every sabbath, and persuaded both Jews and the Greeks" (Acts 18:4). This work of preaching continued with increased urgency when Paul was joined in Corinth by Silas and Timothy: he "devoted himself exclusively to preaching (was pressed in the spirit, KJV), testifying to the Jews that Jesus was the Christ" (Acts 18:5, NIV).

Silas and Timothy brought news of the believers in Macedonian cities where there had been much Jewish opposition, and Paul was heartened to learn from them that the believers were holding fast to the faith (1 Thessalonians 3:5-10). Despite the possibility of stirring up Jewish opposition, the rewards of clear and committed preaching – as evidenced by the ecclesia in Thessalonica – were very attractive. The Jews in Corinth opposed the teaching so forcefully that Paul put into effect the Lord Jesus' advice to his disciples when they met resistance: "Whosoever shall not receive you, nor hear you, when ye depart from there, shake off the dust under your feet as a testimony against them" (Mark 6:11). Paul "shook his garments and said unto them, Your blood be upon your own heads; I am clean: from now on I will go to the Gentiles" (Acts 18:6).

He did not go far. A man called Titus Justus lived in a property adjoining the synagogue, and Paul started preaching from his house. His time amongst the Jews was far from unfruitful, for even the chief ruler of the synagogue, Crispus, believed "with all his house".

But the Jews were not to be thwarted easily. They took advantage of the newly-appointed pro-consul Gallio, and brought Paul before him for judgement on charges of introducing an illegal form of worship. This was a very serious and significant charge and it is highly probable that the case was heard at the place of judgement (the *bema*) which is still visible in the ruins of the ancient city. Gallio was no minor official; as pro-consul he was invested with all the authority of the emperor. An unfavourable judgement could result in the outlawing of the Christian faith throughout the Roman empire.

But even before the case was brought against Paul, he was assured by the Lord appearing to him in a night-vision: "Do not be afraid, but speak, and do not keep silent: for I am with you, and no one will attack you to hurt you" (Acts 18:10). Paul clearly thought, as he stood before Gallio, that as Jesus promised when his followers were brought before kings and governors for his sake, "I will give you a mouth and wisdom which all your adversaries will not be able to contradict nor resist" (Luke 21:15).

The 'bema' or judgement seat with the Acrocorinth in the background

But Paul did not have to speak a word! Gallio summarily dismissed the case against him. Paul was not charged with "wrongdoing or wicked crimes"; it was simply "a question of words and names, and of your own law ... I do not want to be a judge of such matters", Gallio declared (Acts 18:14,15).

This landmark decision gave Paul and the other apostles great freedom to preach anywhere in the Roman empire. Who can doubt that Gallio's appointment was divinely overseen, and that Paul's being "pressed in the Spirit" to spend all his time preaching was intended to provide the impetus for this break with the synagogue so that the message could be taken more directly to the Gentiles?

So many in Corinth responded to the apostle's preaching, he stayed there longer than anywhere else on his previous travels. In Corinth was being established a centre for the gospel whose fame would spread throughout the Roman world. With that fame and the implicit challenge to examine the faith that encouraged so many in Corinth to change the

9

direction of their lives came other challenges too – doctrinal, moral and organisational.

But before considering the message of 1 Corinthians, we must step back and look at the scriptural evidence about all the Apostle Paul's dealings with the Corinthian ecclesia.

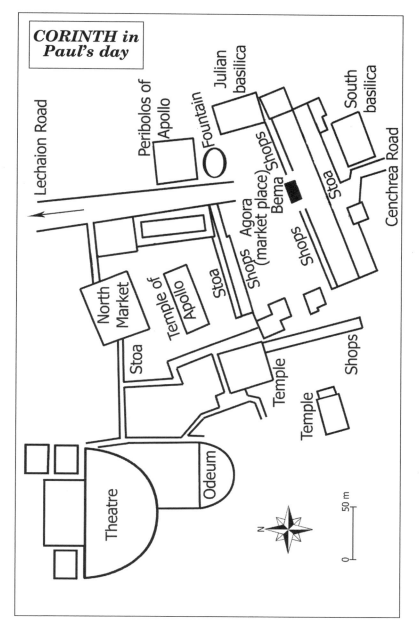

CORINTH in Paul's day

Lechaion Road

Peribolos of Apollo

Fountain

Julian basilica

South basilica

Cenchrea Road

Agora (market place)

Bema

Shops

Shops

Stoa

North Market

Temple of Apollo

Stoa

Shops

Stoa

Temple

Temple

Shops

Theatre

Odeum

N

50 m

0

2

PAUL'S CONTACT WITH CORINTH

THE Apostle Paul left Corinth after his first visit, having spent at least eighteen months there (Acts 18:11,18). He travelled to Ephesus on his way back, to "keep this coming feast (most probably Passover) in Jerusalem", before finally returning to his home ecclesia of Antioch (verses 21,22). He was accompanied as far as Ephesus by his new-found friends Aquila and Priscilla, who remained there while he completed his journey.

This brought to an end his second missionary journey, and it was not long before he left Antioch again with the intention of undertaking pastoral visits in cities where the gospel had started to flourish. While the apostle was travelling through "the region of Galatia and Phrygia in order, strengthening all the disciples" (verse 23), an Alexandrian Jew called Apollos arrived in Ephesus. He was well-versed in the scriptures, and able powerfully to explain his beliefs. Aquila and Priscilla "explained to him the way of God more accurately" (verse 26), and with this improved understanding he was commended by the ecclesia at Ephesus to the brethren and sisters in Corinth when he continued his journey into the province of Achaia. Apollos vastly helped the Corinthian ecclesia, for he was especially effective at convincing the Jews that Jesus was their long-promised Messiah (verse 28).

It was when Apollos was being so effective in Corinth that the Apostle Paul arrived back in Ephesus, where he was going to be based for the next three years. Ephesus was the capital of the province of Asia, as Corinth was capital in Achaia, and there was considerable contact between them across the Aegean Sea. As travellers arrived in Ephesus from Corinth, some of them would bring news of the growing ecclesia there. Equally, travellers from Ephesus would visit Corinth with messages from the apostle.

The two letters to the ecclesia in Corinth have to be seen, therefore, as part of a continuing dialogue between the apostle and his converts. They are just snatches of a longer conversation. Only part has been preserved, and there are places where we have to make educated guesses about what was said.

The First Letter to Corinth, for example, is clearly a response to information Paul received from Greece:

"It has been declared to me concerning you, my brethren, by those of Chloe's household."

(1 Corinthians 1:11)

"I am glad about the coming of Stephanas, Fortunatus, and Achaicus." (16:17)

"It is actually reported that there is sexual immorality among you!" (5:1)

"Now concerning the things of which you wrote to me ..." (7:1)

Channels of Communication

These quotations suggest there were at least three channels of communication reaching the apostle: specific reports from named individuals in Corinth ("Chloe's household"); more general reports from more than one source; and a formal letter to the apostle from the ecclesia as a whole. As a result, even though he was absent, Paul had a very good picture of the situation in Corinth, and he saw the urgent need to do what he could to remedy it.

But there is also evidence within 1 Corinthians that it is not the first letter the apostle wrote to the ecclesia. When he writes to them in chapter 5 about a serious case of sexual immorality, he reminds them: "I have written to you not to keep company with anyone named a brother, who is sexually immoral ... not even to eat with such a person" (5:11). The sense of this passage is that the apostle's appeal was included in a previous communication; one that has not been preserved in the scriptures. It may also have been that earlier letter that gave rise to the questions the ecclesia posed when they wrote to Paul, leading us to draw the following conclusions about the early contacts between Ephesus and Corinth:

- While he is in Ephesus, Paul hears of the moral problems affecting brethren and sisters in Corinth

- He writes to the ecclesia with an urgent appeal to deal with their problems (this letter has been lost)

- Further reports reach him at Ephesus that the problems are continuing and are deep-seated

- He also receives a letter from the ecclesia in Corinth asking questions about a variety of subjects

- He writes another letter of appeal, and tries also to answer their specific questions (this letter appears in the scripture as 1 Corinthians)

Personal Concern for their Welfare

In addition to these communications, Paul added to the urgency of his appeal and showed his personal concern for their spiritual welfare by sending a representative to them: "I have sent Timothy to you, who is my beloved and faithful son in the Lord, who will remind you of my ways in Christ, as I teach everywhere in every church" (1 Corinthians 4:17). This young brother's quiet gentleness was in stark contrast to the robust and abrasive behaviour that was causing such problems in Corinth, where the brethren and sisters needed showing "a more excellent way" (12:31).

Timothy's demeanour was so different from what was common in Corinth that Paul had to issue a sharp warning, "Now if Timothy comes, see that he may be with you without fear; for he does the work of the Lord, as I also do. Therefore let no one despise him. But send him on his journey in peace, that he may come to me; for I am waiting for him with the brethren" (16:10,11).

The seriousness of the problems in Corinth, and the difficulty of their resolution is also marked by the presence with Paul when he writes what we know as 1 Corinthians of three of the ecclesia's leading brethren: Stephanas ("the firstfruits of Achaia", 16:15), Fortunatus and Achaicus (16:17). They almost certainly took the Corinthian letter of enquiry to Paul and may have returned in company with Titus who carried Paul's reply. From first hand questioning of these three brethren, who were almost certainly converted by Paul (and one of them – Stephanas – baptized by him, 1:16), the apostle would quickly discover in detail the difficulties that were preventing the ecclesia going from strength to strength.

What had happened to allow this sorry state of affairs to develop so quickly? First, there was the cultural background in Corinth, for it is extremely difficult to lead a godly life surrounded by extreme worldliness. But, perhaps more seriously, the ecclesia was not well led. In the early days it had undoubtedly relied heavily on the presence of the Apostle Paul, and when he left he took with him Aquila and Priscilla, dealing a double blow to the infant ecclesia. Aquila and Priscilla prepared Apollos before he left Ephesus for Achaia, and he worked effectively when he arrived in Corinth. Yet the problems were still severe. It is only when we discover that Apollos had left Corinth that we realise the ecclesia was like a ship without an adequate rudder: "Now concerning our brother Apollos, I strongly urged him to come to you with the brethren, but he was quite unwilling to come at this time; however, he will come when he has a convenient time" (16:12).

Faced by a series of difficult problems, the inadequacy of the brethren and sisters in Corinth to deal with them was cruelly exposed. They had so many questions, and no-one locally was able to supply acceptable answers, so they turned naturally to the apostle who brought the Truth to their city.

Were Conditions Improved?

Did all these attempts by the apostle bring about an improvement in the conditions in Corinth? To answer this question we need to turn to 2 Corinthians and look for evidence there. What we find is that serious problems still exist, but more worryingly, that relations between the ecclesia and the apostle have dramatically deteriorated. It is clear that much water has passed under the bridge since Paul sent 1 Corinthians, requiring us to piece together the events between the apostle's sending the two communications we know as 1 and 2 Corinthians.

He refers in 2 Corinthians 7:8, for example, to a letter he wrote that made them sorry and which he regretted sending. This does not sound at all like 1 Corinthians. For, though it dealt with the difficulties his brethren and sisters were facing, it concludes with his pleasure at the prospect of seeing them, and confirms his deep affection for them all. Nor does the subject matter of 1 Corinthians seem to be of the character that would cause the apostle to be so agitated as he awaited Titus' return with news of their reaction (verse 6).

No, the letter he wrote to them "out of much affliction and anguish of heart" and "with many tears" (2 Corinthians 2:4) is, we suggest, another missive of the Apostle's that is not preserved in the scriptures. He sent it, hoping that it would achieve a better result than a personal visit, "lest, when I came, I should have sorrow over those from whom I ought to have joy" (verse 3).

This comment of Paul's about his intention to visit Corinth causes us to consider not only his written communications with the Corinthian ecclesia, but also the occasions when he visited the city. The first visit was, as we have already seen, during his second missionary journey, and he stayed there for at least eighteen months. It was his plan, it seemed, to make two separate visits during his third missionary journey: "I intended to come to you before, that you might have a second (literally, 'a double') benefit; to pass by way of you to Macedonia, to come again from Macedonia to you, and be helped by you on my way to Judea" (2 Corinthians 1:15,16).

An Earlier, Sorrowful, Visit

That the apostle did not carry out his plan was through his concern for the ecclesia, "to spare you I came no more to

Corinth" (verse 23). He was sparing them his severe displeasure: "I determined this within myself, that I would not come again to you in sorrow" (2:1). This suggests that he had, in fact, paid one visit "in sorrow", and he had no wish – for their sakes and his – to repeat the exercise. When was this visit made, for it is clear that the intended "double" visit during the third missionary journey was never accomplished? It could not have been his long first visit, for that is only associated in Paul's letters with expressions of joy and thankfulness; never with sorrow.

We do not need to doubt that there was an intermediate visit, for Paul makes it abundantly clear at the end of 2 Corinthians that he is about to make a third visit: "This will be *the third time* I am coming to you" (13:1). But when did the second visit occur? Did Paul go to Corinth before or after writing 1 Corinthians? It is very unlikely that he visited Corinth again before writing 1 Corinthians. He writes there of "reports" that had reached him, of things that were "common knowledge", and never from his own personal observation.

But his references in 2 Corinthians to writing a painful letter, and to a visit made in heaviness of heart supply good reasons for the deteriorating relationships between Paul and the Corinthian ecclesia. They also provide an indication of the reason why it was necessary for the apostle to make a visit to the city. It seems that his authority as an apostle was being roundly rejected; many in the ecclesia were looking elsewhere for leadership; his advice was ignored and ecclesial life was in turmoil. The visit that was made "in heaviness" and which caused Paul such sorrow is probably the one mentioned in 2 Corinthians 9:2 and occurred "a year" before 2 Corinthians was written, and also before he wrote his "painful letter" to the ecclesia.

If this visit occurred during the third missionary journey – and there is no other possibility – it must have been during the "three months" he stayed in Greece (Acts 20:2,3) before a Jewish plot altered his subsequent travel plans.

With all this information, it is now possible to construct a sequence of written communications between the Apostle and the Corinthian ecclesia, and a list of his visits to the city. With this framework in place, we can turn to the text of 1 Corinthians.

CORINTHIAN LETTERS AND VISITS*

First Visit (during Second Missionary Journey) lasting 1.5 years

Letter from Paul to Corinth about serious moral problems

Letter from Corinth to Paul asking various questions about the Christian life

Paul's *First Letter to Corinthians*

Short visit made in sorrow, followed by a

Letter from Paul admonishing Corinthian ecclesia

Paul's *Second Letter to Corinthians*

---

* See also Chapter 22, and fuller description of the apostle's dealings with the Corinthian ecclesia, page 172.

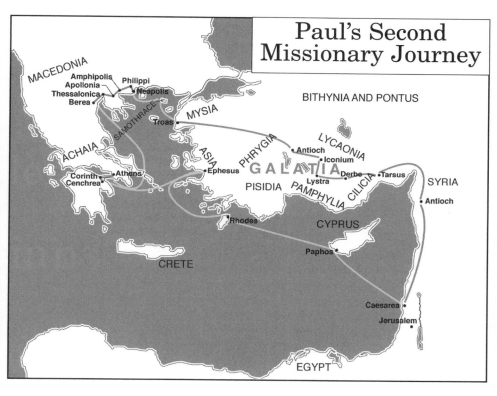

Paul's Second Missionary Journey

Antioch (Syria) to Syria & Cilicia	Acts15:35,41
Syria & Cilicia to Derbe & Lystra	16:1
Derbe & Lystra to Troas	16:6–8
Troas via Samothracia to Neapolis *by sea*	16:11
Neapolis to Philippi	16:12
Philippi via Amphipolis & Apollonia to Thessalonica	17:1
Thessalonica to Berea	17:10
Berea to Athens *by sea*	17:15
Athens to Corinth (& Cenchrea)	18:1 (18:18)
Corinth to Ephesus (on route to Syria) *by sea*	18:18,19
Ephesus to Caesarea (via Rhodes & Cyprus?) *by sea*	18:22
Caesarea to Antioch	18:22

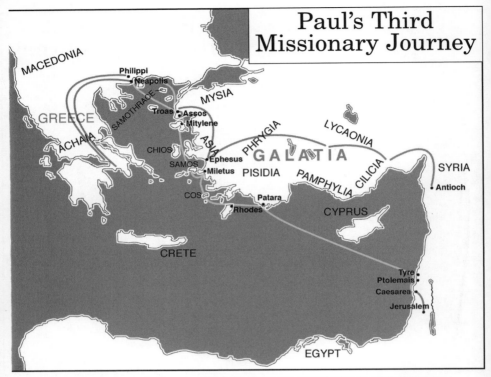

Paul's Third Missionary Journey

Antioch (Syria) to Galatia & Phrygia	Acts 18:22,23
Galatia & Phrygia to Ephesus	19:1
Ephesus to Macedonia *by sea*	20:1
Macedonia to Greece	20:2
Greece to Macedonia (Philippi)	20:3
Macedonia (Philippi) to Troas *by sea*	20:6
Troas to Assos	20:13
Assos to Mitylene *by sea*	20:14
Mitylene via Chios to Samos *by sea*	20:15
Samos (Trogyllium) to Miletus	20:15
Miletus to Cos	21:1
Cos to Rhodes	21:1
Rhodes to Patara	21:1
Patara to Tyre	21:3
Tyre to Ptolemais	21:7
Ptolemais to Caesarea	21:8
Caesarea to Jerusalem	21:15

3

AN OVERVIEW OF 1 CORINTHIANS

THE apostle knew a lot about what was happening in Corinth. He received all sorts of information about the ecclesia, and recently three brethren from Corinth had arrived in Ephesus with a letter from the ecclesia full of questions. They wanted to take back with them the apostle's reply.

But where was he to start? So many difficulties were assailing the new ecclesia in Corinth, it would not be an easy letter to write. An interesting exercise would be to take the list of problems as if they affected your own ecclesia, and decide the order in which you would tackle them. The list that follows shows, as one commentator has said, that whereas the Corinthian ecclesia was in the world – as all ecclesias are – the world was also deeply and almost inextricably imbedded in the ecclesia.

- Some were denying the resurrection
- There was a case of gross immorality
- Brethren and sisters exercising spirit gifts confused ecclesial meetings
- There was no decorum at the breaking of bread
- Sisters were usurping the authority of brethren
- Some were eating food that had been offered to idols
- Paul's position as an apostle was being questioned
- The ecclesia was divided into groups aligned with different individuals
- Members were going to law to resolve disputes with brethren

• There were a variety of different views about marriage

How would you grade these ten problems? Which would head your list as the one most urgently in need of resolution? Would you tackle first of all the case of the man who had taken his father's wife? Or the misunderstandings about the doctrine of the resurrection? Or the chaos at the breaking of bread?

The brethren and sisters in Corinth had established their own priorities, for this is why they wrote to the apostle, and why three brethren were waiting to return with his answers to their questions. But an overall review of 1 Corinthians shows that Paul considered subjects that were not in their letter much more in need of serious attention, and he only touches on their questions after he has dealt with those aspects he believed were the most serious.

There are important lessons to be learned from a careful analysis of the priority the apostle applied to the problems in Corinth. Corinth's problems are unfortunately not completely unique; they can be found in ecclesias all round the world today – though not, one hopes, all in one ecclesia. And we can be guided by the Apostle Paul in setting priorities as problems arise that we have to face.

Sowing Discord Among Brethren

From the order in which he addressed the issues of concern in Corinth, it is apparent that there was nothing more serious in Paul's mind than the existence of deep divisions arising from discord between brethren and sisters. We are reminded of the wise man's words in Proverbs: "These six things the LORD hates, Yes, seven are an abomination to him: a proud look, a lying tongue, hands that shed innocent blood, a heart that devises wicked plans, feet that are swift in running to evil, a false witness who speaks lies, and *one who sows discord among brethren*" (Proverbs 6:16-19).

Without this example in Corinth, it is possible that we would not put this problem at the top of the list. But we should be mistaken. The Lord hates discord among brethren because it is a denial of the redeeming and unifying work of Christ. It may even be that some of the other difficulties arose because of this serious and debilitating schism, so the apostle dedicates almost three chapters in his letter to dealing with it.

The next problem Paul addressed was the serious moral misconduct of a brother who had taken his father's wife. Even in Corinth, famed for its licentiousness, this was an act "not even named among the Gentiles" (1 Corinthians 5:1). But even though the brother's sin was grievous, the apostle was more concerned about the ecclesia's reaction: "you are puffed up, and have not rather mourned, that he who has done this deed might be taken away from among you" (verse 2). There was so little concern, it seems, for each other's eternal salvation that no one was mourning the self-inflicted damage caused by this brother's sin. This was a further indication that the ecclesia in Corinth was not acting in a unified manner, each member was doing what seemed right in his or her own eyes.

This is confirmed by the next issue addressed by Paul, where individuals "having a matter against another, go to law before the unrighteous, and not before the saints" (1 Corinthians 6:1). The authority of the ecclesia (and thus of the Lord Jesus himself) was regarded as of less importance than the Roman provincial courts. This was symptomatic of derisory attitudes towards fellow brethren and sisters, treating them of no account.

The Ecclesia's Letter

Paul mentioned all these problems before he turned to answer the Corinthians' letter, "Now concerning the things of which you wrote to me ..." (1 Corinthians 7:1). These included a number of questions about relationships between men and women, and it is understandable how the immoral Corinthian culture created uncertainty in the minds of some brethren and sisters. The apostle answered on the basis of what he had learned from the teaching of the Lord Jesus. This established certain principles, and it was therefore possible for Paul to speak authoritatively about questions that were not specifically mentioned by the Lord.

The next issue raised in the Corinthians' letter was about "meats offered to idols". This was an exceptionally difficult problem for the early ecclesias, and the Jerusalem conference about four years before had set down some guidelines that were intended to reduce the tensions it caused in ecclesial life.

Part way through his comments about eating food offered in sacrifice to idols, the apostle broke off to assert the grounds of his authority, making it clear that this was being questioned in some quarters in Corinth (1 Corinthians 9). The ecclesia had sent their letter, but some were already seeking to undermine Paul's reply by casting doubt on his apostleship. It was necessary to answer these charges, but Paul did not make it the most important or critical issue, and simply included his rejection of the charges against him within his comments about food offered to idols. He used his work as an apostle, where he never asserted his right to "live from the gospel" (verse 14), to show that the liberties of discipleship must sometimes be forsaken for the benefit of others.

We would probably argue that his authority needed to be established at the outset, so why leave it until this later stage, and why wrap it up in the details of one of his other answers? The fact is that there could be no doubting Paul's authority on this particular issue. He was present at the Jerusalem conference (Acts 15:12), and was one of the bearers of the Jerusalem Accord (verse 25). During the Second Missionary Journey, when the ecclesia at Corinth was established, Paul and Silas "went through the cities, (and) delivered to them the decrees to keep, which were determined by the apostles and elders at Jerusalem" (Acts 16:4). If they questioned Paul's authority on any subject, there were no grounds for questioning his involvement in this case.

Only after Paul had discussed all these issues in his reply did he turn to the problems being experienced in their worship: the prominent part being played by some sisters; and the irreverent behaviour at the breaking of bread. Having denied the apostle's authority, it is clear that some

AN OVERVIEW OF 1 CORINTHIANS

in Corinth were claiming an authority for themselves, based on their possession of certain Holy Spirit gifts. Yet Paul had to tell them that this was just a further manifestation of the lack of unity in the ecclesia; they were not acting as if they were part of the body of Christ.

The Greatest of These is Love

The only way the ecclesia could start to act as "the church of God which is at Corinth" (1 Corinthians 1:2), was if they began to see "a more excellent way", the way of love. This laid a foundation for the apostle to explain the relative lack of importance of Spirit gifts. In everything they should defer to the ultimate good of the ecclesia: "Let all things be done decently and in order" (1 Corinthians 14:40).

The last of the ten serious problems affecting the Corinthian ecclesia that was tackled by Paul was their misunderstanding about the resurrection. Without the apostle's example (perhaps even with the knowledge of what he did) it is unlikely that any modern ecclesia would leave this till last. It is not that the apostle thought doctrines are unimportant, or that moral issues are more serious – for it is impossible completely to separate morality and belief. What is more likely is that the apostle knew the Corinthian brethren and sisters well, and realised that a sound exposition of the subject would soon correct the problem. We must also conclude that questions about the resurrection were included in the ecclesia's letter, or had been reported to him by visitors to Ephesus: "how do some among you say that there is no resurrection of the dead?" (1 Corinthians 15:12).

It seems as if Paul knew the ecclesia well, and correctly assumed that his exposition would be understood and accepted. For there is no further mention of this difficulty in his second epistle, even though some of the other problems persisted.

Paul concludes his first epistle with some personal messages and with an appeal on behalf of the Jerusalem Poor Fund. All in all, it is a model letter, showing how to tackle deep-seated problems. The apostle never abused his authority; he appealed to his brethren and sisters, and regularly showed his love for them. He had a deep concern for their spiritual well being. Surely they would heed his words?

Analysis of 1 Corinthians

Introduction – 1:1-9
Salutation (1:1-3)
Thanksgiving (1:4-9)
Reports that have reached Paul from Corinth – 1:10–6:20
Divisions in the ecclesia (1:10–4:21)
    Rebuke & plea for unity (1:10-17)
    The Gospel is foolishness to Man (1:18–2:5)
    The Gospel contains Divine Wisdom (2:6-16)
    The folly of Division (3:1–4:21)
Discipline in the ecclesia (5:1–6:20)
    The Case of the Incestuous Man (5:1-13)
    A Case of Litigation (6:1-11)
    Fornication is Sin (6:12-20)
Questions in a letter from Corinth – 7:1–15:58
Marriage and Related Matters (7:1-40)
    Advice about marriage (7:1-16)
    Peace in marriage (7:17-24)
    About "Virgins" (7:25-40)
Meat offered to idols (8:1–10:33)
    A question of Conscience (8:1-13)
    Paul defends his apostleship (9:1-27)
    Israel's example applied to Corinth's situation (10:1-33)
Conduct of ecclesial meetings (11:1–14:40)
    Women's conduct & dress (11:1-16)
    Disorders at the Lord's supper (11:17-34)
    Use of Spirit-gifts (12:1–14:40)
        One Lord but many members (12:1-31)
        The More Excellent Way (13:1-13)
        'Prophecy' superior to 'Tongues' (14:1-25)
        Conduct in the Assembly (14:26-40)
The Resurrection (15:1-58)
    Christ is risen (15:1-11)
    The certainty of resurrection (15:12-34)
    The resurrection body (15:35-58)
Final appeal and personal comments – 16:1-24
About the Collection (16:1-12)
Concluding Exhortation (16:13-18)
Final Greetings (16:19-24)

4

NO FLESH SHOULD GLORY

IT has already been shown that an earlier letter not included in the canon of scripture preceded 1 Corinthians (see pages 13,14). We can only guess at its contents, though we do know that it contained strong advice about at least one of the difficulties still troubling the Christian believers in Corinth. Since that letter was written, individuals had been in touch with the Apostle Paul about events in Corinth; and he had received a specific request to answer a series of questions that were troubling the ecclesia. 1 Corinthians was written therefore against a background of various problems where the apostle's advice and counsel were vitally needed by the infant ecclesia.

Divine Perspective

Right from his opening words, Paul leads the Corinthians to the highest possible ground so that their difficulties can be seen from a divine perspective and in relation to the wonder of God's salvation in Christ. This is also sound practice today; for it is so easy to become embroiled in the details of problems, allowing petty and insignificant issues to obscure the Godly principles that should determine our behaviour.

Paul therefore reminds his readers that God does the calling, and His salvation is extended through the work of the Lord Jesus Christ. The effect of this is that it should exclude all boasting, jealousy and pride. Nine times in the first nine verses Paul uses Jesus' name: he was personally called to be Jesus' apostle; converts to the Truth were sanctified in Jesus; and they join in fellowship with all who call on Jesus' name in truth.

Humanly speaking, God's call is indiscriminate. The Corinthian ecclesia was particularly cosmopolitan, being made up of individuals from different races, cultures and backgrounds; but God called them all. Paul himself was like a microcosm of the New Testament church, for he combined Hebrew, Greek and Roman elements in his birth, hometown and citizenship. For this same reason, the letter he wrote was of value not only to those in Corinth but also to all believers wherever they meet. The Corinthians were not therefore to think parochially, but to be conscious of the wider fellowship they now enjoyed as the gospel message was preached in every country under the Roman heavens. Though many of the issues tackled in the letter were extremely serious and some of them were specific to Corinth, the apostle's letter was not written 'In Confidence', as we may have chosen to write it, but was preserved for later generations; possibly it also circulated around other first century ecclesias before it was incorporated in the New Testament canon.

Paul describes the Corinthians as waiting eagerly for Christ's return, and as recipients of God's grace, both in the salvation extended through Christ's sacrifice, and in the spiritual blessings they continued to receive from God. They were particularly enriched in "utterance and all knowledge" (verse 5), meaning that they spoke out about the Truth ("utterance", Greek *logos*) because of their strong grasp of its meaning ("knowledge", Greek *gnosis*). So Paul prayed that, on the day of account, Christ would find them "blameless"*. He wanted them to stand before the Judge with no charge brought against them.

Prayer of Thanksgiving

Verses 4-9 are in the nature of a prayer of thanksgiving to God on the Corinthians' behalf. Despite all the problems they were facing – and the difficulties they created for the apostle himself – Paul could not think of them in any other sense than one of deep gratitude to God for their calling, and for the way His word was working through them. The apostle's attitude is exemplary. The natural man is keen to dismiss anyone he sees as a troublemaker. It is always easier to cut off or destroy, and much harder to encourage

---

* Paul uses a forensic term, meaning unimpeachable.

and build up. But the real lesson from Paul is that he was not adopting a stance towards the Corinthians because he believed it was the one most likely to achieve his desired ends. He wrote in such glowing terms because this was really how he thought of his brethren and sisters, and why he thanked God continually for them, praying for their preservation through every trial of faith.

Faced by a raft of difficult and intractable problems, the apostle follows his prayer of thanksgiving with an urgent appeal. This is at the heart of his letter, flavouring every subject he handles:

> "Now I plead with you, brethren, by the name of our Lord Jesus Christ, that you all speak the same thing, and that there be no divisions among you, but that you be perfectly joined together in the same mind and in the same judgment." (1 Corinthians 1:10)

Perfectly Joined Together

The appeal must not be seen as coming from Paul alone, for he makes it "by the name of our Lord Jesus Christ". This is the tenth time Jesus' name occurs in the opening verses of this letter, thus linking Paul's appeal with all the preceding verses. He calls upon the believers to "speak the same thing", and to cease emphasising their differences. It was not that the ecclesia was divided in the sense of believers being separated from each other, but that there were cliques or parties within the ecclesia with the ever-present danger that this could lead sooner or later to actual division. This was not the Lord's intention when the ecclesia was established. By pleading with them to "be perfectly joined together" (Greek, *katartizo*), Paul used the same word as Matthew when he wrote about James and John "*mending their nets*" when Jesus called them to become his disciples (Matthew 4:21). The Corinthians were like a torn fishing net in need of repair; divisions were making their work ineffective; they were tearing themselves apart. But the analogy of a torn fishing net was insufficient to express fully the seriousness of their behaviour. They were called by God to be Christ's; and by allowing a party spirit to develop and take root they were tearing him apart – their Lord who was "... a body prepared" (Hebrews 10:5, *katartizo*).

Paul was confident in his assessment of the perilous situation, and named his sources of information. Some from "Chloe's household" had described the quarrels that were undermining the new ecclesia in Corinth. Sometimes translated as "variance", "debates", "strife", or "contentions", quarrelling is listed among the works of the flesh in Galatians 5:20. The Corinthians were acting like brute beasts, and not as those who have put on Christ.

Competitive Leaders

In an attempt to show the futility of the different cliques in Corinth, Paul gave them names: "Each of you says, 'I am of Paul,' or 'I am of Apollos,' or 'I am of Cephas,' or 'I am of Christ'" (1 Corinthians 1:12). It is very unlikely that the groups actually associated themselves with these brethren; they would have their own local leaders who attracted disciples around them. But by listing the names of the two apostles, of Apollos, and particularly of Christ, Paul was exposing the utter folly of promoting a party spirit in ecclesial life. "Has Christ been parcelled out?" (Moffatt). He posed the ludicrous suggestion that only one of the groups was related to Christ, or alternatively that the other groups had leaders who were their Saviours: "Was Paul crucified for you? Or were you baptized in the name of Paul?"

The apostle was therefore very thankful that he personally baptized very few of their number – and certainly not sufficient to form a schismatic group. We also know that "Jesus himself did not baptize, but his disciples" (John 4:2), thus indicating the very great care that must be taken even today to ensure that individual brethren are not unduly elevated in the matter of baptism so that converts feel they enter into a special relationship with the one who buries them in water. In baptism, the person who assists is of little importance. Therefore we have always recognised that, in the absence of any more suitable arrangement, immersion can be carried out by anybody: "Dr Thomas ... asked the assistance of a devout acquaintance, on the understanding that the participation of said acquaintance could impart no character or efficacy to the act about to be performed, which was purely an act of obedience rendered ... to God, to which the acquaintance was but mechanically accessory" (Robert Roberts, *Ecclesial Guide*, page 3). Who assists at a baptism is of no importance whatsoever compared to the one into whose name a person is baptized.

At the Name of Jesus

The reason for the great emphasis in these opening verses upon "the name of Jesus" is now glaringly apparent. The contentions and dissensions at Corinth were a travesty of all that is involved in the Name "which is above every name" (Philippians 2:9). Only a few years earlier at the great Jerusalem conference, James said: "Simon (Peter) has declared how God at the first visited the Gentiles to take out of them a people for His name" (Acts 15:14). The Corinthian ecclesia was a prime example of this verse working out in practice: individuals from different backgrounds were brought together in Christ. But their divisive behaviour was denying that call.

How foolish of the Corinthians to give the impression that they were bound more closely to another individual brother than they were to Christ! No one could suggest that Paul tried to encourage the personal allegiance of those whom he converted: his task was to lead men and women to Christ. And though the Corinthians were not apostles, that should be their object too: "For Christ did not send me to baptize, but to preach the gospel, not with wisdom of words, lest the cross of Christ should be made of no effect" (1 Corinthians 1:17).

The Preaching of the Cross

There was a special reason for Paul to speak of *the cross* of Christ; he could have spoken about the Lord's sacrifice, his teaching, his death or his life. But he is building up a careful argument that was intended to show the Corinthians the folly of their current practices. The Romans adopted crucifixion from the Phoenicians as a form of judicial execution because of its effect on those who witnessed it rather than because of its efficiency for the victim. The cross was therefore a symbol of shame, failure and destruction. To all unbelievers – those "who are perishing" – the whole idea of a crucified saviour was beyond their understanding; utter foolishness. But for those who were in the way of salvation, "the message of the cross" had an intrinsic power. It showed God's power, in that through the death of His Son He could save men and women from sin and death. The effects of this power were known and experienced by those "who were being saved".

This created a great gulf between the "wise" according to this world and those whom the world deems to be "foolish". Had not God spoken of this "marvellous work" through Isaiah? "I will again do a marvellous work among this people ... For the wisdom of their wise men shall perish, and the understanding of their prudent men shall be hidden" (Isaiah 29:14).

The divisions in Corinth had doubtless arisen because this worldly thinking was allowed to predominate over the development of the mind of Christ; and the apostle was keen to show how the new mode of thinking required of all believers is totally incompatible with the principles of contemporary society. This is, of course, as true in the twenty-first century as it was in the first!

Jews Request a Sign ...

Whatever human mode of thinking may be followed, the cross of Christ remains an enigma. To Jews who wanted some external or visible evidence of God's miraculous power, the humiliation of crucifixion was actually an enormous impediment to their belief. And it was equally embarrassing to the Greeks, for they could find no explanation for it in their philosophical approach. But if Christ's teaching is to be accepted by men, they must first humble themselves to accept "Christ crucified", and see in his sacrifice "the power of God and the wisdom of God".

How would it have been if the Lord Jesus came with the greatest worldly pomp? Only the rich and powerful could receive him. What if he came as a master of the world's philosophy? Only the learned would understand. But coming as he did, he was accessible to all; he refuted all worldly power, riches and learning. The Corinthians knew this from their own experience: the gospel message when it was preached in Corinth did not attract the so-called leading citizens, who looked down with an air of superiority on the brethren and sisters in the ecclesia.

God's work in Christ had to be powerful to conquer sin – and it was. It had to be wise if there was to be a way opened for forgiveness – and it was. The unenlightened human mind would conclude that all this was weak and foolish, but it would be mistaken. On the contrary, "the message of the cross" shows that the wisdom of this world is weak and foolish. In the scheme of salvation, no credit goes to man, and all boasting is completely excluded. This leads the apostle to state the great principle that denied all boasting, all party groupings and all pride: "No flesh should glory in His presence" (1 Corinthians 1:29).

Glory must always be directed to God, and never to man, as the wonderful words of Jeremiah proclaim: "Let not the wise man glory in his wisdom, let not the mighty man glory in his might, nor let the rich man glory in his riches; but let him who glories glory in this, that he understands and knows Me, that I am the LORD, exercising lovingkindness, judgment, and righteousness in the earth" (Jeremiah 9:23,24). Here lay the problem with the ecclesial divisions. Each group was asserting its claim to superiority over the others, and effectively ignored the supremacy of God. This was a boastful claim, and had no part in the Christian life.

The Example of Paul

The Corinthians only had to look at the apostle's example. He was not a great philosophical orator; he did not appear in a dazzling display of riches or finery. He arrived in Corinth on his own after his brush with the Jews of Thessalonica and the philosophers in Athens! He was of unprepossessing appearance (2 Corinthians 10:10), and may have been suffering from the recurring weakness which was his constant reminder that he must not "be exalted above measure" (2 Corinthians 12:7, cp. Galatians 4:14). And he came with a simple message – "Christ crucified". The ecclesia in Corinth – and hence the faith of its members – was not founded on a silken-tongued message whose effect would soon disappear like froth blown by the wind. They were introduced to "the power of God", and beside that all human pretence swiftly fades.

Imagine the scene as these words were first read aloud to the assembled ecclesia in Corinth. All who had proudly stated their allegiance to one faction or another must have hung their heads in shame as the truth of the argument gradually sank in. Paul led them once again to consider Jesus. He is our wisdom, for the only true wisdom is the message he brought. Through him only can men and women be counted righteous; they are set apart in him, and he is their redeemer (1 Corinthians 1:30).

With this preparation, and after having their petty divisions so completely destroyed, the apostle was ready to show them the elevating wonders of God's work in Christ.

5

WISDOM FROM ABOVE

THE apostle has shown conclusively that human wisdom does not appreciate the gospel, and now he establishes that it is divine wisdom that underpins its message – a wisdom that has existed from "the beginning". The abrupt change of direction is marked by two devices: Paul no longer writes about himself, so the pronoun changes from "I" to "we", referring to all the apostles and teachers; and he writes about a different kind of wisdom – one that he has to define negatively. It is definitely "*not* the wisdom of this age", for that is "coming to nothing" (1 Corinthians 2:6).

This sudden shift of emphasis has lessons for today as well as for the Corinthians; we live in an age of individual expression, but this can easily lead to the kinds of divisions and wrangling that so beset the infant ecclesia in Corinth. Failure to recognise or understand the needs of *the whole* Brotherhood can lead to the development of parochial attitudes which may ultimately tear the body apart. We also live in an age when human wisdom is venerated: man has become his own god, and society is egocentric. This way of thinking, according to the apostle, will come to nothing. For true disciples, the earthly mind must be put aside: they must take on the mind of Christ.

Such wisdom – true wisdom, or "the wisdom that is from above" (see James 3:17) – can only be appreciated by those who are mature. Here the apostle indulges in a gentle rebuke of those who sought prominent positions within the Corinthian ecclesia: for by adopting other methods and upholding human wisdom they were actually immature, just like "babes" (cp. 3:1; Hebrews 5:12-14).

Paul was not seeking to separate the Corinthians into two groups: those who were "mature" and those who were "babes"; for that would be as divisive as the problem he was addressing. He was rather encouraging all the members to strive for a spiritual maturity that has to do with attitude of mind. True believers will receive the message of the cross; it will not be for them either "a stumbling block" or "foolishness" (1 Corinthians 1:23).

The Mystery

Furthermore, divine wisdom is a "mystery". This does not mean it has to be puzzled out, or is intricate or complex; a "mystery" in the scriptures refers to anything that has been generally concealed and is only introduced to selected individuals. The gospel was therefore a *"hidden* wisdom" – the purpose of God was not known by "the rulers of this age": those who conspired to crucify the Lord Jesus and who persecuted his disciples (verse 8, cp. Acts 3:17); but was "revealed ... to *us* through God's Spirit". The apostle was claiming to be a direct recipient of this "mystery". He received by inspiration the message of the gospel which he declared wherever he preached.

This "hidden wisdom" was ordained by God before the world for our glory (verse 7, cp. Ephesians 3:9). It is easy to overlook the point being made here by the apostle. He stresses that the gospel was not a plan framed by the Father *after* man's initial disobedience. The initiative has always been His, and believers are therefore related by the gospel to a timeless purpose. The effect of this is expressed in startling terms: it is "for our glory"! We should not have been surprised if Paul said that the plan of redemption was ordained for *God's* glory. But for ours? How is this to be understood?

One answer appears in the letter to the Hebrews, where the apostle, speaking again about God's purpose in Christ, shows that the intention was to bring "many sons to glory" (Hebrews 2:10). Through bringing the redeemed into fellowship with God and His glory, they are glorified too.

This aspect is mentioned in the context of the widespread failure of mankind to appreciate God's purpose in order to help explain why worldly wisdom becomes a barrier to understanding.

The widespread ignorance of God's ways was mentioned by the prophet Isaiah as he pleaded with God to intervene and further His purpose by delivering Israel. Paul now quotes from Isaiah in order to make the same point: "Eye has not seen, nor ear heard, nor have entered into the heart of man the things which God has prepared for those who love Him" (1 Corinthians 2:9, cp. Isaiah 64:4). It is easy to wrest this scripture out of its context and apply it to those aspects of God's future work that have not yet been revealed in His word. But this is not its meaning. Both the prophet and the apostle were referring to the ignorance of their contemporaries about divine teaching, for Paul continues by saying, "But God has revealed them *to us*" (verse 10).

Divine Wisdom Revealed

Here is the essence of his message. Divine wisdom has to be revealed; it does not come by any other means. The rulers of this world, despite all their self-importance, cannot fathom the deep things of God unless they first humble themselves to receive His teaching. So the message was not sent to them, but to "us", and Paul has already described his own weakness and insignificance in the world's eyes (verses 3,4).

There are therefore two completely opposing philosophies: one is designated by the apostle "the spirit of the world", and is a philosophy based on the natural man which cannot rise any higher than earthly things. The other is "the spirit of God"; so called because it comprises divine ideas revealed by God through His spirit.

The consequence is clear. Man's wisdom can only be expressed "in words which man's wisdom teaches". Divine wisdom has its own means of expression, and God's revelation is also in "words ... which the Holy Spirit teaches" (verse 13). It was not part of the apostle's argument to explain the inspiration of the scriptures, but this section is the more powerful for that reason. It is an undesigned proof that God's revelation of His purpose has been overseen by the Spirit working on those who wrote His word. As David said, "The Spirit of the LORD spoke by me, and His word was on my tongue" (2 Samuel 23:2).

Furthermore, the origin of these two philosophies explains why there is such widespread ignorance: "The natural man does not receive the things of the Spirit of God, for they are foolishness to him; nor can he know them, because they are spiritually discerned" (1 Corinthians 2:14). Once again, this is illustrated by some words from Isaiah: "Who has known the mind of the Lord that he may instruct Him?" (verse 16, citing Isaiah 40:13). Natural thinking will lead only to darkness, for the wisdom of this world concerns itself only with the things of this world. Divine wisdom has a different objective: it instructs about heavenly things. Properly to appreciate these, men and women must strive to "have the mind of Christ".

We could be forgiven for forgetting the object of the apostle's argument. He is seeking to show the folly of schism and division in the ecclesia, and he does so by elevating his reader's minds to higher things. If God's purpose involves "bringing many sons to (His) glory", there is no place for bickering, manipulation or power seeking attitudes. But because these things were present in the Corinthian ecclesia, Paul doubted they would understand his explanation of God's exalted purpose: "I, brethren, could not speak to you as to spiritual people but as to carnal, as to babes in Christ … for where there are envy, strife, and divisions among you, are you not carnal and behaving like mere men?" (1 Corinthians 3:1-3).

Self-seeking Attitudes

Theirs was not an isolated problem, which is why this letter has been preserved in the scriptures. The pressures of the world come thick and fast, and "the flesh lusts against the Spirit … these are contrary to one another, so that you do not do the things that you wish" (Galatians 5:17).

Writing to other believers in different circumstances, the Apostle James also makes the same point: "If you have bitter envy and self-seeking in your hearts, do not boast and lie against the truth ... For where envy and self-seeking exist, confusion and every evil thing are there" (James 3:14-16). The root of the difficulty in Corinth was the self-seeking attitude displayed by those who wanted to be prominent in the ecclesia. Paul previously used his own name and Apollos's to represent two of the different cliques in the ecclesia, so he now asks his readers to assess their work.

We are not leaders, he says, but servants. To think differently betrays a carnal, and not a spiritual mind. When the Corinthians accepted the truth, they responded to Jesus' call and not to Paul's. The apostles and all the other teachers were merely the channels through whom the message of truth was brought to Corinth. The real work was done by God, just as a gardener cannot claim any credit for the fact that plants he sowed or watered grow and increase. But this agricultural metaphor has a further important lesson. Even if the growth of the plant is left out of the equation, who is more important, the person who plants, or the one who waters it? Both are necessary to the process, "and each one will receive his own reward according to his own labour" (1 Corinthians 3:8). But it is also obvious that God cannot be left out of the equation, and both of these necessary tasks are valueless without His input.

Rooted and Built Up

All believers must therefore become "fellow workers". Paul and Apollos shared in the work without rivalry. Neither one sought prominence, or tried to attract disciples who would follow him. There are vast fields waiting for the seed of the gospel to be planted, and everyone is needed if the work is to prosper.

The agricultural metaphor now changes, though the change is not so stark as it first appears. The subject is still about things that grow, but the Corinthians are no longer described as a field of growing plants but as a building in process of erection. The same apparently abrupt change of figure occurred in Jesus' teaching. He ended his parable of the wicked husbandmen by saying that the vineyard will be let out to others "who will render to him the fruits in their seasons", and continued by describing "the stone which the builders rejected (that) has become the chief cornerstone" (Matthew 21:41,42). And Paul himself uses the same two related figures once again in his writings, explaining to the Colossians that they were "rooted and built up" in Jesus Christ (Colossians 2:7).

But the Lord in this new figure is not only "the chief cornerstone" and the framework into which believers are built; he is the foundation: "For no other foundation can anyone lay than that which is laid, which is Jesus Christ" (1 Corinthians 3:11). And this fact imposes a duty of care upon all who build their lives upon the Godly principles he manifested.

The next section in 1 Corinthians 3 is not easy to understand. Paul talks of building upon the foundation of Christ with various materials: "gold, silver, precious stones, wood, hay, straw" (verse 12). These materials obviously represent different values, but what is actually being built? Was Paul speaking of each individual's life in Christ? This is what some commentators suggest, but it creates a difficulty when we continue reading the passage. Verse 15, for example, says: "If anyone's work is burned (i.e., if it is wood, hay or straw), he will suffer loss; but he himself will be saved, yet so as through fire." An individual cannot be destroyed *and* saved!

Another way of looking at the passage puts it in the context of Paul's comments about those who were striving for pre-eminence in the ecclesia and who were by inference critical of Paul and his companions. This view sees "each man's work" as his work of teaching. He builds on the foundation of Christ – not, significantly, on his own foundation! – individuals whose lives may turn out to be golden and abiding, or straw that will not survive the fire of judgement. Those teachers whose work endures will receive a reward, which Paul elsewhere calls a "crown of rejoicing" (cp. 1 Thessalonians 2:19). If their work does not survive the Lord's judgement, it will not necessarily impinge on their own salvation: "he will suffer loss; but he himself will be saved, yet so as through fire" (1 Corinthians 3:15).

You Are God's Temple

We should notice how, in this section, the apostle moves the focus from the individual to his work. If the dissenters in Corinth would only focus their attention on the work of preaching, they would not have the time – or the desire – to bicker, quarrel or posture. And, staying with the figure of building, Paul reminds them that they are component parts of a magnificent edifice still in process of construction: "You are the temple of God and the Spirit of God dwells in you" (verse 16). Of the two Greek words used in the New Testament for temple, *hieron* and *naos*, the apostle here uses the latter, more properly translated as "sanctuary". Believers therefore form the 'throne room' of the God of the Universe when they unite with their fellow believers. Anything that creates a rift in the ecclesia defiles God's sanctuary. The one who is responsible will be punished by God: "God will destroy him" (verse 17, where the word for "destroy" – *phtheiro* – is the same as the word for "defile").

The temple of God is holy by definition. As participants in the temple, believers are also to be holy, and this imposes great responsibilities on them.

Summarising his arguments to this point, Paul returns to the subject of wisdom. Using a favourite phrase, "Let no-one deceive himself" (verse 18, cp. 6:9; 15:33; Galatians 6:7), the main points of his argument are reiterated:

- worldly wisdom is foolishness with God (verses 19,20)

- therefore let no one boast in man (verse 21)

- *all things* can be yours in Christ (verses 21-23)

Now that these matters have been established, the apostle is free to speak about the duties and responsibilities of teachers. He does this by describing his own experiences and those of Apollos, and how teachers must always be ministers: servants of the Lord and of the ecclesias.

6

FOOLS FOR CHRIST'S SAKE

THE last strand in Paul's argument showing the folly of the divisions in the ecclesia forms the subject of 1 Corinthians 4, to which we now turn. The real consideration is not man's judgement of human ministers, but God's. Having already shown the destructive nature of division, and the folly of placing an emphasis on human wisdom, Paul now challenges the whole conception that led to the elevation of certain individuals within the ecclesia who gathered disciples after them. He starts by saying, "So then ..." (verse 1, NIV), i.e., in the light of what has already been discussed, there are certain facts to be recognised about the apostles themselves. They are not leaders of men, but "servants of Christ and stewards of the mysteries of God".

The English translation obscures the two points Paul is making. Describing himself and the other apostles as "servants", he uses the Greek word *huperetes*, meaning the slaves who were given the unenviable task of manning the lowest set of oars in the great Roman triremes: the warships fitted with three decks of oarsmen. Those on the lowest deck had to cope with the foul conditions at the bottom of the boat, and with the waste products of the men who rowed at a higher level.

Changing the figure, the apostles were also "stewards of the mysteries of God" – those entrusted by the master with the running of his household, which required absolute faithfulness (verse 2). These two figures are used by Paul to show first his relationship to Christ – he is the Lord's lowly slave – and his relationship to the ecclesias, to whom he acts as the Lord's representative. But none of this must suggest that it was of any moment to Paul how he was viewed by the Corinthians. They were not his master, nor was any other human court. He has one judge, who is the Lord.

The implication is that Paul and the Corinthians will be judged by Jesus when he comes; and there are some serious matters in Corinth, including some "hidden things of darkness", which will come under the Lord's review. His judgement will "reveal the counsels of the heart", and when praise is given, it will be praise from God and not from men.

The problem Paul was addressing did not only affect the Corinthians. Self-pride and superiority are insidious characteristics of the human make up. These are incompatible with discipleship in Christ, and true believers should seek to control and smother them. They were flourishing in Corinth, and Paul saw the existence of groups associated with different individuals in the ecclesia as a serious indictment of their grasp of his teaching about Christ.

Using the Names "... in a figure"

He explains that he has used his name and Apollos's as a device to show the utter folly of their sectarian spirit. Literally speaking, there were not groups in the ecclesia gathered round Paul, Apollos, Peter and Christ; but there were brethren who had their own band of followers, and those who first received the letter would know who they were. None of them would dare to suggest that they were superior to the apostles, but by encouraging others to associate with them, they were acting in a superior and divisive way.

Paul reminds them "not to think beyond what is written", presumably referring to the Old Testament quotation from Jeremiah 9:23,24 on which he based his great teaching "that no flesh should glory in His presence" (1 Corinthians 1:29). Elevating an individual to a position of prominence is a failure adequately to acknowledge the supremacy of God.

This explains why the apostle spoke of four groups in Corinth, with one named after Christ. It seemed inconceivable that there could be brethren and sisters

43

associating with other leaders, and ignoring the Lord Jesus. But it was equally wrong for there to be a "Christ-group". By including it among the four groups he singled out for rebuke, Paul gives silent witness to the Lord Jesus' submission to his Father. Not even the Son, who is "the head of every man" can draw away individuals from God, who is his head (11:3). And if it would be wrong for there to be a Christ-group, how can any brother or sister "be puffed up on behalf of one against the other" (4:6)? For where did these associations come from? Or, "Who makes you differ from another?" (verse 7). The answer to this rhetorical question is that giving prominence to selected individuals came only from their own conceit.

In a repetition of the argument about worldly and divine wisdom, Paul reminded his readers that any good thing they received came from God, and not as a result of personal achievement. By worldly standards they may have some cause for boasting; but not as disciples of the Lord.

"He who is greatest among you ..."

The situation in Corinth may seem utterly remote from our own experiences. The idea of an ecclesia being divided by individuals drawing away disciples after them can seem alien and strange. But the danger clearly lies in elevating anyone to a position as a leader rather than as a servant or steward. As Jesus himself taught: "Do not be called 'Rabbi'; for one is your Teacher, the Christ, and you are all brethren ... and do not be called teachers; for one is your Teacher, the Christ. But he who is greatest among you shall be your servant" (Matthew 23:8-11).

The danger exists, even today. Brethren should never seek a following, and ecclesias should not allow any of their members to assume such dominant positions. One of the most important guards against this is the role of the whole ecclesia in decision making, whereby issues can be discussed and action taken on behalf of all the members, and not at the whim or desire of a few.

If the so-called leaders in Corinth were actually claiming to be apostles they obviously did not know the rigours of apostolic life. Paul launches into an impassioned and ironic denunciation of the Corinthians' pampered situation. They had all they needed, and in abundance. They were reigning like kings! By contrast, the life of an apostle was hard and dangerous. Turning to a picture that was familiar to the inhabitants of Corinth, Paul likened the apostles to the lowly criminals who were paraded round the amphitheatre to receive derisive abuse from the crowd: "We have been made a spectacle to the world, both to angels and to men" (1 Corinthians 4:9). In this graphic example, if the apostles are the criminals condemned to die, the Corinthians are the crowd – sated with food, elegantly and richly attired, distinguished and with comfortable homes. This was the world's assessment, but not God's.

He looked at the apostles; and they were so different: "we both hunger and thirst, and we are poorly clothed, and beaten, and homeless" (1 Corinthians 4:11). Furthermore, they worked with their own hands, suggesting that there were some in Corinth who criticised Paul for providing for his own "necessities, and for those who were with him" (Acts 20:34).

In worldly terms, the apostles were fools; but they were "fools for Christ's sake". The contrast with the Corinthians is sharp and distinct – as it was meant to be. Paul was trying to shock his readers in the hope they would see their own situation more clearly. In worldly terms, he said, the apostles were simply the filth cleaned off the dishes after the feast, or off the body when it is throughly cleansed. Though the intention was to shock, Paul did not write with the intention of shaming his readers. It was intended as a warning; the sort of warning a father would give to his child to help correct poor behaviour.

Not Many Fathers

Suddenly the mood of the letter changes abruptly. The argument has been incisive, and nothing was held back. All the information needed to correct the situation was provided. But the apostle now makes a strong personal appeal, calling the ecclesia his "beloved children". The leaders they have elevated are not what they need. They are "instructors" (guardians, NIV; tutors, RV; guides, RSV; Greek, *paidagogos*, schoolmaster) when they ought to be "fathers".

There is no exact equivalent in today's society to the Roman pedagogue, and we need to appreciate the cultural background if we are to understand the apostle's message. In a large household, a son was allocated an individual servant who was responsible for his welfare. In particular he accompanied the boy to school, helping him with his lessons and teaching him the manners and customs of the time. Whatever importance this slave had in the boy's life, he was replaceable. The father was different. He bore ultimate responsibility, through his relationship to the child.

This extends the Lord's teaching about the "hireling: he who is not the shepherd, one who does not own the sheep" (John 10:12). It is a warning about times of difficulty, and about who can be trusted when things begin to go wrong. Paul's relationship to the Corinthians was different from that of the other teachers. In a sense they were his children, "for in Christ Jesus I have begotten you through the gospel" (1 Corinthians 4:15).

"Timothy ... my beloved and faithful son"

As their spiritual father, Paul can urge them to imitate his example (verse 16), without asking them to become his disciples or form a schismatic group around him. He was so keen they should do this, he sent Timothy, his own son in the faith, of whom he wrote to the Philippians: "You know his proven character, that as a son with his father he served with me in the gospel" (Philippians 2:22). There was no better example available. Timothy was one of Paul's co-workers. There was no rivalry between them; neither of them sought to draw away disciples after them, but they desired to win disciples for Christ.

In advance of the letter being sent, so it seems (cp. 1 Corinthians 16:10), Timothy was dispatched by Paul to help provide some guidance to the Corinthian ecclesia. He was to show them what was being taught wherever the gospel was preached. Corinth should not be allowed to develop different ways and different practices from all the other ecclesias.

By emphasising the importance of unity in the ecclesia, Paul was naturally speaking also about the need for unity throughout the Brotherhood. It would have been possible for Corinth to be at one in itself, yet at odds with the rest of the ecclesial world. This may seem preferable to the situation where it was being torn apart by party factions. But it would only play out on a larger stage the difficulties Corinth was currently experiencing. When Timothy arrived in Corinth, he was charged with showing them of Paul's "ways in Christ, as I teach everywhere in every church" (1 Corinthians 4:17).

It is apparent that the apostle saw a great benefit in all ecclesias having a common overall method of working. When in later years he sent Titus to Crete, it was with the express intention: "that you should set in order the things that are lacking, and appoint elders in every city as I commanded you" (Titus 1:5).

The message that Paul had sent Timothy to Corinth was taken by some of the brethren there as an admission of his personal timidity. They were prepared to boast about his fear of confronting them face to face. They were growing bold in resisting his teachings. So he advises them not to feel complacent. He will travel to see them, subject always to the proviso, "if the Lord wills". And when he comes, he will be eager to determine, not the words of those who have opposed him, but their power. Preparation for the coming kingdom involves much more than fine speeches or proud statements. Action is needed, and Paul will be looking to see what these self-important teachers have been doing during his absence.

"With a rod … or in love?"

There was an important reason for sending Timothy first to remind them of the apostle's ways. It would give opportunity for the problems to be corrected quietly and away from the glare of publicity which would attend any visit from Paul. The ecclesia was faced by a stark choice, depending on how they reacted to the letter from Paul and Timothy's visit: "What do you want? Shall I come to you with a rod, or in love and a spirit of gentleness?" (1 Corinthians 4:21).

By presenting the choice so starkly before his readers, Paul is preparing for his future relations with the Corinthians. He has some difficult matters to address, and they have difficult choices and decisions to make. "No chastening seems to be joyful for the present, but painful; nevertheless, afterward it yields the peaceable fruit of righteousness to those who have been trained by it" (Hebrews 12:11). The words in the apostle's letter were intended to be chastening. If they were sufficient to train the Corinthians in godliness, Paul would come to them "in love and a spirit of gentleness". But if conditions continued without any correction, he will arrive "with a rod". The choice was theirs.

7

A LITTLE LEAVEN

AFTER discussing the problem of divisions in the Corinthian ecclesia, the next serious matter calling for Paul's attention centred on a specific case. One of the brethren was unfaithful. In an act of gross immorality unusual even in sexually indulgent Corinth, he took his father's wife. Although it is very unlikely the woman was his mother, otherwise Paul would describe her as such, this was still incest under both Roman and Jewish law (see Leviticus 18:8; 20:11; Deuteronomy 22:30; 27:20). Some commentators wonder if the woman was by now divorced from his father, or a widow, making it easier for the man to take her as his wife or concubine. But whatever circumstances were involved, the problem was that an obviously sinful act was not troubling the ecclesia. Even more seriously, there was an element of pride in the situation, presumably from the erroneous belief that life in Christ removes a brother or sister from the restrictions of worldly rule. They were boasting about their ability to accommodate in their midst a person who would be condemned in any other society (see 1 Corinthians 5:2,6). By his actions the brother had separated himself from the things of God. He paid little regard to the hope of life, and chose the way of death.

Put Away the Evil

On a number of occasions in the New Testament, crimes punishable by death under the Law of Moses are described as leading to spiritual death when they are committed by believers. The Law demanded that anyone committing incest should be stoned after a proper and just examination of the circumstances (Leviticus 20:11). So Paul indicates that the ecclesia should apply the Law's underlying principle. It must conduct its own investigation. If the facts of the case as it was reported to him are true, the ecclesia has no option but to: "deliver such a one to Satan for the destruction of the flesh, that his spirit may be saved in the day of the Lord Jesus" (1 Corinthians 5:5). Gross sin was removed from Israel by the death of the sinner, and from the household of faith by the sinner's departure from the ecclesia.

The apostle's command to "put away from yourselves the evil person" (verse 13), quotes from the provision in the law in cases of false prophets, idolaters, rebellious children, and fornicators (Deuteronomy 13:5; 17:7; 21:21; 22:21-24). It is apparent that ecclesial discipline under Christ was to be viewed in the same way as the death penalty under the law.

It must be noted however that the main object is to separate the sinner from his sin, and only secondarily to protect the ecclesia from sin. In an unusual figure, appearing only here and in 1 Timothy 1:20, the apostle describes the world outside the Brotherhood as belonging to Satan, or sin. The brother had sinned. Because he failed to acknowledge and repent of his sin he forfeited his place among "the saints in the light" (Colossians 1:12), and should be "cast ... into outer darkness. There will be weeping and gnashing of teeth" (Matthew 25:30). The language is not inappropriate, and forms part of an extended New Testament metaphor that contrasts light with darkness, and the power of sin (Satan) with the power of salvation (the work of the Holy Spirit).

"When you are gathered together ..."

Whereas some may argue that certain issues are to be left until the Lord returns as judge, Paul makes it clear that the ecclesia has specific responsibilities when the truth is flagrantly denied in principle or practice. Brethren and sisters meet "in the name of our Lord Jesus" (1 Corinthians 5:4). They should bring the man face to face with his sin, "and if he refuses even to hear the church, let him be to you like a heathen and a tax collector" (Matthew 18:17). Jesus made it clear that in these circumstances, "where two or three are gathered together in my name, I am there in the midst of them" (verse 20). So Paul was able to tell the Corinthians: "When you are gathered together, along with my spirit (i.e., they knew the apostle's thinking; and though he was physically absent, his teaching was available to them), with the power of our Lord Jesus Christ, deliver such a one to Satan" (1 Corinthians 5:4,5).

Only after talking about the process that was intended to encourage the brother to repent of his sin does the apostle turn to its effect on the ecclesia: "Do you not know that a little leaven leavens the whole lump?" (verse 6). By ignoring the brother's blatant sin they were allowing a contagious evil to remain in their midst. We must notice, however, that the evil was not simply the brother's gross sin. To be isolated completely from such sins, Paul said, "you would need to go out of the world" (verse 10). The evil they were to put away was the fact that both the brother and the ecclesia failed to regard his actions as serious or in need of amendment. It was this contagion – failing to acknowledge sin when it occurs – that could quietly and completely work its way of destruction throughout the ecclesia, like a small amount of yeast in a lump of dough.

A Clean Sweep

Speedy action was required, and this is reflected in Paul's urgent words, "Purge out the old leaven, that you may be a new lump" (verse 7). The metaphor, as so often in Paul's writings, has Old Testament echoes. Each year as Passover drew near, Jewish houses were swept clean. This was not simply good housekeeping, but taught a strong spiritual lesson about the need for moral uprightness in those who draw near to God.

If the Corinthians were really a new creation in Christ Jesus, as they claimed, they had to be "a new lump". As Christ's body, made up of individual believers, they were to follow his example, "Who committed no sin, nor was deceit found in his mouth" (1 Peter 2:22). In this regard, he was never tainted or defiled, for he did not allow the old leaven of sin to dwell in his mortal body, nor did he obey its lusts (cp. Romans 6:12).

How could they meet together in remembrance of the sacrifice of "Christ, our Passover" – the spotless lamb, for whose sake God is prepared to pass over sins and redeem us from evil – without also denying the sinful aspects of the old way of life they abandoned when they were baptized? To continue the Passover figure, that would be like trying to keep the feast acceptably in the full knowledge that there was leaven in their houses which they had done nothing to remove.

In calling upon the Corinthians to be a "new lump", Paul was speaking in terms his first century readers would understand. The leaven they used in baking was a portion of the previous batch specially kept for the purpose. The natural and spiritual dangers implicit in this practice are apparent. Each fresh batch had leaven from the old batch working in it. This should not be the life of believers in Christ. They were truly a "new creation" (2 Corinthians 5:17; Galatians 6:15). They were to "put off ... the old man which grows corrupt according to the deceitful lusts" (Ephesians 4:22), and "put on Christ" (Galatians 3:27).

The Lord Jesus spurned the old leaven and was completely free from sin: he never allowed the weakness of mortality to gain supremacy over his desire to serve his heavenly Father. By his obedient life he opened up the way of salvation, and his true disciples walk in his steps. As the "new lump" formed by his sacrifice, they too are to forsake the "old leaven"; and in order to become "one bread" – a subject to which the apostle returns later in his letter (chapter 10) – they must be energised by the spirit of Christ. Instead of being motivated by desires that lead to sin, they should follow the Lord's example of "sincerity and truth". As the apostle wrote to Roman believers: "You are not in the flesh but in the spirit, if indeed the spirit of God dwells in you. Now if anyone does not have the spirit of Christ, he is not his. And if Christ is in you, the body is dead because of sin, but the spirit is life because of righteousness" (Romans 8:9,10).

"Christ, our Passover"

The "new lump" was free from the potentially corrupting influence of the "old" leaven, and was to grow according to the influence of Christ who formed it. Paul is urgent in his comments on this subject because commitment to Christ demands that the old life of sin must be completely forsaken when a man or woman enters into covenant relationship with him. Once again, the apostle uses the background of Jewish custom to press home the lesson. The annual search for leaven was always undertaken *before* the Passover lamb was killed (see Exodus 12:15; 13:7). Yet "Christ, our Passover", was already sacrificed (1 Corinthians 5:7), and still there were signs of the old leaven working amongst the Corinthians.

This was not the first time Paul had raised the subject with the Corinthians: "I wrote to you in my epistle (i.e., the earlier letter that has not been preserved, see page 13) not to keep company with sexually immoral people" (1 Corinthians 5:9). The problem of the brother's immorality was longstanding; and the ecclesia knew about it. Their inactivity was inexcusable.

But nor was this particular case the only matter of concern in Corinth, for in his earlier letter Paul alerted the ecclesia to the problem of allowing other serious sins to continue without attention: "I have written to you not to keep company with anyone named a brother, who is sexually immoral, or covetous, or an idolater, or a reviler, or a drunkard, or an extortioner – not even to eat with such a person" (5:11). The repetition here of these offences indicates that those who alerted the apostle to the difficulties in Corinth told him about other situations; not only about the incestuous man. These could result in similar action being necessary, with the ecclesia deciding "not to keep company" with other brothers or sisters too.

Among the sins he lists are ones that were clearly present in Corinth, contributing to problems Paul deals with elsewhere in his letter. Some of them were involved in the schismatic behaviour he has already tackled, and the problems of idolatry and drunkenness are subjects on which he is to comment before he concludes his letter.

Do Not Keep Company

In such cases, when the ecclesia has separated from any who refuse to mend their ways, he says: *do not company* with the sinners, do not even eat with them (verses 9,11). In view of the fact that Paul makes it clear he is not referring to daily contact with sinners outside the Corinthians ecclesia ("since then you would need to go out of the world", verse 10), there has been much discussion about his exact intentions in these cases. Was he meaning that all social contact must be severed? Or more specifically that the former member should no longer be allowed to participate in ecclesial meetings?

The apostle uses a word that occurs only here in Corinthians and in one other place, 2 Thessalonians 3:14: "If anyone does not obey our word in this epistle, note that person and do not keep company with him, that he may be ashamed." It has to be noted that the context is the same in both cases. A member of the ecclesia adopted a way of life that is incompatible with continuing membership, and action was taken by the ecclesia with the hope of restoring him fully to their midst. Paul goes on in Thessalonians to add some further important information that confirms this intention: "Do not count him as an enemy, but admonish him as a brother" (verse 15).

Some religious communities apply these words of the apostle by cutting off completely all contact with the offender. They take the teaching absolutely literally, and refuse to sit down at any meal with someone whom they once counted as a brother or sister in Christ. Paul's intention is revealed by the nature of the word he used to describe the ecclesia's action. They were not to "keep company with" the offender, and the Greek word *sunanamignumi* means not to be mixed up with him or his sinful ways. It is apparent that Paul was still using his metaphor about leaven: continued association with the brother and his sin would allow a little leaven to leaven the whole lump. The real issue is therefore not about eating or drinking, but about the ecclesia declaring by its actions as well as by word that it dissociated itself from the brother and his sin.

Like a Heathen or a Publican

Words already quoted from Matthew 18:17 are helpful in this context. When a brother or sister refuses to listen to the advice of the ecclesia and acknowledge their sin, they are to be treated "like a heathen and a tax collector." Such had no part in the affairs of ecclesial life, though social contact outside the ecclesia was still permissible.

Putting this principle into practical effect may differ from case to case, but in Corinth there is no doubt that the man no longer benefited from ecclesial association with his former brethren and sisters. His case was such that the apostle still has more to say about the Corinthians' lax attitude to immorality, and chapter 6 is part of the same subject, as shown in our next chapter.

But we need first to look ahead into 2 Corinthians to see how the problem of the incestuous brother was resolved. The comments in 2 Corinthians 2:1-9 are generally taken as referring to this case. Paul speaks there about a "punishment (or censure, AV margin) inflicted by the majority" (verse 6). This suggests that the ecclesia discussed the situation following the receipt of his letter, and by a majority vote (one of the very few indications of this ecclesial process in the New Testament) delivered the brother to Satan by withdrawing fellowship from him.

The purpose of this action, as we have already seen, was to "destroy the flesh" by making the brother face up to the consequences of his sin, and "save his spirit" by showing him the benefits of ecclesial fellowship. The action was so successful in this case that there was even the danger that he might "be swallowed up with too much sorrow" (verse 7).

Having considered the harshness of Paul's rebuke of the Corinthians' earlier laxness, we can appreciate their reluctance to welcome the brother back prematurely. They needed the apostle's initiative before they could "reaffirm their love to him" (verse 8). There can surely be little doubt that, in this case, the brother took action to put away the evil from himself, as the ecclesia sought to put away the evil that had entered amongst them, and now wished to become once again part of the "one lump" in the Lord Jesus: the Passover Lamb who "is sacrificed for us".

8

DELIVER UNTO SATAN

THE serious problem of immorality in the Corinthian ecclesia, raises the question of how behavioural problems should be handled by ecclesias today. The details of the difficulties in Corinth were recorded, along with other events in the scriptures, "for *our* admonition, upon whom the ends of the ages are come" (1 Corinthians 10:11).

The Corinthian case provides some very useful advice for any who are facing the difficulties that are created when the high principles of the Truth are denied in practice. As Paul stresses, the prime objective is to recover, if at all possible, the person who has strayed from the way of life.

He is Faithful and Just

The principles apply in *every* case of blatant sin: an adulterer is not to be treated in a different way from an embezzler. Unfortunately, we are inclined to treat some sins more seriously than others, forgetting that any sinful act or thought separates between God and man. Yet there is the wonderful promise that: "If we confess our sins, he is faithful and just to forgive us our sins, and to cleanse us from all unrighteousness" (1 John 1:9).

The problem in Corinth, and when similar problems arise in ecclesias today, is that the man's sin was not confessed by him. The difficulty was made worse in Corinth by the ecclesia's failure to recognise that the brother's behaviour was unacceptable in God's sight. The first requirement, therefore, is for an ecclesia to ascertain the facts of the case and to advise the brother or sister of the seriousness of their position.

It is wrong in such cases to act simply on hearsay, and it has to be acknowledged that clumsy action at this stage often sours relationships, making the objective – the brother or sister's restoration – much harder to achieve.

Though it rarely seems to happen in practice, it is possible that an ecclesia's intervention will actually stop the sinner in his tracks. When he realises how far he has drifted from the way of life, he may show deep remorse for his past actions, and seek help to prevent them occurring again in the future. In such circumstances, it is likely that the ecclesia will recognise that the objective has been secured, and will wish to do everything possible to support the erring member. It is too much to expect that the incident will be completely forgotten, and in many cases it may be inadvisable to expunge the memory completely. Depending on the nature of the offence, the brother or sister's activities in the ecclesia may need to be curtailed. A brother who has shown himself to be untrustworthy with money ought not, for his sake and others, to be given the responsibility of dealing with the ecclesia's finances. If his problem related to inappropriate behaviour with children or young people, he cannot expect to be involved in the future with the Sunday School or Youth Group.

The scriptures teach that sins always have repercussions. Sins can be forgiven by God, and we can be cleansed from their defilement by the blood of Christ; but we may not escape all the consequences that some sins can set in train. There are many examples of faithful men and women in the scripture whose past actions rebounded in different ways throughout their lifetimes.

Making Excuses

Though immediate confession and remorse for past actions are to be sincerely desired, it is more often found that a variety of explanations are given in an attempt to justify sinful behaviour. While it is true that we all suffer the weakness of the flesh, and we all sin, these facts cannot excuse blatant or carefully premeditated behaviour that denies the beliefs we hold.

If this position of denial is maintained, the ecclesia is presented with a considerable difficulty, similar to the one faced by the brethren and sisters in Corinth when a brother took his father's wife. If there is no remorse, and if the sinner refuses to acknowledge or confess his sin, there is no alternative but to follow the apostle's advice and "put away from among yourselves the evil person" (1 Corinthians 5:13).

Withdrawal of fellowship is regulated by the scriptural principles established in the case of the incestuous man: its aim is to cause the sinner to reflect carefully on what he has lost through his folly, and to take full responsibility for his sin. It is no good trying to put the blame on others, as Adam and Eve did when they sinned. According to the proverbial saying, 'Confession is good for the soul'. This is true, for sin is a corrupting influence, and it eats away at the moral framework of a person's being. 'O what a tangled web we weave, when first we practise to deceive.'

Brethren and sisters are not helped in coming to terms with their sin, if the ecclesial action of withdrawal is minimised or undermined by allowing them to continue much as before. The intended outcome of withdrawing fellowship is to cause the offending members to realise what is being denied to them in terms of the benefits of fellowship. Whereas this is primarily the opportunity to break bread in the company of their brethren and sisters, it is not restricted simply to preventing participation in the memorial meeting.

As a Heathen or Publican

Our fellowship involves a number of different aspects whereby we obtain strength and comfort, and the joy of being in the presence of those who share our beliefs and hopes: Bible Classes, Fraternal Gatherings, Bible Schools and Study Days, Campaigns and Special Efforts. Participation in all these different events and activities is forfeited when fellowship is withdrawn. When the action of withdrawal is taken in the hope that it will bring a sinner to his senses, the situation is not helped if every impression is given that very little has occurred to dent his relationship with his brethren and sisters.

A full separation from the ecclesia was certainly the effect of the apostle's letter to Corinth. He was "censured" (2 Corinthians 2:6, AV margin), and "put away from among" the ecclesia, so that he was no longer able to participate in the usual activities. By this means he was "delivered to Satan for the destruction of the flesh" (1 Corinthians 5:5). The language is clear and decisive, and reveals exactly how withdrawal was understood in the first century AD, and therefore how it ought to be understood today.

While not arguing for hasty withdrawal – for that can be equally dangerous – it is often the case today that withdrawal is seen as a last resort, and thus it rarely has the intended effect of bringing the sinner face to face with the serious consequences of his sin. Far too often, it seems, withdrawal either leads to the complete loss of a brother or sister rather than their recovery, or merely acknowledges that they have chosen to leave us. In some cases, it must be admitted, withdrawal of fellowship can prevent someone from seeking to return to fellowship; it does not provide any incentive or encouragement. This may be because ecclesias are rarely faced with such extreme cases as the one in Corinth, or alternatively because a situation has been developing almost unseen over a long period of time. But it may also occur because withdrawal is sometimes considered as a completed action, and not as part of a process of recovery.

It is therefore necessary to consider the question of returning to fellowship. The incestuous man needed the ecclesia's love confirmed to him (2 Corinthians 2:8), which explains that both the action of withdrawing from the brother and the proposed decision to welcome him back were motivated by love. Carried out in the right spirit and for the right objective, withdrawal of fellowship is a loving act to be undertaken by an ecclesia. But, because it is a loving act intended to recover the sinner, it only forms part of the process. The apostle told the Corinthian brethren and sisters to "comfort" the one who had caused so much grief, and he used the verb form of the word *paraklete*, or Comforter. They were now to 'come alongside' him, when previously they were told to "put away ... that wicked person."

Great Sorrow

In this process, where withdrawal forms only a part, the sinner was first "put away" so that a change of heart could occur. This was revealed in the case of the incestuous man by his obvious "sorrow". He grieved because he was separated from the ecclesia; and because his sin placed a barrier between himself and God. He grieved for the sorrow he caused in others, and for his former associations which were now removed from him, as if by death.

There was no boasting now; he was not puffed up, and nor were other members in the ecclesia (cp. 1 Corinthians 5:2,6). All these were signs of deep remorse and contrition, and must have been evident to everybody. If none of these effects were apparent, the brother would have to remain isolated from the ecclesia until he showed remorse, leading to full confession of his sin, and seeking for forgiveness.

In Corinth, this point had been reached, but it was not being acknowledged by the ecclesia. There was the distinct danger that the man would be "swallowed up with overmuch sorrow" (2 Corinthians 2:7). There is a striking echo here of the rebellion of Korah, Dathan and Abiram and their removal from the camp of Israel: "The earth opened and swallowed up Dathan, and covered the company of Abiram" (Psalm 106:17). God's justice did not allow the innocent to be destroyed, so we read that: "Notwithstanding [the destruction that fell on their father and his companions] the children of Korah did not die" (Numbers 26:11).

Satan's Devices

They were not swallowed up, because God showed them mercy. And the man in Corinth was not to be swallowed up, because, in mercy, "God is faithful and just to forgive us our sins". Yet there was a very real danger that, having delivered the man to Satan "for the destruction of the flesh", by their failure to acknowledge its destruction, the ecclesia could create conditions that would send him back headlong into his old ways.

In calling on the Corinthians to restore the erring brother and recognise his contrition, the apostle spoke of the danger of the man falling back again into sin. He warned them to act: "Lest Satan should take advantage of us: for we are not ignorant of his devices" (2 Corinthians 2:11). It is therefore possible for us to put a brother or sister in the way of temptation, by failing to act at the right time.

It must therefore be acknowledged that, save for the sin against the Holy Spirit, there is a way back for every brother or sister who has sinned – however grievous their sin. If this was not true, what hope does the gospel hold for anyone? "For all have sinned, and fall short of the glory of God" (Romans 3:23).

There, but for the grace of God ...

Nor must ecclesial action ever give the impression of superiority or false holiness. No-one rejoices when it proves necessary to withdraw fellowship because of grievous sin, for there, but for the grace of God, we all go. Under the law that is at work in every child of Adam, sin is shown to be exceeding sinful (Romans 7:13). Any situation of moral imperfection arising in the ecclesia should remind all members of their own imperfections and need for forgiveness. Who knows, there may be within others too such a hold on a particular or besetting sin, that only deliverance to Satan will loosen their grip. If we are not, on a daily basis, being washed by the pure water of the word of God, sin will become an inherent part of our lives, until eventually we become swallowed up by it as surely as the rebels in the wilderness.

For this reason, towards the end of the section in his letter about how the Corinthian ecclesia was weighed down by worldly pressures, the Apostle Paul issued a stark warning: "Wherefore let him who thinks he stands take heed lest he fall" (1 Corinthians 10:12).

The incestuous man had fallen, by indulging in a sin that was "not even named among the Gentiles" (5:1). By their initial failure to act, the members of the ecclesia had nearly fallen too. And if they had subsequently failed to acknowledge the man's repentance, it was possible that both he and they could fall once more.

Stablish, Strengthen, Settle

The message is stark and clear: "Be sober, be vigilant; because your adversary the devil, walks about like a roaring lion, seeking whom he may devour" (1 Peter 5:8). Only at our peril do we ignore the problems caused by sin, for they will remain with us throughout our lives: "But may the God of all grace, who called us to his eternal glory by Christ Jesus, after you have suffered a while, perfect, stablish, strengthen, and settle you" (verse 10).

Because this is the hope held out to all faithful disciples, it is incumbent on us now to put the same process into effect when issues arise within the ecclesia. The end of the story in Corinth has not been recorded. There is little doubt that the ecclesia acted on the apostle's advice and restored the man. And there is also little doubt that, because of his contrite and remorseful response, the ecclesia's action achieved its objective. He saw much more clearly what sin does to a believer's relationship with God, and through the support offered to him, he was stablished, strengthened and settled in the faith.

9

DO YOU NOT KNOW?

FROM the way Paul starts 1 Corinthians 6, it is apparent that some in the ecclesia were suggesting that Gentile law courts could settle their disputes. The particular issues he had in mind involved disputes between brethren, not cases where unbelievers were involved – for they would not recognise the jurisdiction of the ecclesia*. It is not clear if the case of the incestuous man fell into this category, even though the overall subject of not properly addressing serious moral issues continues from the previous chapter. But, in any case, that was just an example of the Corinthians' laxity. There was insufficient separation to the things of God, and too much involvement with the concerns of the world; the apostle was seriously concerned about the ecclesia's relationship with general society in Corinth.

This lack of separation was particularly apparent in the failure to address issues falling within the ecclesia's direct control. So the apostle with strong irony asks how they dare place such matters before Gentile courts. This was effectively denying the promise that the saints will rule the nations with the Lord when he returns. Were the Corinthians ignorant of passages like Daniel 7:22: "the Ancient of days came, and judgment was made in favour of the saints of the most High; and the time came for the saints to possess the kingdom"? Had no-one told them the Lord's message to his disciples: "Assuredly I say to you, that

---

* Though the passage speaks specifically of disputes between brethren, and not of those between a brother and an unbeliever, many believe that the principle in 1 Corinthians 6:7 applies in both cases: "Why do you not rather accept wrong? Why do you not rather let yourselves be cheated?"

in the regeneration, when the Son of Man sits on the throne of his glory, you who have followed me will also sit on twelve thrones, judging the twelve tribes of Israel" (Matthew 19:28)?

"We shall judge angels"

Compared with the big issues that will need to be settled when the kingdom is being established, the matters being turned over to Gentile courts by the Corinthian brethren and sisters were minuscule, however serious they may appear in isolation. To stress this point, Paul explains that there was another aspect of the kingdom they were ignoring. He asked, "Do you not know that we shall judge angels?" (1 Corinthians 6:3).

He was referring to other passages about the work of the saints in the millennium, and specifically to Psalm 149, which speaks of the saints executing "vengeance on the nations, and punishments on the peoples; to bind their kings with chains, and their nobles with fetters of iron; to execute upon them the written judgment" (Psalm 149:7-9). When the saints judge the world in the future age, even Gentile rulers will come under their jurisdiction – the same powers to whom the Corinthians were presently deferring in cases of dispute between brethren.

There should be no surprise that Paul refers to these Gentile rulers as "angels". He uses similar terminology in Romans 13 when talking about "the powers that be"; calling them "ministers of God" (Romans 13:4), just as the heavenly angels are sent "to minister for those who will inherit salvation" (Hebrews 1:14).

The essence of his message is that ecclesial life brings before us many difficult situations to test how we respond. Do we apply the mind of the flesh or the mind of the spirit? Are we motivated by the spirit of this world, or by the spirit of Christ? Ecclesial life thus becomes the training ground for the life we hope to live with the Lord when he comes. In that day, we shall be pleased to work under his direction; but it is a denial of that hope if his directions are ignored today, and matters are left to human courts and worldly laws.

To press home his argument, Paul uses an ironic figure. He asks if the Corinthians would ever consider placing these difficult issues before "those who are least esteemed by the church to judge" (1 Corinthians 6:4)*. The question is answered as soon as it is spoken. No ecclesia would leave such matters in the hands of those who are least equipped to handle them. But that was exactly what they were doing when cases were being taken to Gentile courts.

Why Not Suffer Wrong?

If it was true that human courts did not provide the best judges, we must ask why the Corinthians were taking their complaints there. The true reason is revealed in Paul's appeal: "Why do you not rather accept wrong? Why do you not rather let yourselves be cheated?" (1 Corinthians 6:7). This suggests that disputes were being taken to the law courts with the express purpose of obtaining redress and a pecuniary advantage. The courts would impose penalties, and their losses may be restored. This was completely contrary to the Lord Jesus' advice: "If any one wants to take away your tunic, let him have your cloke also" (Matthew 5:40). By going to law, they were actually inflicting wrong, instead of suffering wrong.

This leads Paul to give a long list of acts of unrighteous behaviour, which, if they are continued, will bar a person from God's kingdom. The list starts with "fornicators" (like the incestuous man), and ends with "extortioners", like those who sought redress over their brethren in Gentile courts (1 Corinthians 6:9,10). In between are other sins which deny the message of truth preached by Jesus and the apostles. Unrighteous behaviour like this was characteristic of the former way of life of the members of the Corinthian ecclesia: "Such were some of you. But you were washed, but you were sanctified, but you were justified in the name of the Lord Jesus and by the Spirit of our God" (verse 11).

---

* This is the sense of 1 Corinthians 6:4, NKJV, RSV. Other versions suggest that the Corinthians would be better letting the least esteemed in the ecclesia settle their disputes.

They were washed when they were baptized; sanctified, or set apart to live a holy life; and justified by faith in Christ Jesus, because of the cleansing power of the word of God that was preached to them.

This separation from worldly things was not apparent in practice, and the apostle turns to a comment from his correspondence (in advance of dealing with any of the specific issues raised by the Corinthians). They had written with some pride, it seems, quoting his own words back to him. "All things are lawful", he had said, presumably referring to the Mosaic Law. But this statement was now misapplied. They gave it a universal application, as if Paul was advocating complete license. It seems also as if Paul had written about the question of whether some foods ought to be refused on grounds of conscience (a subject requiring more extensive treatment than the short passage in this chapter, and Paul returns to it in chapter 8). In this reply it is helpful to recognise the dialogue involved. By extending the apostle's comment on law, the Corinthians were justifying fornication. He had to point out that this was returning to the slavery of sin, whereas they should be the Lord's servants: "the body is ... for the Lord, and the Lord for the body"*.

Their Letter	*Paul's reply*
All things are lawful	But all things are not helpful (or profitable)
All things are lawful	I will not be brought under (enslaved by) the power of any
Foods for the stomach	But God will destroy both it and them
(i.e., bodily lusts can be satisfied)	The body is not for sexual immorality but for the Lord

---

* The equation 'body = slave' appears in a number of places in the New Testament. Most notably it is used by the apostle in Hebrews, where he cites Psalm 40:6, "My ears you have opened", talking of the slave who chooses to serve his master "for ever" (Exodus 21:6). In Hebrews, this phrase is recast to express the complete devotion of a loving servant, "Therefore, when He came into the world, He said: "a body you have prepared for me" (Hebrews 10:5).

"Present your bodies"

As faithful servants, Christ's disciples are waiting to present themselves to him, as to their Lord returning from his long journey to receive a kingdom. Nor does it matter if they fall asleep before he comes, for "God both raised up the Lord and will also raise us up by His power" (1 Corinthians 6:14). If they truly believed in bodily resurrection and in the promise that God wishes to live in His people, they must heed the apostle's appeal to the Roman ecclesia: "Present your bodies a living sacrifice, holy, acceptable to God, which is your reasonable service" (Romans 12:1). An understanding of the life promised in the kingdom must have an effect on daily life now.

They could not ignore the effects of discipleship on everyday life. As "members of Christ" they were part of his mystical body; how could they defile his body by joining with a harlot? God's pronouncement about marriage when He provided Eve as Adam's companion should show them the folly of fornication: "for 'the two,' He says, 'shall become one flesh'" (1 Corinthians 6:16). Implicit in this message was the "great mystery" of which Paul spoke to the Ephesian ecclesia, "concerning Christ and the church" (Ephesians 5:32). This is a much higher union than the joining of two fleshly bodies, for "he who is joined to the Lord is one spirit with him" (1 Corinthians 6:17).

Flee Away

The rampant immorality that was so common in Corinth, and which is equally pervasive today must be completely shunned. Paul tells the Corinthians to run for their lives: "Flee sexual immorality" (verse 18). The great scriptural example is the young man Joseph when he was being enticed by Potiphar's wife. His urgency to remove himself completely from the situation was marked when "he left his garment in her hand, and fled and ran outside" (Genesis 39:12).

As well as the urgency of the apostolic command to run away from immorality, the use of the present imperative indicates that fleeing from temptation must become habitual. Unless this attitude is a daily practice, a moment of weakness or a particularly strong temptation will result in disaster.

The importance of this advice for today reinforces its relevance for the Corinthians. For we, like them, are surrounded by sexual immorality in words and illustrations, as well as in reality. The prevalence of sexually suggestive material can easily weaken our realisation of the abhorrence such images should evoke in the minds of the Lord's disciples. With so many unrighteous displays around them, even faithful disciples can become immune to their underlying intentions.

The seriousness of fornication is therefore stressed by Paul: "Every sin that a man does is outside the body, but he who commits sexual immorality sins against his own body" (1 Corinthians 6:18). The first part of this sentence may well be a further quotation by the Corinthians: "All things are lawful ... Every sin that a man does is outside the body". Both of these thoughts are part of the false Greek suggestion that the body can do anything with impunity because it is to be discarded. Paul has already spoken about the importance of the relationship between a believer and Christ, and how this must be reflected in daily life, and has still more to say on the subject; but at this stage he simply and categorically dismisses the theory being promoted in Corinth: "he who commits sexual immorality sins against his own body".

While Paul is speaking primarily about how sexual sins are physical and therefore positively harmful to the physical body, his comment also relates to the damage caused to the Christ-body of which believers are individually members. This is not to say that immorality is the most serious of sins, for it is impossible to categorise sins, though we are often tempted to treat some more seriously than others. Nor is he saying that sexual sins are uniquely "against the body". Other sins, such as gluttony and drunkenness also affect the body and seek to separate the sinner from the union he has with the body of Christ.

Sexual immorality is the outcome of an internal carnal appetite, and involves the body in its execution. To engage in such sins without remorse indicated the Corinthians' failure to appreciate the true nature of their relationship with God through Christ. Paul is once again amazed at the ignorance of some members of the ecclesia in Corinth. On six separate occasions in 1 Corinthians 6, he has to say "Do you not know ...?" (verses 2,3,9,15,16,19). This last occasion introduces the culmination of his argument about the serious consequences of the problems caused by the sexual immorality in Corinth: "Do you not know that your body is the temple of the Holy Spirit ... you are not your own?"

The Temple of God

He has spoken previously about God's temple, noting that the ecclesia is "the temple of God and that the Spirit of God dwells in you?" (1 Corinthians 3:16). But the ecclesia is made up of individual members, and he now speaks of the body of each separate brother and sister: "Do you not know that your body (singular) is the temple of the Holy Spirit?" (6:19). God chose to dwell among His wilderness people in the Tabernacle, and with His nation by His presence in the Temple. Now, through Christ, He dwells individually and communally in His people. The Corinthians were "the temple of God", because God's spirit was in them by virtue of the moral excellencies they embraced at their baptism. They were therefore not their own: "For you were bought at a price" (verse 20). That price was "the precious blood of Christ, as of a lamb without blemish and without spot" (1 Peter 1:19). The only response true believers can make is to "glorify God in your body".

10

MARRIAGE QUESTIONS

FROM the first six chapters of 1 Corinthians, characterised by the apostle's repeated comment, "Do you not know?", we now move to the next section (chapters 7-11) with its key phrase, "We all have knowledge". We also move from the section where Paul deals with issues reported to him "by those of Chloe's household" (1 Corinthians 1:11), to the next which deals with "the things of which you wrote to me" (7:1).

Affairs in the ecclesia since Paul's departure displayed a lamentable ignorance of the basic principles that should guide the life of these believers in Christ. Against this background, the claim that "we all have knowledge" rings very thin. Their complacency was about to be exposed by Paul as he considered the questions they raised with him.

These questions fall into four main areas: marriage and related matters; meat offered to idols; conduct of ecclesial meetings; and teaching about the resurrection. On each of these subjects, the Corinthians asked a series of questions, and these have to be deduced in some cases from the apostle's answer, much as if one was listening to one side of a phone conversation.

Questions About Marriage

On the subject of marriage, there were three main questions troubling the ecclesia:

- Is marriage a desirable thing?

- If one partner is an unbeliever, should the marriage be dissolved?

- Should virgins marry?

Against the background of rampant immorality in Corinth, it is understandable that a view had developed in the ecclesia that "It is good for a man not to touch a woman" (1 Corinthians 7:1). This is probably a direct quotation from the Corinthians' letter to Paul, and at first it seems that he concurred with their view. Indeed there are a number of places within this chapter where he indicates the advantages of remaining single (see verses 7, 8, 11, 26, 27, 32-36).

However preferable it may be to remain alone, Paul was aware of the human need for companionship (cp. Genesis 2:18). "Nevertheless", he therefore writes, "because of sexual immorality, let each man have his own wife, and let each woman have her own husband" (7:2). The Corinthians ought to know from the society in which they lived the power of sexual attraction. This took on perverted forms in the city of Corinth, and these perversions were to be avoided at all costs by the members of the ecclesia. In the divinely appointed relationship between a man and a woman, sexual desires had their proper and natural outlet. So, however desirable it may seem for other reasons "for a man not to touch a woman", the very immorality of Corinth proved that faithfulness in marriage was much more desirable. Paul showed that promiscuity was incompatible with the behaviour required of those who were joined to the Lord, and that marriage is the only acceptable outlet for human sexuality.

Marriage is Honourable in All

Compared to the perversions being practised in Corinth, marriage is based on the selflessness of both partners. Their ruling motive must be a true regard for each other, something that never entered into the immoral society in Corinth: "Let the husband render to his wife the affection due her, and likewise also the wife to her husband" (7:3). A few chapters later, the apostle again stresses the complementary nature and mutual responsibilities of marriage when he says: "Neither is man independent of woman, nor woman independent of man, in the Lord" (11:11).

The apostle chose to remain single himself, but he does not expect that all will wish to be the same, nor is he ignorant of the difficulties created by the degraded morality so evident in Corinth. By saying that each man should have "*his own* wife", and each woman "*her own* husband", it is clear that the apostle was supporting monogamy; yet at the same time his comments about the advantages of remaining single show that he was not advocating that *every* man and *every* woman should be married. In this, he was departing from the Jewish belief that all men should be married, without also forsaking the view that as a God-ordained relationship marriage has special benefits for both husband and wife (see Hebrews 13:4).

By comparison with the flagrant immorality in Corinth, Paul speaks very tenderly about the physical relationship between man and wife, for neither of them has the right to make selfish demands: "The wife does not have authority over her own body, but the husband does. And likewise the husband does not have authority over his own body, but the wife does" (7:4).

The Corinthians probably supported their view that "It is good for a man not to touch a woman", by saying that marriage distracts from the spiritual life they were trying to follow. Paul recognises that there may be occasions when it is necessary to concentrate on intercourse with God in prayer. As human relationships with Him supersede all others, it is not wrong on those occasions to refrain from human intercourse. But he regards this as something exceptional. Man and wife belong so completely to each other that to "deprive one another except with consent for a time" must be regarded as a fraudulent act.

"I say this as a concession"

By commenting that he says this "as a concession, not as a commandment" (7:6), Paul was making it abundantly clear that, within marriage, individuals must make their own decisions based on Godly principles. The Corinthians were trying to lay down strict rules of celibacy or abstinence, and he would not be drawn into being equally dogmatic about exactly how individuals should honour the Lord in their relationships with each other.

He uses his own situation to confirm the advice he has given. Paul had learned the advantages of being single, and was able to "exercise self-control"; he was not tempted by the freedoms of the surrounding society. Yet it is very unlikely that he was never married. As we have already noted, the Jews required men to marry and beget children, and membership of the Sanhedrin was open only to those who were married (cp. Acts 26:10). Paul was therefore either a widower, or perhaps his wife left him when he put on Christ. In either case his later comments about those who are left alone have an extra poignancy when we appreciate his own situation.

Despite his personal example of self-control, Paul is careful not to suggest that everyone must act in the same way: "I wish that all men were even as I myself. But each one has his own gift from God, one in this manner and another in that" (1 Corinthians 7:7).

What Should the Unmarried Do?

Recognising, therefore, that there will be different outcomes from the application of his advice, Paul now speaks about some specific situations. First he considers the unmarried and the widows. Their situation was like his; they were on their own, and his personal experience led him to advise them to remain on their own. But in line with his comments on the general question about marriage, he recognises the pressures they may be under: "if they cannot exercise self-control, let them marry. For it is better to marry than to burn with passion" (7:9).

Turning to those believers who are married*, he starts with the Lord's command: "A wife is not to depart from her husband … and a husband is not to divorce his wife" (7:10,11 cp. Matthew 5:32; 19:3-6; Mark 10:2-12).

---

* As a later section of the chapter looks at cases where only one partner is a believer, the Apostle is here talking of marriages where both partners are believers.

Recognising, however, that situations may arise that result in separation and the breaking of the marriage bond, he says: "but even if she does depart, let her remain unmarried or be reconciled to her husband" (verse 11). Paul is dealing with the overall principles, and does not here discuss the questions of whether there are any grounds for divorce where remarriage is permissible.

Throughout 1 Corinthians 7, Paul confirms the Lord Jesus' teaching about marriage. Acknowledging that there were aspects that did not figure in the Lord's words, Paul's observations were nevertheless inspired, and were the advice that Jesus would have given in those circumstances. It is in this sense that we must understand his comment: "But to the rest I, not the Lord, say ..." (verse 12).

Those With Unbelieving Partners

By referring to "the rest", he was addressing comments to those in the ecclesia whom he has not already described. He has spoken to "the unmarried and widows" (verse 8) and to "the married", where both parties are believers (verse 10). Now he has comments for brethren and sisters whose spouses have not accepted the gospel.

Some of the Corinthians' questions must have arisen because of the special conditions in the newly-formed ecclesia. There would be many whose partners did not accept the truth, and who wondered if the intimate relationship of marriage was still appropriate in their new situation. These feelings would be reinforced by the teaching implicit in a later comment by the apostle about widows remarrying, that marriage should be "only in the Lord" (verse 39). This was a matter of very real concern and Paul did not dismiss it lightly.

It all depended, he said, on the attitude of the unbelieving partners; if they were "willing to live" with a husband or wife whose life had taken a new direction, and who now served and honoured Christ, then the believing partner must not separate from or divorce the unbeliever (verses 12,13). One of the reasons for the Corinthians' enquiry was their concern for the children of such marriages. What was their relationship to the things of God? How did they stand in His sight? Was there any difference between them and the child who had two believing parents?

Paul's answer has given rise to many strange views suggesting some form of substitutionary sanctification, whereby a person's position before God is determined by the faith of their marriage partner or parent. This view is specifically rejected by other passages, most notably in Ezekiel 18 and the teaching that "the soul who sins shall die" (verse 4).

The language Paul uses leads back to passages in the Old Testament that help explain the meaning of this difficult section. "Sanctification" and "holiness" are themes of Leviticus, where the impact of godly service upon families is also discussed. Under the law of Moses, priests were to select their wives carefully, not choosing anyone who was "defiled" (Leviticus 21:7). Equally, their children were not to bring shame on the family, otherwise they were not allowed to share in the "holy things" – sacrificial portions that became meals for the priests (22:10-16).

The teaching under the law was clear. Despite the great responsibilities of priestly service before God, enormous privileges resulted from the work, both for the priests themselves and for their families who benefited from the sanctifying work.

Will God Recognise These Marriages?

This Old Testament background helps resolve the difficulties that exist in the passage, where Paul was effectively answering the Corinthians' question, Will God recognise the marriage of a believer to an unbeliever? Is it, in fact, a marriage? The answer clearly has implications for any children of the marriage. If their parents' marriage is not recognised by God, they are no better than pagans and infidels.

The apostle's comments explain a lot about marriage itself, and why he did not fully concur with the Corinthians' premise that "It is good for a man not to touch a woman".

Because marriage was originally ordained by God, anyone entering into marriage is introduced to the possibility of appreciating its underlying teaching, "concerning Christ and the church" (Ephesians 5:32). This is particularly true when one partner learns and accepts the gospel. For the believer, marriage is viewed as a practical and daily expression of the desire to be united to Christ; and the unbelieving partner will undoubtedly benefit from an approach that honours and practices true Christlike principles.

The marriage, and therefore the unbelieving partner too, is no longer associated completely with worldly things, but is separated to the things of God. This is why Paul talks about them being "sanctified", which does not refer primarily to any moral character, but about a person's standing in relation to the things of God. In the same way the children of these 'mixed marriages' are reckoned as "holy", because they are brought into the ambit of Godly things through their believing parent.

It is apparent that the apostle focuses on the situation of the children to explain why God does not refuse to recognise a marriage between a believer and an unbeliever; and it is possible that such marriages were being treated by some in Corinth as vastly inferior to marriages between two believers. 'Think of the children', he says, 'and of their position, before you condemn a brother or sister who is married to an unbeliever'. This teaching is becoming important again as twenty-first century society takes on increasingly the character of the first century. It is very easy to give the impression that brethren and sisters whose partners are not in the Truth, or who have been left to bring up families on their own are second-class Christadelphians. This passage in Corinthians should cause us to reflect very carefully before making any suggestions of that nature.

Let the Unbeliever Depart

Paramount in all this is the unbelieving partner's attitude to the marriage following the husband or wife's acceptance of the truth. What the apostle has written thus far assumes that the unbelieving partner is "willing to live" under these new conditions. But, what is the brother or sister to do if their unbelieving partner is not willing, and leaves them? Must they consider themselves to be still married to the unbeliever? In this, Paul is categoric. He appreciates that acceptance of the truth by one partner could place unbearable strains on the marriage; and while he counsels brothers and sisters not to initiate a separation, and to do everything they can to keep the marriage together ("For how do you know, O wife, whether you will save your husband? Or how do you know, O husband, whether you will save your wife?" – 1 Corinthians 7:16), he recognises they can do little to stop the unbeliever leaving: "if the unbeliever departs, let him depart; a brother or a sister is not under bondage in such cases" (verse 15).

This advice about what a brother or sister should do when an unbelieving partner will no longer live with them was of a very special nature. The apostle did not want the advice to be applied to other situations; only to cases where an unbelieving partner deserts the marriage. Before continuing to answer the Corinthians' questions about marriage, he therefore digresses to talk about the important principle of remaining in the state in which one was called.

11

REMAIN IN YOUR CALLING

IN the previous chapter, we considered Paul's teaching about marriage, as he set about answering the questions raised with him by the ecclesia at Corinth. The main points were as follows:

- marriage was ordained by God and provides many benefits, especially where immorality is ingrained in society

- there are mutual responsibilities in marriage that should only be suspended for short periods of time, and then only so that greater devotion can be directed to God

- those who are unmarried or widows are advised to remain in that state unless they are sorely tempted – marriage is always preferable to immorality

- married believers are to treat their marriages as inviolable – if they do separate, they are not free to marry anyone else*

- believing husbands or wives must try to live the principles of the truth within marriage, in the hope that their unbelieving partners may be saved

- their marriages are recognised by God, and their children are also acknowledged by Him

- if an unbelieving partner leaves a believing wife or husband, the believing partner is no longer bound by the marriage.

---

* As Paul has already referred to Jesus' commands about marriage, here he also confirms Jesus' teaching about divorce, without entering into the one ground the Lord mentioned where a divorce of believers does not lead to adultery.

"Remain in the same calling"

Paul broke off part way through his answers to these questions about marriage to establish a principle that can be applied in many different circumstances. Corinth was a bustling and cosmopolitan city, and the new members of the ecclesia had a variety of different backgrounds. "Brethren", Paul wrote, "Let each one remain with God in the same calling (the same state, verse 24) in which he was called" (7:20).

This confirms that his teaching about what to do when an unbelieving partner departs is unusual. These were special circumstances, and they were particularly relevant in Corinth where there must have been many in the ecclesia whose spouses did not convert to Christianity. Furthermore, the general society in Corinth was extremely adverse to life in the Truth, as we shall see when we come to consider questions about eating meat offered in sacrifice to idols. Husbands and wives who did not share the same religious beliefs would have very few points of contact. As Paul wrote in 2 Corinthians 6:14, they were "unequally yoked together", and this explains why in such circumstances the general rule of remaining in that state in which each was called need not always apply.

But in other matters the principle should be upheld. On questions of circumcision, the apostles in Jerusalem had made the position plain when they agreed that Gentile converts need not submit to this Jewish rite: "Was anyone called while uncircumcised? Let him not be circumcised" (7:18, cp. Acts 15:24-29). Some were baptized when they were slaves, and Paul gave the same advice to them: "Were you called while a slave? Do not be concerned about it; but if you can be made free, rather use it" (1 Corinthians 7:21).

Legacy of Life Before Baptism

Circumcision and slavery were commonplace problems in first century Corinth, but they do not trouble ecclesias today. However, the underlying principle is very important when we realise that a new convert always brings with him some legacy of his former life. If this conflicts with the highest principles of the truth, he should try to remove them; but if he can't, he should take courage from the fact that, even "he who is called in the Lord while a slave is the Lord's freedman" (7:22), and service for Christ can overcome all worldly barriers.

Paul applied this principle of remaining in the state in which one is called to answer one of the Corinthians' written questions, "concerning virgins". The Lord Jesus did not make any specific comment on this subject, but Paul feels able to "give judgement as one whom the Lord in His mercy has made trustworthy" (7:25). Here is a situation where once again the special difficulties of the day imposed restraints. There was a "special distress" that affected the Corinthians. We do not know exactly what this was, and various suggestions have been made. Some believe Paul was referring to the nearness of Christ's return; others that the impending destruction of Jerusalem was in his mind; and yet others that there were particular local difficulties in Corinth that demanded the single-minded attention of every ecclesial member.

But whatever the nature of this "distress", it caused Paul to apply the general principle of abiding in the state in which one was called to the question about virgins: "it is good for a man to remain as he is" (7:26). However, in just the same way as he upheld the state of marriage when he answered the Corinthians' statement "it is good for a man not to touch a woman" (7:1),* he immediately explains that: "even if you do marry, you have not sinned; and if a virgin marries, she has not sinned" (verse 28).

Aspects to be Taken into Account

There were various factors involved, and some of these conflicted. All were to be considered before a decision was taken about marrying. First, there was the question of "the present distress", as we have already noted. Secondly, marriage brings special responsibilities, and sometimes "trouble in the flesh". No-one should enter into marriage with the romantic thought that it will always be a bed of roses. Thirdly, the advantages for a disciple of Christ of the single life must never be overlooked; someone who is unmarried has much greater liberty for service: "He who is

---

* Note the similarity of wording between 7:1 and 7:26. Were both these statements originally made by the Corinthians?

unmarried cares for the things of the Lord – how he may please the Lord. But he who is married cares about the things of the world – how he may please his wife" (7:32,33). Fourthly, consideration must be given to the personal and individual circumstances of those who are involved; no two cases are ever identical.

The apostle seems to be thinking of a specific case, where a father was forbidding his daughter to marry*. He may have acted in the past on the basis that celibacy is demanded of Christian believers; but now that Paul has shown how this view is not correct, he will realise that he was probably "behaving improperly toward his virgin, if she is past the flower of youth".

Paul appreciated the strain this could place on the young couple, as he did earlier in his comments about the strength of sexual attraction. He therefore introduces an additional factor. The father may have been behaving improperly in refusing permission for the marriage because he was misguided about celibacy, but he could now argue that "the present distress" justified him in maintaining his opposition to the marriage. Paul says that he may also be failing to consider the needs of his daughter and the young man to whom she was promised. If "it must be (if passions are strong, RSV)", Paul says very delicately, "let him do what he wishes. He does not sin; let them marry" (7:36). This is a wonderful blend of principle and practical wisdom that is so much a feature of the apostle's response to the Corinthians' problems.

---

* Other suggestions have been made about 1 Corinthians 7:36-38. AV and NKJV are ambiguous and simply refer to "any man" and "his virgin" (i.e., either his daughter or his fiancée). RV speaks of "any man" and "his virgin *daughter*", to clarify the ambiguity. NIV and RSV go the other way, and take the view that the passage speaks of a young man who has to decide about marrying his fiancée ("the virgin he is engaged to").

One other suggestion finds favour with some commentators who believe the passage speaks of a couple entering into a 'spiritual marriage', with the prior agreement that there will be no physical union. In view of the apostle's comments earlier in the chapter (verses 3-5), this is a very unlikely alternative. Equally, it seems to be a practice that was unknown until almost 200 years after Christ.

The Single Disciple

We must note that Paul's celebrated support for the life of an unmarried disciple occurs in this connection. The Corinthians' mantra was repeated in slightly different forms, but always with the same intent: "It is good for a man not to touch a woman ... it is good for a man to remain as he is" (7:1, 26). On both occasions it was necessary for these statements to be qualified. The phrase "it is good ..." takes our minds back to Adam in the garden when God said: "It is not good that man should be alone" (Genesis 2:18). Because marriage is God-ordained to provide companionship for man who, generally speaking, is not good on his own, no-one can say categorically that "it is good for a man not to touch a woman".

To answer the Corinthians' misguided beliefs about celibacy, it was necessary for Paul to explain the benefits and responsibilities of marriage. But he has been equally careful not to give the impression that all believers must marry. That would go from one extreme to the other. So, just as he has shown the benefits of marriage, he now sets out the benefits of the single life, and the opportunities for unfettered service that it can provide. The Corinthians' attitude was too prescriptive: it sought to legislate and control the decisions of individual brethren and sisters. By contrast, Paul was specifically trying not to circumscribe their actions: "this I say for your own profit, not that I may put a leash on you" (1 Corinthians 7:35). Each man or woman had to assess the situation, and make decisions on the basis of Godly principles and their own conscience.

What About Widows?

This left one situation that was common in other parts of the ecclesial world, even if it was not yet common in Corinth. For completeness, Paul introduces it at the end of his section on marriage, though it is not clear whether he was responding to a specific question from the ecclesia.

Again, he starts with a general principle, which also appears in his letter to the Romans: "A wife is bound by law as long as her husband lives" (verse 39; Romans 7:2). Marriage, under both human and divine law, is a permanent arrangement, and not to be entered into lightly.

We can see in the earlier situations Paul has considered how strongly he supports the marriage bond, though he does recognise that believers are only bound into marriage so long as unbelieving partners are willing to continue living with them.

Equally, he now makes it plain that death ends the marriage. It seems that Paul has in view a marriage between two believers, for he speaks of the husband having fallen asleep (Greek, *koimao*, when used of death always refers to the death of believers). He may therefore have been answering a question from the ecclesia that looked forward to the kingdom age. Perhaps the Corinthians wondered if a sister could have two husbands in the kingdom. It is possible that a view had developed in Corinth about marriage that it is never terminated by any event, including the death of one of the partners.

Once again, Paul does not enter into any other reasons that could end a marriage, but equally his comments here cannot be used to deny that other reasons exist. As we know, the departure of an unbelieving partner ended a marriage with a believer (verse 15), and the Lord Jesus mentioned another reason – "sexual immorality" – when he was answering questions about marriage (Matthew 5:32; 19:9).

What About Widows Remarrying?

Paul's answer is both logical and practical; he refers to the law, and confirms that in this case the law faithfully reflects the true situation, that a marriage is terminated by the death of either the husband or the wife. If the "falling asleep" of a partner ended a marriage, another question arose: Did this mean that the widow (or widower) was free to remarry? The logic of Paul's answer is unassailable, "if her husband dies, she is at liberty to be married to whom she wishes, only in the Lord" (1 Corinthians 7:39). This is, of course, the practical effect when a marriage ends, and it was recognised by the law as Paul mentions. But more importantly, it was recognised by the Lord Jesus in his comments about marriage.

This "liberty", however, must not be taken as a command to remarry. All the previous arguments still apply: the general principle of remaining in the state in which one was called was difficult to apply when a death occurred; but the apostle felt that its application favoured a widow remaining unmarried, rather than seeking a second marriage (verse 40).

Elsewhere in his writings, however, he positively encouraged younger widows to remarry, in order to guard against giving "opportunity to the adversary to speak reproachfully" (1 Timothy 5:14). So, once again, individual circumstances had to be taken into account. Any remarriage must be subject to one proviso; it should be "only in the Lord".

And so Paul returns to where he started – marriage was first ordained by God, and for believers can only be between a man and a woman who both wish to reflect the gospel teaching about the Lord Jesus Christ and his Bride. He will write to the Corinthians in a later letter: "I am jealous for you with godly jealousy. For I have betrothed you to one husband, that I may present you as a chaste virgin to Christ" (2 Corinthians 11:2).

12

THINGS OFFERED TO IDOLS

THREE chapters in Paul's first letter to Corinth (chapters 8-10) are devoted to the subject of meats offered to idols. It was obviously a serious problem in this first century ecclesia, and most probably in others throughout the Roman world at that time. The difficulty is that idolatry, in the form that existed in the first century AD, is not practised today, making the apostle's comments seem meaningless and unimportant for twenty-first century disciples. Yet he writes in 1 Corinthians 10 that "all these things happened to them as examples, and they were written for *our* admonition, upon whom the ends of the ages have come" (verse 11). Unless we restrict these words to those who were living in the closing years of the Jewish age, they explain that the principles surrounding the offering of meat to idols are pertinent to believers in all generations.

But before applying the principles to the modern world, we need to understand the issues as they existed in Corinth. How could there possibly have been any doubt in the minds of the Corinthian brethren and sisters of the need to remain separate from pagan idolatry? Yet there were clearly some differing views about the extent of any involvement, and these views – in common with those on a range of other topics – were being contested by strong-minded individuals.

The Ecclesia's Questions

It will help if we can extract the basic issues, and therefore possibly also the specific questions raised with the apostle by the brethren and sisters in Corinth. They asked first of all about eating food that had been offered in sacrifice to idols when they were invited to a meal with an unbeliever; they asked also about eating actually in the idols' temples;

and then finally they asked about the meat sold in the city, most of which probably was associated with idolatry: would they be defiled by eating it? These questions help to explain why the issue was so difficult, and why there were deeply diverging views about how to react to the problem.

For Corinth, like so many other first century cities, was "wholly given over to idols" (Acts 17:16). This did not mean simply that all the worship was idol-based, but that idolatry was the basis of all aspects of daily life. The nearest we can come to understand the problem is to compare strongly religious countries today, where the involvement of the church, temple or mosque can be seen in every part of life: national and local government, the police and judiciary, hospitals, schools, businesses and commerce. It was the same in Corinth: brethren and sisters were faced with idolatry wherever they turned.

Social Life Centred on the Temple

In particular, social life in the city centred on the idols' temples. Archaeological evidence points to the existence of a consistent pattern. One excavated temple had three terraces: the lower one contained eating facilities, the middle one comprised a theatre, and the highest level was where the idols and images were displayed. "Worship" in idols' temples involved the sating of many fleshly desires, and did not normally comprise the formal and structured services we associate with the word today. Entertainment and feasting were intrinsic parts of idol worship. Those who attended brought their votive offerings, and then joined in many different activities. Immorality in many forms prospered in the temple precincts, and male and female prostitutes abounded.

Food offered to idols was divided into three portions. Some was consumed by fire on the altar; another portion was for the priest; and the remainder went to the offerer and was usually eaten in one of the dining rooms associated with the temple. Thus any social meal in the city was likely to be eaten in the temple courts, and the food was identified specifically with idol worship. The difficulty this created for new converts to Christianity was immense. If they separated themselves completely from everything that was linked to idolatry, their normal daily life would be turned upside down. Regular business was conducted over meals in temple dining rooms; all social gatherings were held there. Invitations to friends and relatives were extended in the name of the deity at whose temple the function was being held. It was a serious and extremely difficult problem, and they sought guidance from the apostle about it.

Knowledge Makes a Man look Big

But it seems as though their approach was strongly influenced by the two opposing groups: "We all have knowledge", was the opening line (1 Corinthians 8:1), and that knowledge led one group to the view "that an idol is nothing in the world, and that there is no other God but one" (verse 4). The conclusion was therefore simple. If there are no such things as idols, and if the images in the temples have no status because there is only one God, there can be no harm in eating in idols' temples! This is a classic case of self-justification, and it was immediately destroyed by Paul's reply, "Knowledge puffs up, but love edifies." J.B. Phillips' paraphrase of this is very graphic, and it captures the sense perfectly: "We should remember that while knowledge may make a man look big, it is only love that can make him grow to his full stature" (verse 1).

Knowledge leads quickly to arrogance and pride: both of these are qualities that elevate human thinking. Love, because it involves self-sacrifice and abasement, elevates God and His ways. This was a stinging rebuke for the group in Corinth who were claiming the right to continue their full social life in the city. What is more, the view promoted by this first group took no account of the effect their actions might have on fellow-believers. Once again, this is the difference between pride and love. Pride is a selfish attribute; "love suffers long and ... is not puffed up" (13:4).

Flee Idolatry

But there was another view held by an opposing group in the Corinthian ecclesia. They saw serious problems if meals were taken in idols' temples. Those engaging in the practice were closely identified with the idols, and surely this was not appropriate for brethren and sisters in Christ. There could hardly be two more different approaches to the problem, and Paul needed the wisdom of Solomon to resolve the difficulty.

Despite his comments about knowledge, the apostle confirmed all the information that led the first group to believe they could visit idols' temples. They were right in saying there is only one God, and idols are "nothing in the world". Furthermore, it was no longer possible to claim that the Jewish dietary laws prevented believers from partaking of temple food. The sacrifices were almost certainly unclean in the Mosaic sense, but these requirements were no longer in force for believers in Christ: "He who eats, eats to the Lord, for he gives God thanks; and he who does not eat, to the Lord he does not eat, and gives God thanks" (Romans 14:6).

Yet the issue of eating meat offered to idols was one that exercised the Jerusalem ecclesia once the gospel message was being accepted by Gentiles. The conclusion of the Jerusalem conference was aimed specifically at the problem of paganism and idolatry. Gentile converts were not to be asked to submit to circumcision and the precepts of the Law of Moses, but they were asked to "abstain from things offered to idols, from blood, from things strangled, and from sexual immorality" – all things that were characteristic of idol worship (Acts 15:29). The reason for this request was the conscience of Jewish believers. It was agreed that Gentile believers must not be asked to become Jews, but they were asked to make it abundantly clear that they were no longer pagans or idolaters.

"Shall the weak brother perish?"

The existence in Corinth of two divergent opinions on the subject shows that this was not simply a question of the Jewish conscience. There were Gentile believers in the city who felt compromised by attending at an idols' temple, or even by buying meat in the city markets which had probably been originally part of an idol sacrifice.

Just as the Apostle Paul confirmed that the information was correct that led some brethren and sisters to feel able to eat in idols' temples, he also confirmed the logic of those who thought differently: "For if anyone sees you who have knowledge eating in an idol's temple, will not the conscience of him who is weak be emboldened to eat those things offered to idols? And because of your knowledge shall the weak brother perish, for whom Christ died?" (1 Corinthians 8:10,11). Some were presumably claiming that the weak brethren and sisters should be encouraged to eat things offered to idols, and thus "build up" their weak consciences*. But what if they are built up only to be permanently destroyed? What is achieved by that?

Both parties could therefore take comfort from his words; but more was needed if the real issue was to be resolved. He therefore addressed them both individually. To those who claimed to be acting on the basis of their knowledge, he warned about the dangers of complacency: "Therefore let him who thinks he stands take heed lest he fall" (10:12). And to those who placed a greater emphasis on the possibility of troubling the consciences of other brethren and sisters, he said: "Therefore, my beloved, flee from idolatry" (1 Corinthians 10:14).

Love in Action

To support these two conclusions, Paul brought forward two examples: one based on his own experiences as an apostle, and the other from Israel's history. Applying 'knowledge' to his own situation, Paul concluded that he had certain rights as an apostle, that should be met by those to whom he ministered: the provision of food and drink, and travelling expenses for himself and a companion (see table facing). "If we have sown spiritual things for you, is it a great thing if we reap your material things?" (9:11). There were some who claimed these rights, and no-one should deny them, "For it is written in the law of Moses, 'You shall not muzzle an ox while it treads out the grain'" (9:9).

---

* "Emboldened" (Greek *oikodomeo*) in 1 Corinthians 8:10 is the same original word as "edifieth" in verse 1.

> **The Apostle's Right to Receive Material Support**
> (1 Corinthians 9:7-14)
> 1. In every day life, soldiers, farmers and shepherds all receive a reward for their toil.
> 2. The Law of Moses even rewarded the corn-treading oxen (Deuteronomy 25:4).
> 3. Ordinary gratitude should cause converts to support materially those who supplied them with spiritual blessings.
> 4. The apostles were more than spiritual teachers, they were their Fathers in Christ.
> 5. In the Temple arrangements, priests were provided with the necessities of daily life.
> 6. Jesus commanded that "a worker is worthy of his food" (Matthew 10:10).

Though others were claiming these rights, Paul never did: "When I preach the gospel, I present the gospel of Christ without charge, that I may not abuse my authority in the gospel" (verse 18). The objective was the winning of as many people as possible for Christ; he did not want to put a barrier in the way of any individual and prevent him or her coming to God: "I have become all things to all men, that I might by all means save some. Now this I do for the gospel's sake, that I may be partaker of it with you" (verses 22,23).

Here was an example of love in action, and not 'knowledge'. Paul was concerned for all, and he deliberately chose not to stand on his dignity: "For though I am free from all men, I have made myself a servant to all, that I might win the more ... I also please all men in all things, not seeking my own profit, but the profit of many, that they may be saved" (9:19; 10:33).

The Example of Israel

Lest his own example was insufficient, Paul then related the history of Israel in the wilderness. Like the Corinthians, they too were baptized and ate "spiritual meat" and drank "spiritual drink". Yet most of them perished in the wilderness because of their love of idolatry. They "sat down to eat and drink, and rose up to play" (10:7, quoting Exodus 32:6). This was the exact counterpart of life in Corinth, where eating at idols' temples led in most cases to extreme licentiousness and immorality.

The food and drink associated with believers in Christ is a potent force: "The cup of blessing which we bless, is it not the communion of the blood of Christ? The bread which we break, is it not the communion of the body of Christ?" (1 Corinthians 10:16). Far from being a dispassionate ritual, believers and their Saviour are wonderfully united. Brethren and sisters are made one both with the Lord Jesus Christ and with their fellow-believers: "for we, though many, are one bread and one body; for we all partake of that one bread" (verse 17).

Paul's message was clear. The question of food offered to idols may seem to be a question of very little moment, so "Eat whatever is sold in the meat market, asking no questions for conscience' sake" (verse 25). But everything connected with idolatry was extremely dangerous. With Israel, it led to the destruction of twenty-three thousand in one day, and "these things became our examples, to the intent that we should not lust after evil things as they also lusted" (verse 6).

Both these examples lead to the same conclusion, and lift the issue onto the highest possible plane. For the problem created by the idea of not harming the conscience of fellow-believers is that there will always be someone who may be offended by our actions. Blindly to follow this course would stifle almost all activity. Though the apostle is clearly sympathetic to this view, saying of himself that "if food makes my brother stumble, I will never again eat meat, lest I make my brother stumble" (8:13), he introduces an even higher principle.

The greatest test the Corinthians could apply to the questions they were asking was found in their relationship with the Lord Jesus Christ. Paul appealed to both parties, the "knowledge" party and the "conscience" party: "I speak as to wise men; judge for yourselves what I say" (verse 15). When they broke bread and drank wine in memory of the Lord's sacrifice they were "partakers" of the body and blood of Christ – of the Lord's table. Those who ate in idols' temples were partakers of the table of devils – *daimonion*, the Greek term used to describe the false gods, who it was claimed were the spirits of dead men and women. "You cannot", he said, "partake of the Lord's table and of the table of demons" (verse 21). This was an answer to both groups. Fellowship with Christ is the aim, and all issues must be determined on that basis. How would Christ act in these circumstances? What would *he* do? And what would his brethren and sisters do if he was in their company?

Applying the Principles

We should be deceiving ourselves if we thought these chapters do not apply to modern disciples. There may not be idols in the same sense as there were in the first century. But the issue was more to do with a believer's association with the world than strictly about idol worship or what to do about meat offered to idols. And in that context, the world is as pressing today as it ever was. There are a variety of different pursuits, many of them seemingly innocuous, that can attract believers and eventually draw us away from Christ. The principles applied by the apostle to the problems in Corinth are very pertinent to all these modern situations as well.

Eating in restaurants, attending concerts, engaging in sporting activities, being entertained by music, dance or drama – all these and many more may not offend an individual's conscience, but still contain the twin dangers mentioned in Paul's letter. Through our 'knowledge' or lack of sensitivity we may lead a brother or sister into situations that will eventually destroy their faith; or we may ourselves, in a moment of weakness, be drawn away from Christ.

The tests to be applied in each situation are simply stated, but not so easily answered. Before engaging in any activity in the world, it is worth asking the following questions, which are all derived from Paul's teaching:

- can I offer thanks beforehand, and thus commit what I am doing to God? (Romans 14:6)

- will it be edifying? (1 Corinthians 8:1)
- will it cause my brother or sister to stumble? (8:11)
- can I do it to the glory of God? (10:31)
- can I share it with my brethren and sisters as an act of fellowship? (10:21)
- would I do it if the Lord Jesus was with me?

The application of these questions, if faithfully under-taken, will determine how disciples will act in the many daily incidents where their standing in Christ is being tested.

13

HEADSHIP AND HEAD COVERINGS

MENTIONING the great contrast between fellowship in an idol's temple and fellowship around the Lord's table led the apostle to tackle some of the other issues that were troubling the ecclesia in Corinth. He had received reports about problems in their meetings, and especially at the breaking of bread: "when you come together in one place, it is not to eat the Lord's Supper. For in eating, each one takes his own supper ahead of others; and one is hungry and another is drunk" (1 Corinthians 11:20,21). There was also a problem relating to the sisters in the ecclesia, for the head coverings worn traditionally by Jewish women and by respectable Greek women too, were being discarded as part of a move for greater prominence. The deep divisions Paul abhorred at the beginning of his letter revealed themselves most particularly on the occasions when the ecclesia assembled, and when unity should be paramount. Human ambitions and tensions were confounding the fact that the ecclesia was God's, and that all its members were "sanctified in Jesus Christ" (1:2).

Paul therefore opened his comments about their meetings by reminding his readers of their great debt to God and to Christ, from whom their fellowship flowed. This was important as an answer to the brethren who were being divisive, and to the sisters who were seeking prominence: "I want you to know", he said, "that the head of every man is Christ, the head of woman is man, and the head of Christ is God" (verse 3). It is often suggested that this verse explains the divine hierarchy. But this is only partly true, and the suggestion may actually mask the underlying meaning. The apostle draws his lesson from the order that is apparent in creation, as he does also in a related passage, saying "Adam was first formed, then Eve" (1 Timothy 2:13). As the Lord

Jesus Christ is dependent on his Father in all things, so man is dependent on Christ in his spiritual life.

Further Information

Thus the apostle encouraged the Corinthians to "Imitate me, just as I also imitate Christ" (1 Corinthians 11:1 – the linking verse between chapters 10 and 11). When this great principle is forgotten troubles are bound to ensue, as they did in Corinth. Some of these troubles were occurring, it seems, despite what Paul wrote in his earlier communication. The ecclesia was trying to "keep the traditions just as I delivered them to you" (verse 2), but further explanation was necessary if they were to understand and implement fully what he had advised.

The difficulties flowed from the Corinthians' failure to appreciate fully the position of Christ, who was their head in supremacy and authority. This position was a consequence of the divine order, beginning with God, who is "from everlasting to everlasting" (Psalm 90:2). Then comes Christ, for "in the beginning was the word, and the word was with God" (John 1:1). Next in the purpose of God was man, made "in the image and likeness of God" (Genesis 1:26, AV); and finally, there was woman, taken from man's side to be his companion when no other was suitable (2:21,22). This order of generation then became the sequence or chain of divine authority. Ultimate authority resides with the Father, who has given to the Son "authority … in heaven and on earth" (Matthew 28:18). In the case of man and woman, man was expected to exercise delegated authority, and thus faithfully transmit God's commands to his companion, woman.

Headship in Family and Society

The relationship between Christ and the ecclesia was echoed in the dealings between man and woman, for just as Christ is the head of man* in the ecclesia, so man is the head of woman in the family and in society. Man is the head of woman: first, because Adam was made in "the image and glory of God", whereas woman in being made from man is

---

* Here *aner*, man, is used generically in the sense of 'mankind'. Elsewhere in the passage it relates to the brethren as males.

his (i.e., man's) glory (verse 7; Genesis 1:27; 2:23); secondly, this was emphasised to Eve after she and Adam sinned: "Your desire shall be for your husband, and *he shall rule over you*" (Genesis 3:16).

For practical purposes (though there were spiritual lessons involved too), God ordained that families should have a head – and under normal circumstances this is the man. A number of Bible passages support this conclusion, including the almost passing comment in Exodus 1:1: "These are the names of the children of Israel who came to Egypt; *each man and his household* came with Jacob." And in society too it was expected that the rulers and judges would be appointed from among the men. These elders were called "their *heads*" (Joshua 24:1).

As we have said, these provisions had a practical purpose: families and society have to be regulated. There needs to be order and a clear process of making decisions that will benefit all. Godly families and godly societies are ordered in accordance with God's word. Ultimately, He is the head of them both, but He has delegated that authority via His Son to the human heads of families and society.

God's Arrangement Challenged

In the first century ecclesia in Corinth, just as in twenty-first century Western society, this divinely ordained relationship between the sexes was being challenged. The equality between brethren and sisters in terms of salvation led some in Corinth to act as if the conventions of the day and the teachings in God's word no longer applied now that they were in Christ. The apostle's reply specifically mentioned therefore the two relationships they could not deny. All true believers accept that God is head over Christ, and that Christ is the head of the Ecclesia (or 'man'). The information that supports these conclusions must also be extended, Paul says, to the relationship between man and woman, and especially between brethren and sisters when they meet to worship.

Quite often, when this passage is being discussed, attention focuses only on the question of head coverings, forgetting that it is introduced by the clear statement about

THE CHALLENGE OF CORINTHIANS

the relationship between man and woman*. To deny that man is the head of the woman is to deny also that God is the head of Christ, and that Christ is the head of man. Another confusion sometimes introduced into this passage is the suggestion that it relates only to husband and wife, and not to man and woman generally. Now it is true that the original Greek words for "man" and "woman" (*aner* and *gune*) can also refer to husband and wife (as in Ephesians 5:33); but the meaning always depends on the context. So what about the context in Corinthians? Marriage questions were dealt with in an earlier chapter (1 Corinthians 7), and chapter 11 and the latter half of chapter 10 focus on ecclesial meetings. There is no doubt that in this context the words can only properly refer to "man" and "woman", not husband and wife**.

The apostle emphasised the divinely appointed order because it was being forsaken by an element in the Corinthian ecclesia. It is probable that some of the schismatic brethren were forgetting that God's authority has a clearly defined channel, which must not be over-turned. Paul therefore argued for their return to the principles of headship he described, and explained that this should also be shown outwardly by the proper use of head coverings.

Different Practices

Corinth was a cosmopolitan society, with Jews, Romans and Greeks, as well as members of other races. Each of these had their own customs and practices: among Jews, for example, the use of a head covering by wives was considered to be so important that a man could divorce his wife if she appeared bareheaded in a public place. Under the Law of Moses, a woman charged with unfaithfulness had to remove her head covering; if she was unfaithful, she had disgraced her "head" – her husband (Numbers 5:18). Among Greeks, both men and women worshipped with bare heads; while

* Note that "the head of woman is man" is placed centrally in 1 Corinthians 11:3, between the other two statements: "the head of every man is Christ", and "the head of Christ is God".

** Verse 12 cannot apply to husbands and wives. Men are born to women, but no husband was ever born to his own wife!

Romans – men and women – covered theirs when they worshipped. In general society, prostitutes went about bareheaded and respectable women were covered, whereas wealthy Greek women had elaborate and fashionable hairstyles to mark their status, causing the Apostle Peter to deplore the practice entering the ecclesial world (1 Peter 3:3). With this great variety of different traditions, none of which he endorses completely, it is clear that Paul was not simply referring to the customs of the day; there was more involved.

He starts by mentioning the brethren: "Every man praying or prophesying, having his [natural] head covered, dishonours his [spiritual] head (i.e., Christ)" (1 Corinthians 11:4). The brethren in the ecclesia, if they worshipped with covered heads, would be denying that God's authority was delegated to them by Christ, and would be seeking to impose their own authority over the ecclesia. There were groups in Corinth that wished to do this, and Paul sternly rebuked this dominant attitude.

He then turned to the sisters, and some of these were taking part in the ecclesial meetings. At this stage Paul does not give his opinion on that aspect of the problem; he leaves it to a later chapter*, confining his comments at this stage to the matter of dress and the relationship between sisters and brothers: "Every woman who prays or prophesies with her [natural] head uncovered dishonours her [spiritual] head (i.e., man)" (verse 5). For a woman to appear bareheaded at ecclesial meetings was the equivalent of arrogantly refusing to acknowledge the delegated headship of the brethren, and effectively also denying the 'chain' of delegated authority that begins with the Father. Paul is obviously concerned about the attitude of sisters seeking prominence in the ecclesial meetings, but it is apparent that the real problem lies with the denial of Christ's authority. He tries to show that this behaviour is unseemly by saying that the sisters might just as well

---

* 1 Corinthians 14:34,35, (see Chapter 17, page 131ff). However, we should note at this point that it is unreasonable to build an argument on Paul's comments in chapter 11, if the conclusion is not in accord with his comments in chapter 14.

appear shaven headed, a practice linked with idolatry and immorality. If it was shameful for the sisters' heads to be shaved, surely they could also realise how shameful it was for them to appear uncovered at ecclesial meetings.

It was important for the Corinthians, and also for ecclesias today, to realise that the practice Paul was advocating has a scriptural basis. He sets it out as follows:

"A man ought not to cover his head, since he is the image and glory of God";

"A woman [ought to cover her head, since she] is the glory of man" (verse 7).

The ecclesia is the house of God; His glory and not man's should be evident at all times. So man should appear bareheaded, for he was made in the image of God. Because woman is "the glory of man", man's glory must be covered in the assembly by her adoption of a head covering. There is no place in the ecclesia for human pride or authority.

When the practice of head coverings for sisters is questioned, it is usually on the basis that in Christ both men and women are equal. But it will be seen from Paul's comments that this is not the issue. He does not speak about equality or inequality between men and women, but about the differences between divine and human glory. God is elevated, he says, when both brethren and sisters seek only to reverence Him, and to subdue human pride. Brethren appearing bareheaded, and sisters covering their heads in communal worship are marks of these attitudes.

Because of the Angels

This is further confirmed in the case of sisters by the order of Creation, as we have seen. Because "woman (was created) for the man" (verse 9), sisters should symbolise their acknowledgement of this by covering man's glory. They should do this, "because of the angels" (verse 10). Various tortured explanations have been given of this phrase, including the suggestion that the angels' lustful thoughts must be prevented; that angels were present during communal worship; and that until the time when saints will judge angels, believers are under their jurisdiction. The most logical and satisfactory explanation, however, is that Paul was referring to the angelic decree to woman in Genesis: "Your desire shall be for your husband, and *he shall rule over you*" (3:16).

This decree arose because of the disobedience of Adam and Eve, and it raises a secondary – but no less important – aspect of the use of head coverings by sisters. Again, by divine arrangement, the relationship between man and woman in Christ is modelled on the one between Christ and the ecclesia (Ephesians 5:32). By this arrangement, sisters symbolise the ecclesia, and brethren symbolise Christ. When the sisters wear a head covering, the ecclesia as a whole (brethren *and* sisters) acknowledge that they are in need of a covering, and that that covering has been provided by the sacrifice of the Lord.

It seems as though it was recognised that the apostle's teaching about headship and head coverings might appear to validate the continued domination of women by men, and that even in ecclesial life brethren would seek to impose their will (as opposed to God's will) upon the sisters. So Paul continued immediately to correct this potential mis-application of Bible teaching. The divine channel of communication by means of devolved authority must not be abused by the brethren; nor must the sisters usurp it. Man needs the woman, as much as woman needs the man; neither can be viewed independently. This is true naturally, but also "in the Lord" man and woman are mutually necessary to each other. While Eve, the first woman, "came from man", all other men have "come through woman". As God ordained it, woman is the channel both of man's fall ("woman being deceived, fell into transgression", 1 Timothy 2:14), and of his rise again: for salvation comes by means of woman through the birth of the child Jesus. How can any brother say, therefore, that he does not need the woman? And how can any sister say that she does not need the Man?

Argument from Nature

To round off this section of his letter, Paul introduces two more reasons for his teaching. First he asks his readers to consider nature. As a general rule women have long hair, and men have short hair. Long hair is part of a woman's femininity*, but a man who has long hair loses his masculine appearance. This is a confusion of the sexes, and that has always been abhorrent with God (Deuteronomy 22:5). Lastly, Paul refers his readers to custom and practice: "If anyone seems to be contentious, we have no such custom, nor do the churches of God" (1 Corinthians 11:16). This comment is much more significant than may at first appear. The Apostle was never a traditionalist; when necessary, he challenged the way things were done if he felt there was no scriptural support (e.g., Galatians 2:11). But his comment also reveals that the instructions about head coverings were not limited to the specific problems in cosmopolitan Corinth. His teaching was being followed in other ecclesial centres; indeed the practice was consistent across the ecclesial world, and Corinth's problem was virtually unique.

Conclusions

Because so much has been written at different times on this subject, often with conflicting conclusions, it will be helpful to summarise the Bible teaching introduced by the apostle:

1. The divine order (God, Christ, Man, Woman) becomes the chain of delegated authority;
2. Man is the God-appointed head in the family, in society, and in the ecclesia;
3. In ecclesial life, all must be done to elevate the glory of God, and to suppress the glory of man;
4. Against the background of varying conventions in cosmopolitan Corinth, the apostle explains the Christian convention of head coverings, practised by all ecclesias in the first century;
5. This convention is based on scriptural principles, and on natural law;
6. The apostle reserved until later in his letter, any comment about sisters "praying or prophesying" in ecclesial gatherings.

---

* "Her hair is given her for a covering" (11:15), i.e., to adorn her. See use of same Greek word (*peribolaion*) in Hebrews 1:12, and Peter's comment, 1 Peter 3:3,4.

14

THE BREAKING OF BREAD

SOLEMN remembrance of Christ's sacrifice is the central focus of a believer's life. The privilege of meeting with others who share the same faith, in order to "proclaim the Lord's death till He comes" (1 Corinthians 11:26), should never be taken for granted. But in Corinth, from the reports he had received, Paul concluded that their memorial meetings were doing "more harm than good" (see verse 17, NIV). This was the ultimate disgrace.

Paul therefore issued "instructions" (NKJV, RSV) about the breaking of bread. He did not advise, or offer academic comments, but gave a "charge" (RV), a "declaration" (AV), a "directive" (NIV), about their future arrangements. But first of all, he specified the root cause of the problem: "I hear that there are divisions among you, and in part I believe it" (verse 18).

The deepest disgrace in the Corinthian ecclesia involved partisanship, envy and pride, and this impacted on the breaking of bread. Division and schism in an ecclesia will always manifest itself at the Lord's Table. A brother or sister may even choose to stay away, rather than eat and drink with one who has caused them some offence. In Corinth, the deep divisions that possibly carried over from the cosmopolitan nature of the surrounding society were flagrantly perpetuated, so that they were no longer eating the Lord's Supper, but their own.

First Be Reconciled

The root cause must be tackled; the disease, and not just the symptoms; and the apostle was following the Lord's advice in such matters, who said: "if you bring your gift to the altar, and there remember that your brother has something against you, leave your gift there before the altar, and go your way. First be reconciled to your brother, and then come and offer your gift" (Matthew 5:23,24). The problem in Corinth flowed from the divisions and factions in the ecclesia, and Paul had already given commands about them at the beginning of his letter. How individual brethren and sisters respond to such situations becomes an important test of their discipleship. When difficulties lead to intemperate behaviour, a person is shown in his or her true colours. Those who hold fast to God's word, and continue to act in a brotherly fashion towards all, are the ones that are "approved" – they are manifested as faithful ones.

As a whole, the ecclesia was not celebrating the Lord's Supper; each group was celebrating on its own. The almost unique use of the phrase "the Lord's" (Greek, *kyriakon*, only here and in Revelation 1:10) emphasises what Paul is about to declare to them. Because the meal is held at Christ's command – "This do ... in remembrance of me" (1 Corinthians 11:25) – they must be careful to follow his instructions, and not introduce their own arrangements. That they were celebrating something of their own arrangement, and not the Lord's Supper, was revealed by the chaotic circumstances reported to Paul: "in eating, each one takes his own supper ahead of others; and one is hungry and another is drunk" (verse 21).

The Love Feast

In those early days of the infant ecclesias, the remembrance of the Lord's sacrifice was accompanied by, or formed part of a larger meal: what Jude called "love feasts" (Jude 12). These started after Pentecost with all good intentions: "Breaking bread from house to house, they ate their food with gladness and simplicity of heart" (Acts 2:46). They also had "all things in common" (verse 44), sharing out as each had need. In Corinth as well as elsewhere, the richer brethren and sisters would provide most of the food to ensure everyone was catered for. But the possibility of corruption was very strong, and the original "simplicity" did not last long. Both Jude and Peter mention that the feasts were infiltrated by so-called brethren who were "serving only themselves", and "carousing in their own deceptions" (Jude 12; 2 Peter 2:13). So Corinth was not the only place where the Lord's Supper was turned into an orgy of selfish greed. It could well be that the problem started when some tried to take advantage of the generosity of the richer members, who reacted by refusing to share out their own food and drink.

Paul did not pull his punches, and soundly castigated their crude and unthinking behaviour. There could be, he said, only two reasons for their practice. Either they did not have houses of their own to eat in, or they despised the ecclesia and deliberately shamed those members who had less of this world's goods. There was clearly some pride in the lavishness of their meals, and it is possible that some received praise of men as they took the "best places" and the "best seats" (cp. Matthew 23:6). But Paul could not praise them. They stood condemned by the Lord himself, whose commands about his Supper left no room for their arrogant behaviour.

A range of unbrotherly actions compounded the problem. The meal was not eaten together – "each one takes his own supper ahead of others". Some were gorging themselves, and not sharing the provisions among all – "one is hungry". Wine was drunk to excess – "another is drunk" (1 Corinthians 11:21). The poor were hungry, the rich were drunk. What sort of "love feast" was this, where no love was shown but love of self? They mocked the Lord's Supper.

Guilty of the Body and Blood of the Lord

In recounting the information he received directly from the Lord about when the first breaking of bread occurred, the apostle pointedly drew a parallel between their behaviour and that of Judas: "the Lord Jesus *on the same night* in which He was betrayed took bread ..." (verse 23). The feast which was designed to bring strength and comfort to generations of believers was actually initiated when human wickedness and evil schemes were being directed at the Son of God, and when one of his own disciples was preparing to betray him. By behaving unthinkingly and without regard for their brothers and sisters, the Corinthians were following in Judas' footsteps; they were "guilty of the body and blood of the Lord" (verse 27).

It is difficult to imagine a more scathing or comprehensive criticism of their behaviour at the breaking of bread. This was a shock tactic intended to shame them. But before we sit back complacently with the thought that nothing like that happens today, each brother or sister needs to look carefully into his or her own heart to see if the Lord's sacrifice is being denied in any way by similar behaviour.

Paul's comments about the breaking of bread are not the first time the Corinthian brethren and sisters were properly informed about its details. When he wrote, "I received from the Lord that which I also delivered to you" (verse 23), he revealed that they already knew about the Last Supper; he had instructed them personally when he was there. And by saying "I received ... I delivered", he was declaring that the message was not his, but the Lord's. They were not altering Paul's arrangements, but those of the Lord Jesus himself.

Very graphically, the broken bread was designed to show the need of brethren and sisters to be "one loaf", "one body". In Corinth, the body was broken – it was divided and not united. And this was being manifested on the very occasion that should have reminded them of the reconciliation achieved through Christ's death and resurrection.

Proclaim the Lord's Death

The reiteration of how the feast was instituted in the Upper room emphasises its essential simplicity. Paul tells them to concentrate on what the Lord's Supper symbolises. This will draw their attention away from a physical meal to the spiritual sustenance provided by a remembrance of what the Lord achieved on their behalf. His example of selfless giving should both shame and inspire them to keep the feast more acceptably in the future. "Do this in remembrance of me", means much more than simply to take bread and share it among themselves. After breaking the bread, Jesus said, "Take, eat; this is my body". "For as often as you eat this bread and drink this cup, you proclaim the Lord's death till he comes" (verses 24, 26). He was challenging all his disciples to take up their cross daily and follow him. It is the surest antidote to bickering, schism and division.

As they took the cup they were to remember that it is "the new covenant in my blood" (verse 25). They were forgetting in all their surfeiting and drunkenness that when they were baptized they entered into a covenant with God: a covenant announced before to Abraham, promising the forgiveness of

---

This is my body ... Broken for you

TWO specific difficulties are introduced in 1 Corinthians 11:23,24: Jesus "took bread; and when he had given thanks, he broke it and said, Take, eat; this is my body which is broken for you; do this in remembrance of me."

1. According to Catholic commentators, the bread becomes literally the body of Christ when it is shared among partakers at the communion meal. But this is an assertion without a proof. The Lord claimed also to be "the door" and "the true vine". The apostle says in the previous chapter in 1 Corinthians that the rock in the wilderness "was Christ". In all of these passages, the sense is that the thing mentioned symbolises the Lord and an aspect of his work. So too in 1 Corinthians 11:24. The bread symbolises or represents his body.

2. The second problem is found in the words, "which is broken for you". These occur in the KJV and NKJV, but other translations (NIV, RSV, AV) have "which is for you", sometimes with a footnote explaining that the words "broken for you" exist in some, but not all, manuscripts. The textual evidence is not clear one way or the other; but even if the words are not in the text, it is difficult to see how the idea is not there. The syntax of the sentence seems to demand a verb: "this is my body, which is ... for you". If the word "broken" is not in the text, it is natural to supply it from earlier in the verse.

For many the difficulty turns on another verse, which declares about the Lord's sacrifice: "Not one of his bones shall be broken" (John 19:36, cp. Exodus 12:46). As with the Catholic view of trans-substantiation, it is possible to treat scripture too literally. It is true that the Lord's legs were not broken, like those of the criminals who were executed beside him. But his flesh was pierced, and he broke the power of Sin—in his flesh (Romans 8:3).

Even the Passover lamb, whose bones were not to be broken, had to be broken in order to be eaten by each redeemed family.

---

sins. "This is the covenant that I will make with the house of Israel after those days, says the Lord: I will put my law in their minds, and write it on their hearts ... I will forgive their iniquity, and their sin I will remember no more" (Jeremiah 31:33,34).

When these words are quoted in the Letter to the Hebrews, it is significant that the apostle emphasises the need of those who are bound in this covenant to "consider one another in order to stir up love and good works, not forsaking the assembling of ourselves together, as is the manner of some, but exhorting one another, and so much the more as you see the Day approaching" (Hebrews 10:24,25). These responsibilities were being denied in Corinth. They were "trampling the Son of God underfoot, counting the blood of the covenant by which he was sanctified a common thing, and insulting the Spirit of grace" (verse 29).

Each brother and each sister was to take personal responsibility to improve the situation in Corinth: "Let a man examine himself ..." (1 Corinthians 11:28; note the singular, *a man*). Each was to undertake sober self-examination before attending the Lord's Supper. Paul brings together here both practical and spiritual solutions to the problem. They were to "wait for one another", before starting the symbolic meal; and those who were hungry should eat at home beforehand "... lest you come together for judgment" (verses 33,34).

Chastened by the Lord

The letter explains that this judgement was already being felt in Corinth – "many are weak and sick among you, and many sleep" (verse 30) – so the comment does not refer solely to the future judgement when the Lord returns. The exact nature of these illnesses is not revealed, but it seems that the ecclesia was abnormally affected. Some had even fallen asleep. We cannot be certain how these results occurred. The tensions and stress of divisions and disputes in an ecclesia can cause physical illnesses, as some brethren and sisters know to their cost. But from Paul's use of the word "judgment", we cannot deny that the illnesses were a divine chastening intended to bring the ecclesia back to the Lord's commands (see verse 32).

The answer, as we have seen, for was for each individual to engage in sober self-examination, "For if we would judge ourselves, we would not be judged" (verse 31). Paul's response to the riotous behaviour at the breaking of bread was threefold:

1. To give the remembrance its original character and emphasis, as defined by the Lord's words.

2. Each brother and sister should attend only after carefully considering their relationship to the sacrifice that is symbolised by bread and wine.

3. The meal itself should be regarded as wholly symbolic. Anything more than this would be likely to detract from its true significance.

There were, apparently, other concerns. But to deal with these by letter would detract from the important issues. Paul promised to deal personally with them when he next visited the ecclesia: "The rest I will set in order when I come" (verse 34).

15

GIFTS FOR EDIFICATION

FROM the list of items raised specifically by the Corinthians themselves (see 1 Corinthians 7:1), the apostle turns in chapters 12-14 to the question of how Holy Spirit gifts were to be used within the ecclesia. He opens his remarks on this subject by reminding his readers of their past life. Corinth was a city, like Athens "given over to idols" (Acts 17:16), and the Corinthians before their conversion "were Gentiles, carried away to these dumb idols" (1 Corinthians 12:2). As pagans they had frequented the idol-shrines and participated in the worship that took place there. Pagan priests often acted in a frenzied state, claiming to be under the inspiration of their particular deity. Some indication of the extent of this activity is apparent in the account of the confrontation on Mount Carmel between Elijah and the prophets of Baal: "they cried aloud, and cut themselves, as was their custom, with knives and lances, until the blood gushed out on them" (1 Kings 18:28). Life in Christ, and worship of the one true God was to be distinctly different from the other forms of religion practised in Corinth. Paul therefore sets the brethren and sisters a test: "No one speaking by the Spirit of God calls Jesus accursed, and no one can say that Jesus is Lord except by the Holy Spirit" (1 Corinthians 12:3).

"Confess with thy mouth"

Persecuted Christians were asked to renounce their faith by using a specific form of words. They had to make the declaration, "Jesus is accursed" (Greek, *Anathema Iesous*), if they were to escape torture, imprisonment or death. There quickly grew up therefore a contrary declaration used by those who remained faithful under persecution, and more generally to epitomise their beliefs: "because if thou shalt confess with thy mouth 'Jesus as Lord' (*Kyrios Iesous*), and shalt believe in thy heart that God raised him from the dead, thou shalt be saved" (Romans 10:9, RV). It is quite probable that in first century pagan temples, just as today, great pleasure was obtained from abusing terms close to the hearts of believers in Christ. Men and women involved in ecstatic and frenzied worship would take the name of Christ in vain, and rejoice to shout out, "Anathema Jesus", or even "Jesus is Lord" to the embarrassment and shame of any Christian believer who heard them.

For the pagans themselves, who had "many gods and many lords" (1 Corinthians 8:5), there was no embarrassment. Yet those who truly acknowledged "Jesus as Lord" roundly repudiated pagan beliefs in a pantheon of deities. Only someone could honestly make this statement who had separated from his or her former way of life, and who was trying to live after the example of the Lord himself. The words may have been simple, but they expressed belief in the saving work of Christ and all that had been learned about him through the teaching of the apostles. So Paul was absolutely correct when he said, "no one can say that Jesus is Lord except by the Holy Spirit" (literally, "*in* a holy spirit", 12:3). And the reverse was also true, "no one speaking by the Spirit of God calls Jesus accursed". Then, as now, the real test of anyone who claims spirit-possession is sound doctrine: "To the law and to the testimony! If they do not speak according to this word, it is because there is no light in them" (Isaiah 8:20).

In circumstances where it was possible that idol-worship and true worship could be confused, the existence of spirit-gifted men and women acting in the ecclesias in the same way as pagan priests was a mixed blessing. This may have been the reason why in Thessalonica the brethren and sisters suppressed all manifestations of the spirit, leading the apostle to comment: "Do not quench the Spirit. Do not despise prophecies" (1 Thessalonians 5:19,20). A different problem existed in Corinth; the spirit was not quenched at all, but was rather abused, to the detriment of the ecclesia as a whole.

"The manifestation of the Spirit"

The first century gifts of the spirit were passed on only "through the laying on of the apostles' hands" (Acts 8:18), and one of the problems in Corinth was caused by the fact that not every member of the ecclesia possessed spirit-gifts. Their possession thus became a matter of pride, contention and potentially of schism. The Corinthians therefore asked Paul "concerning spiritual(s)" (Greek, *pneumatikon*, 1 Corinthians 12:1). Note that the word "gifts" is not in the original, and "spiritual(s)" therefore refers either to those things that come by the spirit – the gifts or some other spiritual blessing; or to those individuals who are spiritual*. Though the apostle will go on to talk specifically about spirit-gifts, it seems that in 1 Corinthians 12:1-3 he speaks primarily about the spiritual lives which the Corinthians should be living, now that they have put away carnal things (cp. 1 Corinthians 3:1).

Against this background, which applied to every member of the Corinthian ecclesia – those who had spirit-gifts, and those who had not – the apostle can explain about their right use. He used two main arguments, and these are considered in the rest of this chapter. Other aspects of the subject, including the treatise on the importance of love (chapter 13) are dealt with in chapters 16 to 18.

The two arguments used by Paul are:

• Though the gifts were given to individuals, they were not to benefit individuals but the whole ecclesia; in order to be effective, the full cooperation of every member was necessary

• Gifts had a limited application and importance. They were a passing phenomenon, supplied for a special purpose; and they only had a limited life.

* Of the twenty-four other occurrences of *pneumatikon* in the New Testament, only one specifically refers to spirit-gifts (14:1), four refer to 'spiritual people' (1 Corinthians 2:15; 3:1; 14:37; Galatians 6:1), and the rest describe a variety of different spiritual things.

"For the profit of all"

The first of these arguments is introduced by stating an important principle: "the manifestation of the Spirit is given to each one for the profit of all" (12:7). We should note carefully what this verse does not say. It does not say that gifts were given to everybody, but that each person who received a gift was to use it for the benefit of everybody. Here lay Corinth's particular problem. There were tensions between brethren who sought prominent positions within the ecclesia, and some sisters were abusing the freedom of fellowship in Christ. To add to these problems, the clamour of those exercising spirit-gifts was causing confusion within the ecclesial assemblies, and Paul set out to show how this was radically opposed to the purpose of the gifts.

There were various gifts (Greek, *charismata*), but they all came from the same source – the Spirit of God (verse 4). The gifts served different purposes, but they all involved the service of one Lord (verse 5). The nature of their operation varied, but all was according to God who was working in them all (verse 6). It should therefore be obvious that the gifts were being exercised incorrectly if they were causing confusion; their whole object was to edify and unify the body of Christ.

The list of the various gifts explains their different modes of operation:

1. *The word of wisdom*, or practical instruction;

2. *The word of knowledge*: truthful teachings;

3. *Faith*: not general faith, but one to perform miracles (Matthew 17:20; 1 Corinthians 13:2);

4. *Gifts of healing*, to perform cures of sickness;

5. *Working of miracles*: wider in scope than healing;

6. *Prophecy*: making known God's purpose and will;

7. *Discerning of spirits*: the ability to know the true from the false;

8. *Different kinds of tongues*: the ability to speak in other languages;

9. *Interpretation of tongues*: the ability to interpret other languages.

The order of this list is also important, with "tongues" and "the interpretation of tongues" relegated to the end. It was the abuse of these two gifts within the ecclesial meetings that caused the greatest problems in Corinth, and Paul was keen to show their relative unimportance to the needs of the ecclesia. But, whatever form the gift took and whatever ability it gave to the individual believer, all the gifts had the same source and were distributed according to God's will (verse 11).

"Many members ... one body"

The best analogy that could be used to describe the phenomenon of a variety of gifts with a common purpose was the human body. This is a frequent figure in the apostle's writings, and he uses it in his letters to the ecclesias at Rome (12:4,5), Ephesus (4:16; 5:30) and Colosse (2:19). Throughout this section of his letter to Corinth (12:12-27), the apostle shows the importance of having a common aim and purpose: "all the members ... are one body"; "by one spirit we were baptized into one body"; "the body is not one member but many". He reminds his readers of when they were baptized; they were all animated by one mind, the desire to be reconciled to God. There is a unity of thought and sympathy between all who submit to baptism, because all are displaying the mind of Christ (see Philippians 2:1-6). This unity of mind, which is marked by a harmony of belief, Paul compares to a human body. But it is not only the unity of motive that leads him to draw this analogy; there was a single source of nourishment and guidance, poured out for the benefit of everybody: "all have been made to drink into one Spirit" (1 Corinthians 12:13).

The analogy teaches other lessons too. All the different parts are necessary if the body is to function correctly. Not all the parts have prominent functions; but each part is necessary. The parts on show might appear more important

– hands, feet, eyes – but there are other parts, which because they are not on view may seem less important, yet they are vital to the body's existence. The dependence this creates means that the whole body is affected by an injury to one part.

How did this apply to the Corinthians' situation? Together they were Christ's body; individually, they were his members (verse 27). The different spirit-gifts were like the different body members: each gift had its own importance, but it was not unique, nor was it to dominate all the others. Most notably, some gifts were less important in the Corinthian situation than others. The ecclesia needed apostles, prophets and teachers; and it needed these more than it needed miracle workers or those who could speak in other tongues (verse 28). "Earnestly desire the best gifts", was Paul's concluding advice (verse 31).

"That which is in part shall be done away"

Paul's second argument relates to limitations of the gifts, for the emphasis on spirit-gifts in the Corinthian ecclesia displayed an ignorance about their true position in the overall scope of God's purpose. Because the gifts of the Spirit were only passed on by the apostles, Paul said there would come a time when they ceased: "But whether there are prophecies, *they will fail*; whether there are tongues, *they will cease*; whether there is knowledge, *it will vanish away*" (13:8). This message is as important today as it was in the first century. Many religious communities around us claim spirit-possession, and therefore deny this aspect of the apostle's teaching. They claim that these words speak about the future – after the Lord has returned, and when faith is replaced by sight. But this cannot be, for Paul speaks eloquently of the situation when the gifts have passed, when he says: "*And now abide* (i.e., after the spirit-gifts have been "done away") faith, hope, love, these three; but the greatest of these is love" (verse 13). It is true that he also speaks of the kingdom age, for he says, "Love never fails". Faith and hope will both be realised when the promises are all fulfilled; they are qualities firmly rooted in the time of our probation. But "love never fails", and is therefore the greatest of them all because it is enduring.

It is possible to show this teaching in tabular form:

	Apostolic Age	Before Christ's Return	Kingdom Age
Spirit Gifts	Yes	No	?*
Faith	Yes	Yes	No
Hope	Yes	Yes	No
Love	Yes	Yes	Yes

It will be argued that Paul's reason for showing the passing of spirit-gifts was his emphasis on the coming of "that which is perfect" (verse 10); a time when we shall see "face to face", and "know just as I also am known" (verse 12). Surely, it is suggested, this refers to the kingdom age? And if it does, then the gifts must last throughout the Christian era. But to what was Paul referring when he spoke of "that which is perfect"? It is a strange way to talk of the coming of Christ. When he spoke two chapters earlier about the need to remember the Lord's death and resurrection, "till he comes", he spoke with absolute clarity (11:26). And whenever he speaks of the second coming, he usually talks about it as a person coming rather than as an event that will occur. The context in 1 Corinthians 13:10 is that "that which is perfect" replaces what was formerly "in part" – tongues, knowledge and prophecies. Indeed, the original word for "perfect" (Greek, *teleion*) means literally

---

* It is not strictly part of the apostle's argument in Corinthians to discuss the question of the presence of spirit-gifts in the kingdom age. But there is a strong body of thought, on which the Pentecostalist movement is based, that Peter's quotation at Pentecost from Joel 2 pointed to a "latter rain" (i.e., last days) outpouring of the gifts, "Before the coming of the great and awesome day of the Lord" (Acts 2:20). Paul's emphatic language in 1 Corinthians 13 about "that which is in part" being "done away" or destroyed, indicates that there would be no more spirit-gifted mortals. While undoubtedly the spirit will be active in the kingdom, its powers will be available only to Jesus and the immortal saints.

"complete". What was partial will become complete; and when it is complete the partial will no longer be needed.

It is difficult to resist the conclusion that Paul was looking forward to the completed written revelation of God's word, that which is "able to make you wise for salvation through faith which is in Christ Jesus" (2 Timothy 3:15). The gifts were supplied for the purpose of building up, or edifying the ecclesia – a function that is accomplished in these days by the written word of God.

An Old Testament Example

An Old Testament incident helps to explain the limited timescale of the first century spirit-gifts. In the time of Israel's wilderness wanderings, Bezaleel and Aholiab were spirit-gifted craftsmen who led the construction of the Tabernacle and its furniture "according to the pattern" (Exodus 35:30-35). Their gifts were specifically "for edification" – they "built up" the place where God intended to dwell among His people. When their work was finished, the Tabernacle was completed, and "that which is perfect" had come. For the nation of Israel, the Tabernacle, the Law and the sacrifices provided eloquent instruction about God's plan of salvation. The counterparts in the Christian era are obvious:

- Bezaleel, Aholiab and the spirit-empowered workforce were the equivalent of the apostles and spirit-gifted members of the early church.

- The Tabernacle was the equivalent of "the house of God, which is the church of the living God" (1 Timothy 3:15).

- With the law and sacrifices ministered from its precincts, the Tabernacle was the equivalent of the Word of God, providing instruction in holy things.

Before looking at the apostle's teaching about the use of spirit-gifts in Corinth, we must consider the dramatic occurrences at Pentecost, and what they meant for new disciples of the Lord Jesus Christ.

16

THE TEACHING OF PENTECOST

THE beginning of the New Testament ecclesia can be identified with the events of the Day of Pentecost as recorded in Acts 2. At the start of the chapter there was just a comparatively small group of frightened men and women, gathered together into one place. But by the time the day was over, there were over three thousand souls who: "continuing daily with one accord in the temple, and breaking bread from house to house, they ate their food with gladness and simplicity of heart, praising God, and having favour with all the people" (Acts 2:46,47). Obviously something dramatic and decisive occurred during that twenty-four hour period to bring about such changes, and we do well to reflect on what it was.

After Jesus' resurrection, and before he ascended to his Father, he explained to the disciples: "Behold, I send the promise of my Father upon you: but tarry in the city of Jerusalem, until you are endued with power from on high" (Luke 24:49). This power would compensate for his leaving them, and they would be comforted by its presence just as they had benefited from the presence of the Lord himself both before and after his death and resurrection. Jesus guided them in the Truth, and so would the power that was to be given to them: "It is to your advantage that I go away: for if I do not go away, the Helper will not come to you ... when he, the Spirit of truth, has come, he will guide you into all truth ... he will shew you things to come" (John 16:7,13).

In a Visible Form

The coming of this "power from on high" was accompanied by a physical manifestation. In the case of the disciples, it was "divided tongues, as of fire, and one sat upon each of them" (Acts 2:3). In Jesus' case, when he was baptized, it "descended in bodily form like a dove upon him, and a voice came from heaven, which said, You are my beloved Son; in you I am well pleased" (Luke 3:22). The forms were different in each case, but singularly appropriate. The Prince of Peace received power in the form of a dove of peace; and those who were to turn the world upside down with teaching that scorched across the first-century world received it as cloven tongues of fire. That the power was seen as fiery tongues was also significant, as the disciples were to be witnesses by their words to the life and teachings of their Messiah.

The effect on them was instantaneous: "they were all filled with the Holy Spirit, and began to speak with other tongues, as the Spirit gave them utterance" (Acts 2:4). Humanly speaking, the task that lay ahead of them was impossible. How could the world of that day be evangelised by a small group of "unlearned and ignorant men"? What the gift of the Holy Spirit provided was effectively the continuing presence of the Lord in their midst, so that the Jewish rulers – and many others also – "marvelled; and they realised that they had been with Jesus" (Acts 4:13).

The Benefits of Receiving the Holy Spirit

In considering what the gift of the Holy Spirit provided, it is necessary also to discuss what it did not do for the apostles. So many claims are made by the churches around us, especially those of a charismatic and Pentecostalist nature, that some confusion can exist about this important passage. Did the Holy Spirit work directly on the hearts of those who gathered on the day of Pentecost so that they would respond to the apostles speaking? Did the gift of the spirit bring to the apostles a complete change of outlook? Did it give them a new vision? For these are some of the claims that are made.

If they are true, they must presumably also be true for the Lord himself when he received the spirit at his baptism. Was his outlook changed and was his vision renewed? The thirty years before Jesus stood before John the Baptist in the Jordan were a period of intense preparation for the mission his Father had for him. When he stood in front of John, and before the Holy Spirit descended upon him, he declared: "thus it is fitting for us to fulfil all righteousness" (Matthew 3:15). This was a direct reference to his death and resurrection, which were being prefigured by his impending immersion in the waters of the Jordan (cp. Luke 12:50). He knew before ever he approached John what the task would entail, for his familiarity with his Father's word had prepared him for every step of the way. The "powers of the age to come" (Hebrews 6:5) acted as the Lord's credentials; they did not assist him personally to accomplish what his Father had in store for him.

The opposite would be more true – that the powers were a potential hindrance to his accomplishing God's will. In a lesser man, the availability of the spirit "without measure" would undoubtedly lead to the misuse and abuse of the gift. We see the intense struggle, even in the mind of the Son of God, when he was driven of the spirit into the wilderness of temptation (Mark 1:12). The same was true in the experience of the apostles. Simon the sorcerer was prepared to pay good money in order to obtain the power of the spirit, and brethren and sisters in the ecclesia in Corinth did not use the gifts as they were intended, for the edification and benefit of all, but to indicate an alleged superiority over those that did not have them.

The Joy of Shared Hope

Furthermore, the presence of the spirit-gifts did not make the believers better people. There was no increased joy because the gifts were present in the first century ecclesias. The fellowship that characterised the ecclesia in Jerusalem immediately following the day of Pentecost was a consequence of the shared beliefs and common faith of those who were baptized, and not the transforming effect upon them of the Holy Spirit. Knowing that their past sins were washed away: "All that believed were together, and had all things common ... So they, continuing daily with one accord in the temple, and breaking bread from house to house, they ate their food with gladness and simplicity of heart, praising God, and having favour with all the people" (Acts 2:44-47).

What then was the importance of the disciples waiting in Jerusalem until they received the Holy Spirit, before they commenced their work of going out to: "make disciples of all the nations, baptizing them in the name of the Father, and of the Son, and of the Holy Spirit" (Matthew 28:19)? Surely the importance was that their message would become authoritative; they would speak in Christ's name, with the confidence that the message was true. The prophecy of Joel indicated that those on whom the Spirit was poured forth would be truly God's "menservants and maidservants" (Joel 2:28-32, Acts 2:18). Miraculous signs would support their teaching, just as Jesus' words were reinforced by his wonderful works of healing (cp. John 10:38).

This chapter reviews the evidence about the limited period when such spirit-gifts were available. They spanned the gap between the ascension of Jesus, and the completion of the written New Testament account of his works and teaching. Once their work was completed, the gifts "vanished away". This focuses attention on what was taught, rather than on those who taught it, or on the means by which that teaching was received.

The Promised Gift

When the great crowd meeting in Jerusalem on the Day of Pentecost heard the teaching of the apostles, "they were cut to the heart, and said to Peter and to the rest of the apostles, Men and brethren, what shall we do?" (Acts 2:37). What affected them was not the sudden presence within themselves of a heavenly power, but the awful realisation that they were responsible for putting to death their Messiah. Furthermore, the Apostle Peter's response to their anguished request, "What shall we do?" was to tell them to "Repent ... be baptized ... for the remission of sins", and then they would receive the gift of the Holy

Spirit. The gift was a consequence of their repentance and commitment, and not its cause.

Nor was this a promise that they, their children, and "as many as the Lord our God will call" out of every generation, would all receive spirit-gifts. Peter was referring to a comment he made when he was telling the crowd of their involvement in Jesus' cruel death. Jesus was raised from the dead by the power of the Father, "and having received from the Father the promise of the Holy Spirit, he poured out this, which you now see and hear" (Acts 2:33). What Jesus received from the Father after his resurrection cannot possibly have been the spirit-gifts; for these were imparted to him over three years earlier when he was baptized. What he received was the gift of immortality, the great promise of God that was fulfilled because of his work of salvation. As it is impossible to separate the Holy Spirit from this work, it is appropriate to describe resurrection and immortality as "the promise (or gift) of the Holy Spirit".

David made a similar point in the Psalm composed after his sin with Bathsheba. He pleaded with God, "Do not cast me away from your presence; and do not take your holy spirit from me. Restore unto me the joy of your salvation; and uphold me by your generous spirit" (Psalm 51:11,12). David knew the promises of God, for He had "spoken of thy servant's house for a great while to come" (2 Samuel 7:19). He therefore looked for reassurance that God's salvation – His free gift – was still extended to him, and that his sin was forgiven.

This conclusion about "the gift of the Holy Spirit" in Acts 2 is reinforced by the words that are used. The usual word for spirit-gifts in the New Testament is *charismata*, from which we get our word 'charismatic'. But this is not used in Acts 2. When those who were baptized were promised "the gift of the Holy Spirit", the word "gift" translates the Greek word *dorea*. Now while it is true that this word is used occasionally to refer to spirit-gifts, it has a much wider meaning relating it to the fulfilment of God's purpose (see, for example, Romans 5:15,17).

The Blessing of Abraham

The Apostle Paul in his letter to the Galatians further reinforces the importance that belief plays in the process of salvation. Abraham is the great example of faith: "Abraham believed God, and it was accounted to him for righteousness. Therefore know that only those who are of faith, are sons of Abraham ... that the blessing of Abraham might come on the Gentiles in Jesus Christ; that we might receive the promise of the Spirit through faith" (Galatians 3:6,7,14). In this context, once again, "the promise of the Spirit" refers to the forgiveness of sins, and to resurrection and immortality: the transforming message of the gospel of Christ that so pricked the hearts of men and women on the Day of Pentecost. The "promise of the Spirit" is also equated in this passage with "the blessing of Abraham". Peter made the same connection when, shortly after the Day of Pentecost, he spoke to another crowd in Jerusalem: "You are the sons of the prophets, and of the covenant which God made with our fathers ... to you first God, having raised up his Servant Jesus, sent him to bless you, in turning away every one of you from your iniquities" (Acts 3:25,26).

Of course their lives were changed. They experienced something similar to the emotions of the disciples who were downcast by the crucifixion of the Lord Jesus Christ, but who leapt for joy once they realised he was raised from the dead. The knowledge that he is now "alive for evermore", and the guarantee of resurrection to eternal life became a motivating force in their lives, just as it can in ours. We too are assured of the forgiveness of sins: at baptism of all the sins of our former life; and after baptism, when we confess our sins, knowing that God "is faithful and just to forgive us our sins, and to cleanse us from all unrighteousness" (1 John 1:9).

The change comes about through the work of the Holy Spirit, for "if Christ is not risen, your faith is futile; you are yet in your sins" (1 Corinthians 15:17). Faithful believers have a new spirit within them, one that is related to the mind of Christ they seek to develop. So the apostles speak about acting "in a holy spirit", when they describe behaviour that is motivated by the knowledge of Christ's work of salvation (for example, Romans 9:1; 14:17; Jude 20).

Nor does our understanding of what happened at Pentecost and afterwards suggest that God does not work today in the lives of believers. Such criticisms are a travesty of our beliefs. The passages we have considered all show the importance of accepting and embracing the relevance of the promises vouchsafed through the work of Christ, but the Father promises too that He will comfort the weary, and give strength to the weak and frail: He is constantly their strength and stay.

Our Situation is not Deficient

The important lesson to be learned from Pentecost is that we must not feel our situation is deficient compared with that of first century brethren and sisters. The gospel message is not different today from the one that caused so many to ask, "Men and brethren, what shall we do?" The same commitment is required from today's disciples as from those who "continued daily with one accord ... Praising God, and having favour with all the people" (Acts 2:46,47). We can have the same assurance about the truth and accuracy of God's word of salvation as was provided by the miraculous powers given to and through the apostles.

The joy of following faithfully in the way of salvation is not an effervescent feeling of pleasure, created only by our emotions; but something that is much more soundly based. Our emotions should be motivated by the truths we have learned, and by our convictions that these are sound and trustworthy. In simple terms, we become different people, no longer burdened by sin or by the worries which so beset our friends and neighbours. But looking forward confidently to the coming of the Lord, and to the hope of everlasting life with him in his Father's kingdom.

This is the message Paul wished to convey to the brethren and sisters in Corinth.

17

CONFUSION OF TONGUES

HOLY SPIRIT-GIFTS, given for the benefit of the whole ecclesia, were being abused in Corinth. We have seen (pages 114,115) how Paul used the example of the different parts of the human body to show the interdependence of all the varying members of the ecclesia, with their distinct skills and abilities. What is more, spirit-gifts would not always be available; they could only be transmitted by the apostles, and would die with them. The fact that they were a passing phenomenon should stop the Corinthians using them as matters of pride and conflict. This applied particularly to the gift of speaking in tongues, and Paul now gives advice about the proper use of this and other spirit-gifts, and shows the importance of order and submission in ecclesial life.

In Corinth the gift of tongues was being used almost exclusively, and the other spirit-gifts were hardly being used at all. Whenever the ecclesia gathered together, it was dominated by those who spoke in tongues. Brethren and sisters vied with each other in the exercise of this gift. And though the proper use of this gift was to speak in another language to assist the spread of the gospel, it seems that even in these early days, a form of ecstatic speech had entered the Corinthian meetings: "For he who speaks in a tongue does not speak to men but to God, for *no one understands him*" (1 Corinthians 14:2). The words being spoken were unintelligible to those who heard, "For ... *he utters mysteries* with his spirit" (NIV). Without divine interpretation, the words were only of emotional value. To the uninitiated onlooker, ecclesial meetings would appear ludicrous: "will they not say that *you are out of your mind?*" (verse 23).

The real purpose of the gift of speaking in tongues was shown at Pentecost, when the crowds of people assembled in Jerusalem "were all amazed and marvelled, saying to one another, Look, are not all these who speak Galileans? And how is it that we hear, each in our own language in which we were born?" (Acts 2:7,8). What was happening in Corinth did not conform to this description, and the apostle had to remind the brethren and sisters that "There are ... many kinds of languages in the world, and none of them is without significance" (1 Corinthians 14:10). If the "tongues" being spoken in Corinth were unintelligible, they were either in a language unknown to the inhabitants of the city – and we should remember the cosmopolitan nature of this important seaport – or it was a form of ecstatic speech similar to that used by the priests in idols' temples elsewhere in the city, and in charismatic gatherings today.

But it seems that the members of the ecclesia who spoke in tongues claimed they were speaking the language of angels (cp. 13:1); a claim that it would be difficult for non-gifted members to refute or deny.

Tongues or *'Glossolalia'*?

All that the apostle has to say on this subject indicates that the spirit-gifts were being seriously abused, not simply by their being used in inappropriate situations, but by brethren and sisters pretending to have the gift of tongues when in fact they were probably indulging in the practice of 'glossolalia' – emotionally-charged speaking using words that have no known meaning. The term *'glossolalia'* is actually built up from the two words used by Paul to describe a person who "speaks in tongues" (*laleo glossa*), terminology he only uses in 1 Corinthians 14 and nowhere else. 'Glossolalia' has been defined as "vocalisation that sounds language-like but is devoid of semantic meaning or syntax" (Nicholas P. Spanos, *Journal of Abnormal Psychology*, 1986).

Paul's approach to the problem is of great interest to us, because speaking in tongues has become a modern-day phenomenon in Christian circles, though there are examples of ecstatic speech in some ancient cultures. The

Pentecostal movement was virtually unknown before the twentieth century, but has sustained a rapid growth since revivalist meetings started in the USA in the early years of the last century, and now most of the main Christian denominations have Pentecostal members. The apostle sets out a way of dealing with the problem, when it arises. He says that two criteria are important:

- Speaking in tongues is only edifying if the message is interpreted, "But if there is no interpreter, let him keep silent in church" (1 Corinthians 14:28).

- "Tongues are for a sign, not to those who believe but to unbelievers" (verse 22).

If what was happening at Corinth was a display of unintelligible ecstatic speech, the need for interpretation would create difficulties. And because speaking in tongues was disturbing meetings of the Corinthian ecclesia, the sign was being directed towards believers and not unbelievers. The Corinthian brethren and sisters were therefore not following either of the requirements mentioned by Paul. The apostle did not encourage some in the ecclesia to be tongue-speakers and others to be interpreters; he said: "let him who speaks in a tongue pray that he may interpret", so that the message could be given "with the understanding" (verse 15). This is a further indication that the problem related to a form of ecstatic speech. And as regards the circumstances in which the gift of tongues should be used, Paul said: "in the church (i.e., in ecclesial meetings) I would rather speak five words with my understanding, that I may teach others also, than ten thousand words in a tongue" (verse 19).

A Contemporary Example

Some idea of the conditions in the Corinthian ecclesia can be gained from the following description by a pastor who opened his church to "both those who speak in tongues and those who do not". This, of course, was the situation in Corinth: some claimed to have the gift of tongues, and some had no spirit-gifts at all. This is the pastor's description of what happened:

127

"Professing to be filled with the Spirit of humility and holiness, these persons expressed the opposite. The subtle but real spiritual conceit became more apparent until the words 'Spirit-filled' came to have a regrettable taint. Other pastors with whom I have talked have had similar experiences. There is often a 'know-it-all' attitude among those who speak in tongues that exactly contradicts what they profess in testimony. They definitely give the impression that those who do not speak in tongues have not 'arrived' spiritually, do not have the sensitivity to interpret the Scriptures, do not have prayer power that can bring results. These persons are insensitive to the concept of Christian discipline. In many of them, habits of worldliness remain while the tongue-speaking flourishes. They are unteachable. Again the spiritual superiority complex rears its ugly head. The tongues-speakers apparently believe that they know it all." ("A Plea to Some Who Speak in Tongues", *Christianity Today*, February 28, 1975)

As we have already discovered, the root cause of many of the problems in Corinth was the tension between those who clamoured for supremacy. The ecclesia was deeply divided by schismatic groupings, and the confusion created by tongue-speaking was another manifestation of this serious difficulty.

When the Apostle James wrote about the need for individuals to control their tongues, he could have been describing the conditions in Corinth. What is true of insensitivity in normal speaking was also true of the competitive nature of some in Corinth as they vied with each other to be the most prominent speaker in tongues: "the tongue is a little member and boasts great things ... the tongue is a fire, a world of iniquity. The tongue is so set among our members that it defiles the whole body" (James 3:5,6).

"They will not hear me ..."

Paul used an Old Testament incident and quotation to show the seriousness of this behaviour: "In the law it is written: 'With men of other tongues and other lips I will speak to this people; and yet, for all that, they will not hear me,' says the Lord" (1 Corinthians 14:21, quoting Isaiah 28:11,12). The background to this quotation was the irreverent attitude of the nation of Israel. Drunken revellers mocked and derided the prophet's message, likening it to childlike instruction. Through Isaiah, God promised to speak to the nation by means of a language and a people they would not understand – the Assyrians. This message would be a sign to people who did not understand.

Applying this to the situation in Corinth was a strong condemnation of the ecclesia. Paul had already noted that there was drunkenness at the memorial meeting (11:21); the attitude of superiority that existed was probably couched in terms that described some in the ecclesia as "children" (see 14:20); and if tongue-speaking was considered to be so important that much of their time together was engaged in that way, it was actually an admission that they were "unbelievers". "Tongues are for a sign, not to those who believe but to unbelievers; but prophesying is not for unbelievers but for those who believe" (verse 22).

Covet the Best Gifts

The apostle's main advice was therefore to "desire earnestly to prophesy" (verse 39). Prophecy – the speaking forth of God's will and purpose – was infinitely more beneficial to the ecclesia than the gift of tongues: "he who prophesies speaks edification and exhortation and comfort to men" (verse 3). The great test of the value of spirit-gifts, according to the apostle, was whether they were used to benefit the ecclesia as a whole, or simply to satisfy the pride of those who were using them.

Even Paul himself, who said: "I thank my God I speak with tongues more than you all" (verse 18), would not use the gift if he visited Corinth. Other gifts – "knowledge, prophesying, teaching" – were much more suited to their needs (verse 6). So, "in the church I would rather speak five words with my understanding, that I may teach others also, than ten thousand words in a tongue" (verse 19).

Practical Advice to Control Spirit-Gifts

There were practical consequences for the ecclesia in Corinth, and the apostle established some guidelines, which, if they were followed would restore order to the ecclesial meetings:

1. Choose from the material that is offered only those contributions that are edifying (verse 26).

2. If this includes any tongues-speakers, "let there be two or at the most three" (verse 27).

3. No tongue-speaking should occur unless there is an interpreter present (verse 28).

4. Other gifts – including prophecy – should be subject to similar constraints (verses 29-32).

If this advice was followed, the confusion of the past should cease. By using the word "confusion", there is an interesting echo of the Babel story when God said, "Come, let us go down and there confuse their language, that they may not understand one another's speech" (Genesis 11:7). This confusion of speech led to the scattering of the ancient earth's population; and the gift of tongues was specifically given so that those who went out into all the world with the gospel message would be able to call out men and women from the confusion of the world with its clamouring sounds to the calm and comfort of God's family: "For God is not the author of confusion but of peace" (1 Corinthians 14:33).

It was possible that the Corinthians, receiving this advice from the apostle, would react by completely stifling the use of the gift of tongues. But that would not be right – it was one of the gifts God gave for the furtherance of His purpose at that time, and it had an important part to play. So Paul summarised his advice by concluding: "Therefore, brethren, desire earnestly to prophesy, and do not forbid to speak with tongues" (verse 39).

What about the Sisters?

There was one further aspect of the problem. It was mentioned earlier in connection with the disturbances in the ecclesial meetings when some sisters were seeking leading roles for themselves; but at that stage only the questions of headship and head coverings were addressed. Now, as it was closely associated with the problem of the confusion arising from the abuse of the gift of tongues, Paul considers the position of sisters when the ecclesia gathered together. It is apparent that they too were involved, and Paul follows up his comments about headship to talk specifically about the part sisters could play in ecclesial meetings. Were they included, for example, in the new arrangement that allowed the involvement of no more than two or three with a specific spirit-gift?

Paul makes it abundantly clear that they were not: "Let your women keep silent (Greek, *sigao*) in the churches, for they are not permitted to speak" (1 Corinthians 14:34). They were in exactly the same position as brethren who wanted to speak in tongues, but no interpretation was available: "let him keep silent (*sigao*) in church, and let him speak to himself and to God" (verse 28). Just as he explained when he was talking about head-coverings, this requirement for sisters followed the general principle in the scriptures that divine authority has been devolved through Christ to man and then to woman: "they are to be submissive, as the law also says" (verse 34).

What the Law Says

Most marginal references direct the reader to Genesis 3:16 and God's words to Eve after her disobedience, "Your desire shall be for your husband, and he shall rule over you". This is also reinforced in the Law itself when it deals with the subject of oaths. A woman's vow was subject to the control of her husband, or, if she was unmarried, her father (Numbers 30:3-8). That the Edenic situation provides the backdrop to all the apostle's comments about the position of sisters is apparent on every occasion he refers to the subject (1 Corinthians 11 & 14; 1 Timothy 2). When he says, "it is shameful for women to speak in church" (1 Corinthians 14:35), we are being reminded of the shame felt by Adam and Eve when they discovered their nakedness. Paul wished to ensure that sisters did not feel ashamed, or become exposed in ecclesial meetings, and therefore told them that the home is the place for further and specific instruction.

The reference to the law of the oath helps to explain why this provision was made. If a married woman in Israel "bound her soul" by an oath, her oath would stand only if her husband did not countermand it. We can imagine the embarrassment for a woman who made a public oath, only to have her husband nullify its effect. How much better for these things to be dealt with "at home", and out of the public eye. And so in the ecclesia, sisters were asked to keep silent, and thus signal to every member – male and female – the consequences of sin's entry into the world, from whose effects all have been saved by the sacrifice of Christ.

"Let all things be done decently and in order."
(1 Corinthians 14:40)

18

A MORE EXCELLENT WAY

IN the heart of the section in his letter where the apostle Paul comments on the right use of spirit-gifts is his chapter on love. It has been described as "a pure and perfect gem, perhaps the noblest assemblage of beautiful thoughts in beautiful language extant in this our world" (Alford). Yet beautiful though it is, the chapter has a context that is often overlooked. It is directly connected with the particular problems the brethren and sisters in Corinth were facing, and it puts firmly in their place the gifts that had become vehicles for so much pride and disruption in the ecclesia. The apostle wanted to show them "a more excellent way" (1 Corinthians 12:31), the way of love.

He had previously pointed out that their emphasis on human knowledge was of no lasting benefit: "Knowledge puffs up, but love edifies" (8:1). When they were not boasting about superior knowledge, they were vying with each other over whose spirit-gift was best. All of this led directly to the divisions that plagued the ecclesia and held back its growth. They were pretending to be mature, but in reality they were still children. If they were going to grow to full maturity they needed to know and walk in the way of love. Love is lasting, where the gifts and knowledge that propped up their present boastfulness would soon pass away.

'Love', not 'Desire'

But first of all, Paul needed to explain what he meant by love. Corinth knew all about one form of love, for Venus was the Corinthian goddess and eroticism was one of the city's main pastimes. The love Paul wished them to follow was not the love of Venus or Eros, related only to the fleshly senses and their satisfaction. Nor was it the kind of weak sentimentality that it has become in today's currency, describing simply an emotional liking, or sometimes just a personal preference for one person, activity or product over another. The love Paul wished the Corinthians to practice is much more than affection and emotion. This love is shown in action and flows from an appreciation of the love of God that has been showered upon His creatures. It is directed by the mind and will as much as it is by the heart, though it is substantially more than the result only of an intellectual exercise.

Paul uses the Greek word *agape* to describe this love, but gives it an altogether richer and more unique meaning than it has in classical Greek. He is inspired to use it to describe the love that flows from a person's association with God's purpose in Christ, a principled love that is not free from passion, but is not driven by passion. There is another Greek word, *philia*, to describe the personal feelings of fondness and longing with which we are more familiar. These are the emotions we feel towards friends, and particularly the love a bridegroom has for his bride. The word is often extended in its New Testament use to become *philadelphia*, "love of the brethren" (e.g., 1 Peter 1:22). Yet when the apostle was talking about marriage, he said: "Husbands, love your wives, just as Christ also loved the church" (Ephesians 5:25), and he used the word *agape*, not *philia*. There is a duty in marriage, and it goes beyond the natural feelings between a man and a woman. This responsibility endures, even if other feelings wane.

The Duty of Loving

When Jesus said, "love your enemies" (Matthew 5:44), he also was speaking about loving them on the basis of principle. It is a disciple's duty to love his enemies; true followers of the Lord will sincerely try to "do good to those who hate" them, because that is what he did throughout his life. Jesus did not mean, love your enemies more than you love your friends, but love all men; *even* your enemies. If by love he meant the emotional regard we all have towards our nearest and dearest, it would be impossible to love our enemies. If we were fond of them, it is unlikely they would be our enemies. But it is possible to "bless those who curse you, do good to those who hate you, and pray for those who spitefully use you and persecute you." These are the hallmarks of the kind of love that both Jesus and the Apostle Paul expect of true believers. Its application in the ecclesia at Corinth would make all the difference and resolve most of its problems.

Paul also touches on this subject in his first letter to the Thessalonians. He warned them against the kind of love practised so widely in Corinth, and told each brother, "to possess his own vessel in sanctification and honour, not in passion of lust, like the Gentiles who do not know God" (1 Thessalonians 4:4,5). And he encouraged them to increase their love for each other. The situation was clearly different from the one that existed in the Corinthian ecclesia. The brethren and sisters in Thessalonica were already showing love to each other, and did not need reminding of their duty: "Concerning brotherly love (*philadelphia*) you have no need that I should write to you, for you yourselves are taught by God to love (*agapao*) one another" (verse 9).

If this situation could develop in Corinth, all their problems would be resolved. If the members of the ecclesia could start by showing love for each other because they realised their responsibility as disciples in Christ, this could eventually develop into a true fellow-feeling and all would be edified. Paul even urged the Thessalonians, who were already practising "brotherly love", to "increase more and more" (verse 10). The progression he described would never reach its limit.

Transferred to Myself – for Your Sakes

On the basis of what he has already written in 1 Corinthians 4:6 – "These things, brethren, I have figuratively transferred to myself and Apollos for your sakes, that you may learn in us not to think beyond what is written, that none of you may be puffed up on behalf of one against the other" – Paul pretends he has all the attributes that were so prized within the ecclesia. He shows how bereft he would be if, even having all these, he had not got the true

Christian love that he encourages them to develop. He starts with the gift of tongues – either the ability to speak in a foreign language, or the ecstatic speech that some in the ecclesia were claiming was angelic language. This was no better than the noisy brass foundries for which Corinth was renowned, or the cymbals made by the city's craftsmen for the priests of Cybele. The way tongues were being abused in the ecclesia was disturbing and distracting, and destructive of harmony. Without the positive principles of love even the best gifts were useless. The same would be true if Paul used his gift to "remove mountains", the act by which the Lord challenged the disciples' faith (Matthew 17:20; 21:21). Unless it was motivated by love this would be purely dramatic and achieve nothing of lasting value.

Charity and Sacrifice

What if he gave all he possessed to feed the poor, which in modern times we call 'charity'? He said that this too, unless it is motivated by love, is of no profit. These are harsh words, and they challenge a widespread belief that good works are above all else the mark of Christian discipleship. The act of giving, the apostle says, brings no lasting benefit unless it is accompanied by love. As we have seen, this is not love bred only by fellow-feeling or by compassion, but from a sincere desire to share what God has given, particularly the word of salvation.

But what if someone went beyond giving away everything he possessed, and gave his body by self-immolation? Paul would be aware of the notorious case of an Indian fakir who burned himself to death in the streets of Athens. His tomb is inscribed: "He made himself immortal". It is a bold claim, but completely untrue. He gained notoriety and brief fame, but certainly not immortality: his action profited him nothing, and it was of no benefit to anyone else. Even the Lord's sacrifice would have been valueless, unless it was an expression of God's love to man. However great or outstanding the act, without love it is equivalent to a row of zeros. These can be multiplied indefinitely and still have no value whatsoever. But add any other figure, at the beginning, middle or end of a row of zeros, and it makes all the difference. The figure has value itself, and it gives value to all the rest. Love is like that; it makes the meaningless meaningful.

The Christian love of which Paul speaks is the antithesis of what was happening in the Corinthian ecclesia. The brethren and sisters were impatient and rude; they were buoyed up with pride, and strutted round full of self-importance; they were concerned only with their own business, and reacted vehemently to any real or imagined opposition. By contrast, "Love suffers long and is kind; love does not envy; love does not parade itself, is not puffed up; does not behave rudely, does not seek its own, is not provoked, thinks no evil; does not rejoice in iniquity, but rejoices in the truth; bears all things, believes all things, hopes all things, endures all things" (1 Corinthians 13:4-7).

The test of a true disciple of Christ is not therefore the magnificence of his spirit-gifts, or the wonder of his knowledge, the oratory of his speech or even the generosity of his spirit. It lies in whether he bears, believes, hopes and endures. The qualities of love that should be developed recognise God's love bestowed through the work of the Lord Jesus Christ.

Love Endures

If the Corinthians were to begin walking in this "more excellent way", they had to be shown that the grounds of their present confidence were ill-founded. Other things will come to an end, but not love, for "Love never fails" (verse 8). The spirit-gifts that seemed so important to their individual self-esteem and to ecclesial life, "will vanish away". However magnificent they seemed, and despite the fact that they were given by God for edification, the spirit-gifts were limited. Each gift was virtually useless on its own; it needed to be associated with others, and motivated by love. The brother or sister gifted in tongues was of little use, for example, to the person who needed healing. The very existence of the gifts cried out for something that was more complete, more perfect and more enduring.

By describing the process of his own natural growth from childhood to maturity, Paul was teaching the Corinthians about their own need to "put away childish things" (verse 11). We might feel that this is an unusually gentle approach given the severity of the problems that affected Corinth, but had not the apostle just said that "Love suffers long and is kind … does not behave rudely … is not provoked, thinks no evil"? How could he possibly act any differently as he sought to encourage them towards a better and more excellent way?

Now	Then
We know in part and we prophesy in part	When the perfect is come, what is in part is done away
I spoke as a child, I understood as a child, I thought as a child	When I became a man, I put away childish things
Now **We** see in a mirror dimly	Then face to face
Now **I** know in part	Then shall I know just as I am known

When his comments are set out in a table, as above, it is possible to see quite clearly what the apostle was teaching. In order to make his point, Paul changes from speaking about all believers (*"We"*), to his personal situation (*"I"*). He also likened the Corinthians to the nation of Israel, who criticised Moses and, by implication, God Himself who had chosen him to lead the nation. God had to reprove them: "I speak with him (Moses) face to face, even plainly, and not in dark sayings; and he sees the form of the Lord. Why then were you not afraid to speak against my servant Moses?" (Numbers 12:8). In just the same way, the brethren and sisters in Corinth were not seeing clearly; their self-importance was getting in the way and obscuring the reality of their standing before God. Their boastful claims about "knowledge" ignored the fact that they had not understood the reality of God's work on their behalf; only by displaying the divine qualities that motivated the life of the Lord Jesus would they begin to know, even as they were known.

"Make love your aim"

The Corinthians' self-satisfaction was almost boundless. They were arrogant about their supposed "knowledge", and needed to develop a much greater humility if they were to get any closer to knowing God and knowing themselves. Their selfishness acted as an almost impenetrable barrier, like a hardened outer shell; they showed virtually no interest or concern for anyone other than themselves, and they were resistant to the necessary changes that exposure to the gospel should bring.

Paul was encouraging them to develop the true hallmark of discipleship: "God is love, and he who abides in love abides in God, and God in him" (1 John 4:16). As we have seen, love is not an abstract or nebulous philosophy; the apostle was not giving them a choice between the spirit-gifts and love; he was showing how all they did must be motivated by love. Love only manifests itself when it inspires Godly behaviour. It is "the greatest"; so Paul pleads with them to "pursue love" (1 Corinthians 14:1) with the intensity of a hunter ("Make love your aim", RSV).

19

QUESTIONS ABOUT RESURRECTION

BEFORE concluding his letter with various practical issues, Paul deals with the subject of resurrection. It is not clear if this was in the ecclesia's list of questions, or whether the apostle learned of the problem from other sources. Clearly it was a serious matter, and the ecclesia needed to be of one mind on the subject. The apostle therefore preceded his comments on resurrection by reminding his readers of the privileges and responsibilities of ecclesial life, and how each must play his or her part, working toward a common goal. For this to be effective, there had to be right attitudes – hence the emphasis on the "more excellent way" of love – and a right basis. So Paul opens his comments on resurrection by declaring to them "the gospel which I preached to you, which also you received and in which you stand" (1 Corinthians 15:1).

Sound Doctrine

The idea of there being a firm foundation for faith, a body of belief giving confidence and assurance, appears elsewhere in the apostle's letters. He wrote to Timothy, for example, about "sound words" and "sound doctrine" (1 Timothy 1:10, etc.), and explained that anyone who does not assent to this basis, "is proud, knowing nothing, but is obsessed with disputes and arguments over words, from which come envy, strife, reviling, evil suspicions, useless wranglings of men of corrupt minds and destitute of the truth" (6:4,5). This is a very apt description of the unbrotherly behaviour that plagued the Corinthian ecclesia, and may well have been the illustration Paul had in mind when he wrote to Timothy, who also had first-hand experience of the situation in Corinth from his own visit there during their time of trouble (1 Corinthians 4:17, etc.).

This foundation of sound teaching leads to saving faith. To the Romans Paul wrote, "the gospel of Christ ... is the power of God to salvation for everyone who believes" (Romans 1:16). It is "*to* salvation" because believers are being saved: a process that commences with hearing the word of the gospel. As the Lord explained in the parable of the Sower, this word takes root in good and honest hearts to bring forth fruit unto life eternal. The true nature of the gospel-fruit will only be revealed when the Lord comes to gather in the harvest. The most important part of this gospel-word concerns the Lord Jesus Christ and his work. Our familiarity with the scriptural definition of the gospel in Acts 8:12 – "the things concerning the kingdom of God and the name of Jesus Christ" – can obscure the fact that there is an aspect of this twin-teaching that comes "first of all", and is "of first importance" (RSV): namely, "that Christ died for our sins according to the Scriptures" (1 Corinthians 15:3). According to the apostle, this is what motivated the first Corinthian preaching campaign: "I, brethren, when I came to you ... determined not to know anything among you except Jesus Christ and Him crucified" (2:1,2).

Two Witnesses

An intrinsic part of this message was the proven fact of the resurrection of Christ. There are two strands of evidence: the Word of God and human witnesses. The scriptures prophesied that it would occur on "the third day"; and both the law and the prophets testified to this truth (for example, Genesis 22:4; Leviticus 23:11; 2 Kings 20:5; Hosea 6:2; Jonah 1:17). Furthermore, Jesus "presented himself alive after his suffering by many infallible proofs" (Acts 1:3), first to the apostles – "the twelve" – "then last of all he was seen by me also, as by one born out of due time" (1 Corinthians 15:8). The original words are much sharper. Paul was probably referring to a coarse term of abuse that some were using against him: "this abortion of an apostle, as some call me" (F. F. Bruce, paraphrase). The way of flesh would quickly produce a scathing retort to a comment like this; the more excellent way of love required that Paul admit his unworthiness "to be called an apostle, because I persecuted the church of God" (verse 9).

141

What really mattered was not what he had been, but what God had made him. Through him and the work he was allowed to accomplish, there was much fruit – including the Corinthians themselves if only they would admit it. That they were actually in a position to criticise him was a proof of God's grace towards him. The message he – "the abortion" – preached, was the same gospel preached by all the other apostles, and rested completely on the certainty of Christ's resurrection: "so we preach and so you believed" (verse 11).

Exactly what was being taught in Corinth about the resurrection can only be deduced from the apostle's comments. He reports two statements that were common in the ecclesia:

"How do some among you say that there is no resurrection of the dead?"   (verse 12)

"Someone will say, 'How are the dead raised up? And with what body do they come?'"   (verse 35)

From the first of these comments, it appears there was a denial of bodily resurrection, so probably Greek ideas about the immortality of the soul were not fully abandoned when the gospel truth was accepted. There is evidence of the same difficulty occurring in Ephesus, from where Paul was writing. For, when he wrote at the end of his life to Timothy who was then in Ephesus, Paul mentioned Hymenaeus and Philetus, "who have strayed concerning the truth, saying that *the resurrection is already past*; and they overthrow the faith of some" (2 Timothy 2:18). This was not therefore an isolated case, and there needed to be a robust explanation of true Bible teaching. Having shown the certainty of Jesus' physical and bodily resurrection, Paul proceeds to list ten serious consequences of failing to accept the evidence about resurrection:

(Verses 14-19)

1. Nothing can be gained from preaching the gospel, as all future hope is effectively removed.

2 The believer's faith is based on a lie.

QUESTIONS ABOUT RESURRECTION

3. The apostles (who taught them the truth) were false witnesses.

4. Faith has no purpose, because there is nothing to believe in.

5. Sins cannot be forgiven if Jesus was not raised.

6. The sleeping dead, resting in hope of awakening, are actually perished.

7. If the Christian hope only applies to our present existence, we are to be pitied.

(Verses 29–31)

8. Baptism is a symbol of death and resurrection. Why were the Corinthians baptized if there is no resurrection?

9. Why do the apostles continually risk their lives to preach the gospel if man's position is hopeless?

10. Paul particularly suffered daily in hope of their eventual exaltation.

A Passage of Epic Grandeur

Inserted into this closely reasoned and logically developed argument is a lengthy parenthesis (verses 20-28) that has been described as "a passage of epic grandeur" describing the important place accorded in God's plan to the resurrection of Christ. Because of the evidence for Christ's resurrection, and because of the consequences for all believers, Paul declares: "now Christ is risen from the dead, and has become the firstfruits of those who have fallen asleep" (verse 20). He does not use the word "now" in a temporal sense (now, as compared with previously), but more in the sense of "therefore", as the logical and reasonable conclusion of the evidence. Equally logical is the fact that, through resurrection Jesus is "the firstfruits" (see also verse 23).

The Lesson of Israel's Calendar

This likens resurrection to the stages in Israel's agricultural life, for the first sheaf of harvest was cut three days after

143

the Passover lamb was slain and waved "before the Lord" (Leviticus 23:11), and Paul identifies this sheaf with Christ (1 Corinthians 15:4). The other two major feasts can also be identified with stages in God's purpose and with resurrection. At Pentecost two loaves baked with leaven were waved. They too were "firstfruits" (Leviticus 23:17), and represented Jews and Gentiles who are now one loaf in Christ: their resurrection is "afterwards ... at his coming" (verse 23).

The last feast in the agricultural year was the feast of tabernacles held at harvest time in the seventh month. "Then comes the end", Paul says, speaking of the final resurrection at the end of the thousand years before sin and death are finally removed from the earth.

Continuing his logical explanation about resurrection, Paul now explains why it was necessary in God's plan of salvation. Until Christ was raised from the tomb, death reigned completely over all mankind, and had done so ever since Adam was disobedient to God's word. Death entered the world "by man", so resurrection also had to come to the world through a man (verse 21). This is further explained in a most important verse: "For as in Adam all die, even so in Christ all shall be made alive". The information was not simply of academic interest to the Corinthians, as it would be if it referred only to Adam and Christ. The whole human race (the Lord Jesus Christ included) was born "in Adam"; all are related to him by physical descent. The race is an Adamic race, and therefore all die. Writing at greater length to the ecclesia in Rome, Paul explained: "death reigned by the one man's offence" (Romans 5:17). This "one man" was Adam.

There is another group among Adam's race – a small group within a larger group (see diagram facing). These are the men and women who are "in Christ" through faith and baptism. "All" of these (not the "all" who are in Adam, but just a portion of them) "shall be made alive" when Jesus returns to establish the kingdom. The "all" who are "in Adam" inherit death; the "all" who are "in Christ" are heirs of life. It will be noted that, though the apostle speaks of

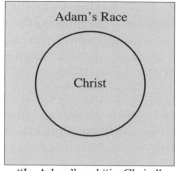

"In Adam" and "in Christ"

resurrection, he looks forward to the granting of everlasting life. It is not part of his subject to explain the need for judgement, or that some will be raised only to condemnation (cp. Daniel 12:2). His aim is to explain the hope of life which all who are truly "in Christ" will obtain. Again this is explained in Romans 5:17: "those who receive abundance of grace and of the gift of righteousness will reign in life through the one, Jesus Christ".

Each in His Own 'Troop'

As we have already considered from the connection with Israel's three annual feasts, this work of making alive has stages that are separated in time: "each one (is made alive) in his own order (Greek, *tagma*, a military term meaning a group, company or battalion)" (1 Corinthians 15:23). The first group contained only one person, the captain of our salvation: "Christ the firstfruits". "Afterwards ... at his (Christ's) coming", there will be a much larger troop of fellow-soldiers comprising all who in their lives acknowledged their need for God's saviour. Finally, there will be a group who live faithfully during the millennium. This last battalion will "be made alive" at "the end, when he delivers the kingdom to God the Father" (verse 24).

Only then, after "he has put all enemies under his feet" in fulfilment of prophecies made through David long before his birth (Psalm 8:6; 110:1), will "the last enemy" be destroyed. Death, which entered into every man's experience through Adam will finally be conquered when "all in Christ (are) made alive".

The only being who is not comprehended in the Adamic condemnation of death is God Himself; so when "all things are made subject to Christ", it is obvious that the Father is not included. The ultimate stage in His purpose is when "God is all in all": a perfect harmony and unity.

Baptized for the Dead

Paul, having explained the importance to God's plan of the resurrection of Christ, returns in verse 29 to his list of the serious effects of not believing in a physical or bodily resurrection. Taken out of this context, 1 Corinthians 15:29 can be difficult to understand, and has been wrested by some, particularly the Mormon church, to teach that it is possible to be baptized by proxy for someone who has died. In its context, however, the verse is easily understood; it only seems difficult when considered in isolation. Baptism is a symbol of death and resurrection. Anyone who is baptized acknowledges their relationship to Adam, and that they are under the reign of death. In seeking to become associated with the living Lord Jesus Christ, they "die" with him in water to show belief in the promise of being raised by him at his coming. Jesus' own resurrection is the guarantee of a greater resurrection when he returns to the earth.

Given this understanding of baptism, which is again expanded in his letter to the Romans, Paul asks why the Corinthians were being baptized if they were now doubting the certainty of a physical resurrection. Baptism is "for the dead"; literally it is for "dead ones", members of Adam's race (the word "dead" is in the plural form throughout verse 29). If "dead ones" are not going to be raised, why should anyone be baptized?

Furthermore, if there is no bodily resurrection, why should the apostles continually risk their lives to "go into all the world and preach the gospel to every creature" (Mark 16:15)? The "jeopardy" of their position was particularly marked in Paul's case, so that he was able to say with complete truthfulness: "I die daily". He only took these risks because of his firm hope in the eventual resurrection of all faithful believers to new life with the Lord in the kingdom. As an example of the predicament he faced daily, he was able to cite a recent event that occurred in Ephesus, which he described as "fighting with beasts". The temper of the inhabitants of Ephesus is shown in Acts 19:29, when "the whole city was filled with confusion, and rushed into the theatre with one accord".

It is likely that Paul was describing an event that preceded the disturbance recorded in Acts 19, explaining why, on the later occasion, the disciples would not allow him to enter the arena (verse 30). Possibly it was also when he "fought with beasts at Ephesus" that Priscilla and Aquila, whom Paul describes as "my fellow workers in Christ Jesus", risked their own necks for his life (Romans 16:3,4). But why should he or they take such risks unless they were convinced about the bodily resurrection of Jesus and all his faithful followers? "If the dead do not rise, 'Let us eat and drink, for tomorrow we die!'" (1 Corinthians 15:32).

Bad Company Ruins Good Morals

This was a scriptural proverb (Isaiah 22:13; Ecclesiastes 9:7-10), and a group in Corinth may have used it to justify their hedonistic behaviour. Paul warns against being deceived in this way, and quotes in response a well-known Greek proverb: "Evil company corrupts good habits" ("bad company ruins good morals", RSV). The evil company in Corinth comprised those who denied the truth about the resurrection, and the moral evil of this denial was seen in the serious immorality that was evident in the ecclesia – corruption, greed, fornication, drunkenness, extortion, and the like.

Paul exhorts them to come to their senses. They were like drunken revellers who needed to "return to a sober mind, and cease to sin" (1 Corinthians 15:34, Moffat). The false ideas about resurrection showed their ignorance of God. They boasted about knowledge, but really their ignorance was shameful.

This comprehensive treatment of resurrection was surely sufficient to restore the ecclesia to a right position. But there was still a second aspect to consider. Some were asking, "How are the dead raised up? And with what body do they come?" (1 Corinthians 15:35). We shall look at Paul's reply to this question in the next chapter.

20

HOW ARE THE DEAD RAISED?

"But someone will say, 'How are the dead raised up? And with what body do they come?'"

(1 Corinthians 15:35)

DENIAL of the resurrection among some in Corinth centred on its mechanics. They could not understand how a body that has mouldered into dust can be restored to full vigour. There were possibly other subsidiary questions concerning the nature of the body that is raised, and its 'age' compared with the years a person lived before his death. As this line of thought was followed, more and more difficulties were discovered. It became easier for the Corinthians to reject the whole concept of resurrection than to ignore or answer the difficulties. This is not a problem confined to Corinth or to the first century. There are many today that mock belief in the resurrection by asking how anyone can possibly live again after the body has completely decomposed.

The answer is that the promise of resurrection at the return of Christ has to be accepted in faith. Though there are compelling reasons for belief, and strong evidence that the Lord Jesus Christ himself rose from the dead, it is not something that can be proved conclusively. The difficulties that were being discussed in Corinth therefore arose from the lack of faith of some brethren and sisters, and Paul sought to provide secure grounds on which their faith could be founded.

Analogy from Nature

First of all, he chastened the Corinthians for their blindness, explaining that an answer to their difficulty was right under their noses. They all knew about planting and harvesting; it was part of everyday life. The seed they planted each year was destroyed in the process of reproduction and growth; it died so that it could live! Paul was picking up words of the Lord himself: "Most assuredly, I say to you, unless a grain of wheat falls into the ground and dies, it remains alone; but if it dies, it produces much grain" (John 12:24). In dying – and only through that process of decay – a seed produces new life. What this process produces is not the seed that was sown, but something very closely related to it. Familiarity with this agricultural principle may well dull the marvel and wonder of what is achieved; yet careful thought soon shows that the promise of resurrection is essentially the same.

The example helps answer the Corinthians' "foolish question" about the nature of the resurrection-body. "Each seed" has "its own body"; there is an identity of kind between what is sown and what is produced. A grain of wheat produces a wheat plant when it develops through being sown. You do not get a barley plant from a wheat seed, or oats from corn-seed. We can term these two bodies the seed-body and the plant-body. They are related, even though there are distinct differences. The seed is bare, dry and brown; the plant is green, moist and vigorous. Furthermore, "God gives it a body as He pleases" (1 Corinthians 15:38). Plants do not grow by themselves, or solely by human agency. All the farmer can do is plant the seed, provide the most helpful conditions, and then trust in God. It is the same with the resurrection; it is God's work, and it demonstrates His power.

Each According to Its Kind

The farmer has a choice of different seeds to sow, and each will provide a different plant. In the same way, there are different flesh-bodies: "All flesh is not the same flesh, but there is one kind of flesh of men, another flesh of animals, another of fish, and another of birds" (verse 39). It is worth noticing here that the apostle provides an undesigned testimony to the special creation of the main species: each was formed by a separate creative act "according to its kind" (Genesis 1:11). Furthermore, everything in God's creation is fitted to its purpose, and this is not limited to things on earth: "There are also celestial (heavenly) bodies and terrestrial (earthly) bodies; but the glory of the celestial is one, and the glory of the terrestrial is another" (1 Corinthians 15:40). Even the heavenly bodies – sun, moon and stars – are not all the same: "for one star differs from another star in glory" (verse 41).

These examples from the natural world must be applied to the promise of resurrection: just as there is a seed-body and a plant-body, and amidst a variety of "kinds" and "glories" an identity between a seed and the plant produced from it, so it is with resurrection. The key passage that influenced the apostle's thinking is John 12:23-25, where Jesus talks about his approaching glorification. He envisages a man who chooses not to plant his seed; and he loses it by the natural process of decay. If he chooses instead to plant it in his field, he sacrifices it, and still it 'decays', but he gains a harvest. This process can be applied to human life. One man chooses not to commit his life to God – he lives entirely for himself, and in the end he perishes. Another man 'loses' his life in following Christ, but gains it everlastingly.

"Sowing" and "Reaping"

Because the apostle likens death and resurrection to planting and harvesting, some have thought that when he refers to "sowing" he is speaking about putting bodies in the grave. His use of a similar figure in his letter to the Galatians makes it abundantly apparent that this was not his intention: "Do not be deceived, God is not mocked; for whatever a man sows, that he will also reap. For he who sows to his flesh will of the flesh reap corruption, but he who sows to the Spirit will of the Spirit reap everlasting life" (Galatians 6:7,8).

Paul is not saying here, or in Corinthians, that the nature of a man's resurrection-body depends on the state of his natural body when it is placed in the ground. If that were the case, it would be better to die in the full vigour of youth; there would be no glory in old age. He describes instead two ways of life available to man: selfishly "sowing to the flesh", or faithfully "sowing to the spirit" (note that he does not say "sowing *in* the flesh or spirit", but "sowing *to*" one or the other). "Sowing to the spirit" can only be understood as a moral process. It describes how a man can live with the intention of serving God to the best of his ability, despite the fact that he is mortal. He is "in the flesh", but he "sows to the spirit", in full expectation that he will eventually live "in the spirit". He anticipates a change that will alter a body adapted to natural life to one that is fitted for spiritual life.

By a series of stark contrasts Paul explains the nature both of the "sowing" and of the harvest. There is a sowing in corruption, in dishonour, in weakness – a natural body. There is a raising in incorruption, in glory, in power – a spiritual body. One is a body adapted to natural life; the other is fitted to spiritual life. If we wish to be part of the resurrection to everlasting life, there must be a "sowing" now, during our lifetime. This "sowing" is done "in corruption", referring to our mortal bodies; it is done "in weakness" – the condition of our mortality (as it was of Christ's, see 2 Corinthians 13:4); and it is done "in dishonour", referring to the frailty and unworthiness of mortality (cp. 1 Corinthians 15:50). We "sow" during our lifetime in "a natural body", or what Genesis 2:7 describes as "a living being" (cp. 1 Corinthians 15:45).

Still applying the agricultural metaphor, Paul cites the case of the first man Adam and contrasts him with Jesus: the last Adam. Adam was the first of the human race, and was made a "living soul (or being)". Earlier in 1 Corinthians 15, Paul explained about Adam as head of the race and how all humanity is encompassed "in Adam" (see previous chapter), sharing the mortality that came about through his disobedience (verse 22). Adam's origin was "of the earth, made of dust"; he was related naturally to earthly things. When he disobeyed God's Word he was told that he would "return to the ground, for out of it you were taken; dust you are, and to dust you shall return" (Genesis 3:19).

Of the Earth … of Heaven

Jesus, though born "in Adam" and sharing the weaknesses of mortality, was of a very different origin. He "proceeded forth and came from God" (John 8:42; 13:3; 1:1,14). Using virtually identical language to that used by Paul in Corinthians, John the Baptist spoke about the origins of the two Adams: "He who is of the earth is earthly and speaks of the earth. He who comes from heaven is above all" (3:31). Because he was true to this heavenly calling throughout his life, Jesus was *the last* Adam"; he showed the end of the Adamic state in mankind, and "became a life-giving spirit" (1 Corinthians 15:45). This further explains the apostle's earlier statement that "as in Adam all die, even so in Christ all shall be made alive" (verse 22). Jesus *became* a life-giving spirit": he gives life, while all that Adam ever gave is death. Adam is the physical head of creation, and all born after him are like him. But there is a new creation in Christ; all who are subject to that new creation, even though physically bearing Adam's impress or "image", partake of Christ's character. Furthermore, they become related to the hope of sharing in the new nature to be granted at the resurrection – "the image of the heavenly".

The present nature of Adam's race, which Paul describes as "flesh and blood" (verse 50) is not adapted for God's kingdom – it has no enduring qualities, being corruptible, weak, and lacking in inherent honour. An incorruptible nature is necessary to inherit a place in God's eternal kingdom. This can occur only through the influence of the Word of God, which Peter later describes as *incorruptible seed … which lives and abides forever"* (1 Peter 1:23). Therefore there must be a change from mortality to immortality: from corruption to incorruption. For this to happen, the dead saints must be raised, and to deny the promise of resurrection is to consign oneself to eternal oblivion.

"We shall be changed"

The change will occur at Christ's return – the life-giver will bring life. When he comes, some saints will be alive, and some will be asleep, "but we shall all be changed" (verse 51).

Just as in verse 22, Paul ignores those who "shall awake ... to shame and everlasting contempt" (Daniel 12:2); he is only concerned with those who are "in Christ", and who "shall be made alive". He therefore speaks of the change as if it is instantaneous, "in a moment, in the twinkling of an eye, at the last trumpet. For the trumpet will sound, and the dead will be raised incorruptible, and we shall be changed" (1 Corinthians 15:52). In Old Testament times, the trumpet was sounded to gather together the assembly of Israel. At Christ's coming it will call together those who are accepted, and their bodies will be changed.

Some have seen these verses as teaching that sleeping saints will emerge from the grave in an immortal state. But this ignores the general teaching of scripture that we shall all have to stand before the judgement seat of Christ before receiving life or condemnation (notably in Paul's second letter to Corinth, 2 Corinthians 5:10). It also ignores the implicit message of 1 Corinthians 15 about the process of "sowing" and "planting". The Lord uses this same analogy in his parables. He follows the well-known story of the sower by explaining that "the kingdom of God is as if a man should scatter seed on the ground" (Mark 4:26); and he shows that a process is involved: "first the blade, then the ear, after that the full grain in the ear" (verse 28). In other parables – wheat and tares, sheep and goats, and the great fishing net – Jesus refers to a process of selection and separation "at the end of this age. The Son of Man will send out his angels, and they will gather out of his kingdom all things that offend" (Matthew 13:40,41). As a result of this selection process, the unfaithful "will go away into everlasting punishment, but the righteous into eternal life" (25:46). All these stages are comprehended in the apostle's elliptical statement in Corinthians, "the dead will be raised incorruptible" (1 Corinthians 15:52).

After the judgement, when the righteous are changed, it will be "in a moment, in the twinkling of an eye." Paul immediately acknowledges the need for this change: "For this corruptible must put on incorruption, and this mortal must put on immortality" (verse 53). He was especially conscious of the burden of mortality, and wished desperately to be free from it. In his second letter to Corinth, he speaks of mortal human nature as a frail tent: "our earthly house". He goes on to say: "we who are in this tent groan, being burdened, not because we want to be unclothed, but further clothed, that mortality may be swallowed up by life" (2 Corinthians 5:1-4).

Swallowed Up

The same figure of putting on clothing fitted for the new life in the spirit occurs in 1 Corinthians 15, and in both passages Paul uses the same Greek word, *enduo*, to describe what happens. When our present mortality is "clothed upon" with immortality, and corruption with incorruption, "Death is swallowed up in victory" (1 Corinthians 15:54, quoting Isaiah 25:8). There is an echo here of the destruction following Korah, Dathan and Abiram's rebellion, when "the earth opened its mouth and swallowed them up ... with all their goods" (Numbers 16:32). The same finality is indicated for death itself at the last day.

Reference to mortality and corruption is not duplication of terms; there are two distinct and separate concepts involved. When Adam was told that he would die, it was a gracious word from God. The concept of an immortal yet corruptible sinner is awful to comprehend. So the resurrection-body will be both immortal and incorruptible. All the effects of mortality will be removed, and death and the grave will no longer be any threat. It is as the prophet Hosea declared: "O Death, where is your sting? O Hades, where is your victory?" (1 Corinthians 15:55, see Hosea 13:14). As the apostle reflected on this prospect, he asked himself about death's sting, and recognised that the idea could be confusing; surely death is the punishment inflicted by sin. So in a brief verse he captured Bible teaching about sin and death. Death entered the world because of man's disobedience. It is therefore possible to describe sin as death's weapon; remove sin, and death has no power – it is disarmed. And the way sin continues to inflict death is through Law, for "sin is lawlessness" (1 John 3:4).

The great prospect of victory over sin and death also caused Paul to reflect on how it would be achieved. Men and women will not become victorious by their own endeavours; for by themselves they are powerless to overcome. This is where the resurrection of Christ is all-important; he was victorious over sin throughout his life, and by resurrection he showed that the grave could no longer hold him. The captain of our salvation has therefore conquered both sin and death; and we can share in this victory through God's goodness: "the gift of God is eternal life in Christ Jesus our Lord" (Romans 6:23).

"Be ye Stedfast, Unmoveable"

Although the way has been prepared, and the victory has been won, something is still required from us. Paul concludes his comments on resurrection by encouraging the Corinthians to stand firm, and not to be moved. It seems they were liable to be disturbed by novel ideas and suggestions, and the apostle has therefore taken them back to the simple truths that can underpin a robust faith. Be assured, he says, "that your labour is not in vain in the Lord" (1 Corinthians 15:58). Thankfully, the same is true for disciples in every generation – "Life is the time to serve the Lord, to do His will, to learn His Word ..." (Hymn 396).

21

PRACTICAL ENCOURAGEMENT

AFTER all the perplexing difficulties covered earlier in the letter, the question about collections towards the Jerusalem Poor Fund was very straightforward, and so is the apostle's answer. He tells the Corinthians, as he had told the ecclesias in Galatia, that it is best to make regular, weekly, collections. In the course of his reply, we learn that the ecclesia normally assembled "on the first day of the week" (1 Corinthians 16:2), a custom still followed by ecclesias round the world today. This is a pattern started, it seems, by the apostles immediately after Christ's resurrection, to commemorate his victory over sin and death, and it is very appropriate that reference to it occurs in Paul's letter immediately following his treatise on resurrection and its fundamental importance.

This strong connection between the end of chapter 15 and the beginning of chapter 16 (emphasised in the original where there are no chapter divisions) brings together the need for steadfast resolve and the practical arrangements for providing financial help to those in distress. In just the same way today, collections for different funds should form an integral part of our faith and worship; they are not necessary evils that have no justifiable place in our memorial meetings. The pattern was helpfully set in the first century, reminding us of the important part that is played by practical expressions of concern for the welfare of others.

Paul's Personal Obligation

Paul had committed himself fully to the collection for the poor saints, assuring the other apostles of his readiness to undertake the task when they gave him and Barnabas: "the right hand of fellowship, that we should go to the Gentiles and they to the circumcised" (Galatians 2:9). There was a special urgency for Paul, as it is highly likely that the poverty of the brethren and sisters in Judea arose, at least partially, from the "persecution that arose over Stephen" (Acts 11:19), for which the apostle would feel a great personal responsibility. Wherever he went, therefore, he made arrangements for contributions to be sent back to the needy in Jerusalem.

A significant aspect of the arrangements was that ecclesias were made responsible both for the collections from their own members and for forwarding the combined sums to Jerusalem. Although it is not mentioned in his letter to Corinth, this shift of responsibility from the individual to the ecclesia would follow the Lord's strictures about almsgiving: "do not let your left hand know what your right hand is doing" (Matthew 6:3). Because the combined amounts of individual contributions could grow to considerable proportions, it was also necessary to introduce some control into the process. The Corinthians were therefore to nominate representatives who would travel to Jerusalem with the ecclesia's contribution – and possibly with the apostle as well. The scrupulous attention to detail indicated that the money was never intended to be in the apostle's hands at all; he was organising the collection, but he was guarding carefully against any charge that it – or some of it – was intended for his own personal use. In ecclesial financial matters this is a good precedent to follow; there has to be transparency and accountability at the same time as providing for the anonymity of the donor.

Commitments in Ephesus & Macedonia

Whether Paul would be able to accompany the contributions as they were taken from Corinth to Jerusalem depended on any intervening events that may arise. It was his clear intention to visit Corinth for an extended stay, and perhaps to spend the next winter there – the months between October and February during which sea travel was especially hazardous (cp. Acts 27:9-12). He did not intend to travel directly from Ephesus to Corinth, for there was something needing his attention in Macedonia; and in any case he would stay in Ephesus at least "until Pentecost", because "a great and effective door has opened to me, and there are many adversaries" (1 Corinthians 16:9)*. Paul was obviously writing against the background of exciting and dangerous times in his Ephesian ministry. Acts 19 shows the difficult circumstances in Ephesus, a city that was deeply superstitious and devoted to the worship of Diana, and Paul has already mentioned how he "fought with beasts at Ephesus" (1 Corinthians 15:32). The situation was too fluid for him to consider leaving there immediately, and the Corinthian brethren and sisters and their problems must await his later arrival.

Paul's Representative, Timothy

In the meantime, Paul has dispatched his travelling companion Timothy. Timothy was still very young, and was a relatively inexperienced missionary. But he was a young brother of great promise, "well spoken of by the brethren" in the locality of his home city, Lystra (Acts 16:2). Paul placed every confidence in Timothy's ability. He was able to write at a later date to the brethren and sisters at Philippi about him: "I trust in the Lord Jesus to send Timothy to you shortly, that I also may be encouraged when I know your state. For I have no one like-minded, who will sincerely care for your state" (Philippians 2:19,20). The same need existed in Corinth's case; Paul was concerned about the situation in the ecclesia, and if he could not go himself, there was no better person he could send than Timothy: "for he does the work of the Lord, as I also do" (1 Corinthians 16:10).

Timothy's visit to Corinth was not, however, assured of success. His youth and inexperience would militate strongly against his acceptance, particularly by those puffed up by their own self-importance whom Paul strongly criticised in his letter. Some would despise Timothy's youth (verse 11; see 1 Timothy 4:12), and try to overturn his authority, so Paul made it plain that the Corinthians would have to answer to him for Timothy's safety.

* This verse confirms that the letter was written from Ephesus, and not from Philippi as suggested by the postscript in the AV.

Another reason why everyone would not accept Timothy's visit is that the Corinthians had specifically asked about Apollos, who was obviously well regarded in the city. After Aquila and Priscilla "explained to him the way of God more accurately" during his time in Ephesus (Acts 18:26), Apollos travelled to Corinth and helped the ecclesia considerably: "for he vigorously refuted the Jews publicly, showing from the Scriptures that Jesus is the Christ" (verse 28). Paul explains how, after receiving the Corinthians' letter, he urged Apollos to return to Corinth, but without success. The decision not to go was thus Apollos's and not Paul's: "he will come when he has a convenient time" (1 Corinthians 16:12).

There is an important message here, both for the Corinthians and for us. Paul's presence was required in Ephesus and Macedonia ahead of any need in Corinth; Apollos was also engaged on other work. Both men determined their priorities, and reckoned that Corinth's needs were not greater than these other tasks to which they were committed. It is very easy to feel that our needs demand immediate attention, when a longer view will soon show that those of others are vastly more pressing. The fact that neither Paul or Apollos planned immediately to travel to Corinth would be a blow to the brethren and sisters there, but it should also teach them not to depend upon others at every turn. Paul's letter gave replies to their urgent questions, and it encouraged them to take the necessary decisions themselves about each different issue.

Concluding Exhortation

Knowing in advance that the members of the ecclesia in Corinth would have to apply his advice, Paul concludes his letter with a clear and compelling exhortation, based on five simple points:

1. **Watch** – Each member was to be alert. The problems in the ecclesia had not arisen overnight, but they developed over a period of time. By watching out for danger, it is possible that some serious difficulties could be averted. Laziness and disinterest allowed unscrupulous members to build up a following and start to lead others astray.

2. ***Stand fast in the faith*** – Linked with the previous point, this indicates that the brethren and sisters were to be on their guard against serious errors. Only a sure foundation in the fundamentals of the faith would help them to recognize error when it arose, and to be unmoved by its deceptive ways.

3. ***Be brave*** ("Quit you like men", AV) – The brethren and sisters in Corinth were like soldiers on active service. They faced an enemy that was often unseen, and who fought unconventionally. Paul uses the words of the Philistine commanders who reassured their troops when the ark of God was brought into the Hebrew camp in Samuel's day (1 Samuel 4:9). The soldiers recalled with fear all they knew of God's victory four centuries earlier against the Egyptians. They were ready to submit or flee, but their commanders encouraged them to bravery. Members of the ecclesia were facing a similar threat. The easiest course was the one of least resistance; but they should choose to resist in view of the rewards of victory.

4. ***Be strong*** – Any sign of weakness would be exploited, so the faith in which they stood was to make them strong against all forms of evil.

5. ***Be charitable*** – None of the earlier points provide any excuse for worldly responses or reactions. No one should forget "the more excellent way" of love, the surest antidote to a factious spirit.

Dependable Elders

In the absence of Paul and Apollos, and knowing that neither would be present in Corinth for some time, the ecclesia had to know on whom they could depend. Paul appealed personally to each member of the ecclesia to recognize the worth and experience of their founding members – "the household of Stephanas ... the firstfruits of Achaia" (verse 15). This group of brethren and sisters "devoted themselves to the ministry of the saints" so fervently that the AV describes their attention as an "addiction" – the fully committed practical and outward expression of their firmly held beliefs. "Ministry of the saints" suggests that they had a desire to undertake lowly rather than prominent service, in contrast to those who sought the "best seats" and the "best places" (cp. Luke 20:46). Here in Stephanas' household was a dependable group, who had proved themselves in service, through working and labouring with the apostle.

They and others like them formed the backbone of the true ecclesia, and could be trusted to act selflessly on behalf of all others. They had the scriptural qualifications for elders, on the basis of the apostle's lists in his later letters to Timothy and Titus. His comments about them are similar to words used in Hebrews 13:17 about elders: "Obey those who rule over you, and be submissive, for they watch out for your souls, as those who must give account. Let them do so with joy and not with grief, for that would be unprofitable for you" (cp. 1 Corinthians 16:16). In the original, there is a play on words that does not come through in English translations. Paul speaks of Stephanas and his household "addicting" themselves to service (Greek, *tasso*), and asks the ecclesia to "submit" to them (Greek, *hupotasso*). A similar conscious effort must be made to be submissive, as those good examples provided in their complete dedication to service.

What a contrast they revealed to the carping and destructive criticisms of those who sought positions of leadership in Corinth! The critics were so self-centred that they gave no thought to the needs or welfare of the apostle and his team. Paul clearly missed his friends in Corinth and wished to feel closer to them. By their travelling to Ephesus, Stephanas, Fortunatus and Achaicus gave him a little taste of the ecclesia's fellowship: "what was lacking on your part they supplied" (verse 17). Personal visits, letters, notes and (in our day) telephone calls can mean an enormous amount to anyone separated by distance from loved ones, and their value ought never to be underestimated. The benefit is much greater than the time and effort expended; and it is not difficult – because of this example – to see the reason. Such communication is an expression of a person's deep regard; if it is absent, serious doubt exists as to whether there is any real concern.

The Value of Practical Concern

Paul was so encouraged by the brethren's visit that he felt physically as well as spiritually refreshed; but he suggested that there was also an equal benefit for those – even his critics – whom they represented: "they refreshed my spirit *and yours*" (verse 18). When Jesus warned his disciples to be on their guard against false prophets, he explained that men and women are to be tested by their actions as well as by what they profess: "by their fruits you will know them" (Matthew 7:20). Paul therefore told the Corinthians about the visit of Stephanas and his companions, concluding on the basis of their actions: "Therefore acknowledge such men" (1 Corinthians 16:18). This is a resounding endorsement of the small group who travelled from Corinth to Ephesus. When they returned in the company of Timothy and with Paul's letter, all possible resources were available to the ecclesia to tackle its serious problems.

It would also be helpful for the Corinthians to realize that they were not alone; other believers in other countries shared the same fundamental truths, and faced similar difficulties. So Paul sends greetings from the ecclesias in the Roman province of Asia, where Ephesus was the leading centre. Only Aquila and Priscilla of the brethren and sisters in that province would be well known to the Corinthians, so he specifically names them, and explains that they opened up their home to the ecclesia in Ephesus, as they did later when they moved to Rome (verse 19, Romans 16:5). This practice most probably started in Corinth where they were closely involved with the first preaching mission in the city (Acts 18).

Sincere and Honourable Greetings

The fellowship that exists between ecclesias, as evidenced by the warm expressions Paul was able to extend in his letter to Corinth, should also exist within each ecclesia. Unfortunately, Corinth's problems acted against the existence of such a climate, so Paul encouraged them to

"Greet one another with a holy kiss" (1 Corinthians 16:20). This simple command is often misunderstood, and some wonder why brethren and sisters do not always greet each other today with a kiss – in the Western world, for example, a handshake is much more common. But Paul was not instructing brethren and sisters to kiss each other, as if the most important thing was the kiss; the emphasis is on the word "holy". Judas showed how treacherous a kiss can be: "Judas", Jesus said, "are you betraying the Son of Man with a kiss?" (Luke 22:48). Something similar probably occurred in Corinth, where brethren were expansively greeting members of the ecclesia whom they clearly despised and opposed. So Paul told them that their greetings must be sincere and honourable – something that is true for all disciples, whatever form the greeting may take.

To show that the letter was authentic, Paul followed his usual practice and personally signed the letter (1 Corinthians 16:21, cp. 2 Thessalonians 3:17), though an amanuensis wrote the main part. Possibly the last section of the letter (1 Corinthians 16:21-24) was all in his hand-writing. This would give added significance to verse 22, which otherwise seems out of place. Despite all that has gone before, Paul will not close the letter with his usual greetings and prayer for the recipients, without issuing a last stern and fateful warning: "If anyone does not love the Lord Jesus Christ, let him be accursed." We have mentioned before, in connection with 1 Corinthians 12:3, that *anathema Iesous* ("Jesus is accursed") was the formal recantation required by those who persecuted the early Christians, yet many replied with the contrary declaration, "Jesus is Lord" (*Kyrios Iesous*) (pages 110, 111). Now Paul challenges each reader of his letter to indicate where he or she stands. Unless there is true love for the Lord Jesus Christ, the believer will be "accursed". And in order to focus their minds on this challenge, he reminded them that the answer will one day have to be made in the Lord's presence: "O Lord, come!" (Greek, *Maranatha*).

Paul's love for the Lord was shown by his love for his brethren and sisters (1 John 4:21). Despite all the criticism

163

personally levelled at him, and the harsh comments about him, Paul is a large-hearted individual. He prays sincerely that the grace of the Lord Jesus will be evident among them – the awareness of what has been achieved on their behalf being shown by a gracious attitude towards each other and by sincere thanksgiving to God.

22

PREPARING FOR A THIRD VISIT

THE scriptures provide only a partial and sketchy account of the apostle's contacts with Corinth. In chapter 2 we concluded that Paul sent at least one letter to the ecclesia prior to writing from Ephesus what we know as 1 Corinthians. And there are hints in 2 Corinthians that he visited the ecclesia with a heavy heart, and also wrote a severe letter in the period of time that passed between writing the two New Testament epistles. Before looking in detail at 2 Corinthians it will help to put it in context if we can bring together as much information as possible about this intervening period.

From the information provided in the Acts of the Apostles, we learn that the ecclesia in Corinth was founded during the second missionary journey, when Paul and his companions spent nearly two years in the city (Acts 18:1-17). According to Acts, he did not return until late in the third missionary journey (20:2,3). This all seems straight-forward until it is recognized that Paul, writing 2 Corinthians from Macedonia during the third journey, refers to that return visit as his third – not his second – visit to the city (2 Corinthians 12:14; 13:1). Therefore there must have been another visit that is not mentioned in Acts, and this visit must also have been the one he describes as being made "in sorrow" (2:1). This is hardly a way of describing the exciting occasion when he was first there. He stayed during that initial visit for over "a year and six months", because the Lord had "much people in this city" (Acts 18:10,11), and the response to his preaching must have filled him with joy. The visit "in sorrow" is therefore almost certainly the "missing" second visit, and this must have occurred for a reason that was not foreseen when Paul wrote 1 Corinthians.

This all seems relatively straightforward until we try to make sense of Paul's various descriptions of his intentions to revisit Corinth. The relevant passages (all written during the third missionary journey) are as follows:

> "Now I will come to you when I pass through Macedonia (for I am passing through Macedonia). And it may be that I will remain, or even spend the winter with you."   (1 Corinthians 16:5,6)

> "I intended to come to you before, that you might have a second benefit – to pass by way of you to Macedonia, to come again from Macedonia to you, and be helped by you on my way to Judea."   (2 Corinthians 1:15,16)

> "Now for the third time I am ready to come to you. And I will not be burdensome to you."   (12:14)

> "This will be the third time I am coming to you."
> (13:1)

Changing Plans

The problem arises if we assume these comments relate strictly to the chronological order in which they were written. In other words, if it was Paul's intention first of all to travel to Corinth via Macedonia (1 Corinthians 16:5); then, after a change of plan, to make a visit to Macedonia from Corinth (2 Corinthians 1:15,16); and finally to change his mind yet again – despite making an unspecified visit "in sorrow" (2:1) – and plan a third visit late on in his third missionary journey (12:14; 13:1).

But his comments should not be read as if they follow this pattern. The clue appears when Paul speaks of his intention to make a second visit – an intention that was not fulfilled, despite the fact that he made a visit to them "in sorrow". We need therefore to rearrange the quotations above. 1 Corinthians 16:5,6 describes the visit Paul actually made (cp. Acts 20:1-3). 2 Corinthians 1:15,16 explains an original plan that was soon discarded. This intention to travel to Corinth must have been his immediate reaction to the information he received in the Corinthian ecclesia's own letter and from the verbal reports given him by members of Chloe's household and others. But instead of travelling to Corinth personally, he sent Timothy as his representative and the letter we know as 1 Corinthians. This enabled him to spend a longer time in Ephesus (three years in total, Acts 20:31), where there was clearly a great need for his presence: "for a great and effective door has opened to me, and there are many adversaries" (1 Corinthians 16:9).

Paul's objective in sending Timothy, even though he decided not to go himself, was to "remind you of my ways in Christ, as I teach everywhere in every church" (4:17). This would prepare the ecclesia for the advice contained in the first epistle, even if Timothy was not the actual postman. Paul presumably felt it better that the ecclesia should have opportunity to think carefully about the points he would be making in his letter. A visit from him could have been confrontational, and less likely to remedy the serious problems that existed. Timothy's task was therefore far from easy, and the concern the apostle had for his young protégée is apparent in the closing section of the first epistle. Paul realised that the task was almost impossible in view of the swirling currents of conflicting problems in the ecclesia (16:10,11). When Timothy returned with a report of conditions in Corinth, there was indisputable confirmation that some of the ecclesia's difficulties were deep-seated.

The ecclesia, or at least those members who were highly critical of the apostle, saw Paul's failure to travel to them as a sign of serious weakness, and he wrote 2 Corinthians partly to answer this criticism: "Therefore, when I was planning this (i.e., the visit he originally intended), did I do it lightly? Or the things I plan, do I plan according to the flesh, that with me there should be Yes, Yes, and No, No?" (2 Corinthians 1:17). But he did not only respond in writing; as we have seen there was another apostolic visit that must have taken place at some time during his three-year stay in Ephesus. What we now wish to discover is when this visit occurred, any details it is possible to glean about its purpose, and what it achieved.

When was the painful visit made?

While not every commentator accepts that the visit "in sorrow" must have been made during Paul's stay in Ephesus, the reasons set out above lead almost certainly to that conclusion. But exactly when during that period did Paul travel to Corinth? It must have been after he sent his first epistle, and after Timothy returned with his report of conditions in the city. This leaves only a comparatively small window of opportunity, as it appears that 1 Corinthians was written in the early part of the year when Paul left Ephesus (1 Corinthians 16:8).

This period of time occurs in Acts between 19:9, where Paul's preaching in the school of Tyrannus is described, and 20:1 when he leaves Ephesus to go into Macedonia. From the information in Acts of his activities in Ephesus he could not have been away for an extended period – weeks, rather than months.

What caused this quickly arranged and hasty visit? It can only have been an extremely disturbing report from Timothy about the situation he found in Corinth. Are there any clues in 2 Corinthians that help us to construct the message Timothy brought back to the apostle?

The Changing Scene

Though it is impossible to be certain about the contents of the 'severe letter', or the subject of the hasty visit, the changing scene revealed by differences between 1 and 2 Corinthians helps to indicate the subjects that must have exercised Paul's mind. When he wrote 1 Corinthians the major problem in the ecclesia was the existence of factions. This lack of internal unity impacted on other matters: the ecclesia had failed to deal adequately with a serious case of immorality; there were disputes between brethren being settled in Gentile law-courts; there was not a common approach to marriage problems; it was doubtful if all the members of the ecclesia had made a clear break with idolatry; the breaking of bread meetings were disorderly; some sisters were ignoring the injunction to be submissive, and other members were abusing the spirit-gifts. On top of all this was a misunderstanding about the resurrection.

By the time Paul wrote 2 Corinthians some of these issues no longer troubled the ecclesia, while others had developed and deteriorated. There was no longer a problem with their understanding of the resurrection; the memorial meetings were not a cause for concern; and the ecclesia had tackled the case of immorality. But the problem of the different factions had grown into a different and more sinister issue. One faction in particular had become even more outspoken, and was directly opposing the apostle and his teachings. He was criticised for being fickle and light-hearted; his credentials as an apostle were questioned and ridiculed; and he was charged with taking advantage of the hospitality of some members of the ecclesia, and of collecting money for his own private purposes.

2 Corinthians therefore contains basically three parts, and was written to prepare the brethren and sisters in Corinth for the third visit Paul planned to make to the city, the visit recorded in Acts 20:2,3:

- Paul defends himself against the charges made about his conduct towards the ecclesia (chapters 1-7).

- He explains the details for the collection he is organising on behalf of the poverty-stricken ecclesias in Judea (chapters 8,9).

- He makes an impassioned defence against those who have personally opposed him (chapters 10-13).

It is probably this last section that gives the clue to the content of the severe letter and the reason for Paul's hasty visit. Timothy must have returned from Corinth with news of how some in the ecclesia were growing forthright in their criticism of the apostle, challenging his apostleship and seeking to negate the advice he gave in his first epistle. It would be natural for Paul to respond to this by making an immediate personal visit to reinforce what he had written in his first epistle. He found the situation just as bad as Timothy described it, and he met severe opposition. The visit seemed to achieve no useful purpose. If anything, the situation was worse afterwards than it was before he went.

The Severe Letter

After Paul returned to Ephesus, he therefore wrote an extremely severe letter, marshalling all his best arguments and strongest points. He put all Gamaliel's training to good use, and used all his powers of advocacy. His objective was to expose his fiercest opponents, and encourage the continuing support of the majority of the ecclesia. Titus, who had returned from Corinth after delivering the first epistle, was most probably also the bearer of this direct and blunt letter. Titus was a good choice, for he had first-hand knowledge of the situation; and he was an older brother than Timothy, whose natural diffidence had allowed Paul's opponents to continue almost unchecked in their slanderous comments. Furthermore, Titus had started the collection for the poor saints in Judea, and would be able to explain from first-hand experience how it was organised.

No sooner had Titus left Ephesus, bearing this severe letter, and Paul began to wonder if he had been too stern. Would his approach be counter-productive? There was a time when he actually regretted sending the letter (2 Corinthians 7:8), and was anxious to learn if it was effective. To stay in Ephesus became impossible, for it would only further add to the delay in Paul receiving Titus' report. So the apostle started to travel towards Corinth by the route Titus would be using to return. He reached Macedonia, and was still restless and anxious. "Nevertheless God, who comforts the downcast, comforted us by the coming of Titus, and not only by his coming, but also by the consolation with which he was comforted in you, when he told us of your earnest desire, your mourning, your zeal for me, so that I rejoiced even more" (2 Corinthians 7:6,7).

Rejoicing

How this must have cheered Paul! His regrets evaporated immediately, and the second epistle was the release of all his pent-up feelings. It is thus among the most personal of all his letters, showing his deep emotions and his intimate concern for every member of the Corinthian ecclesia. These intense feelings, oscillating between frantic concern and ecstatic joy, and the deeply personal nature of the letter, make it sometimes difficult to understand. One commentator has called it "the most letter-like of all the letters of Paul"; and its various allusions and personal references were probably only fully appreciated by the first recipients. The task of translators is thus made particularly difficult, and literal English translations such as the 1611 Authorised version (KJV) are almost unintelligible in places. Therefore it is often helpful to read the letter through first in a good paraphrase to get a flavour of the apostle's message before using a dependable translation for study purposes*.

The table overleaf suggests a possible order of events, providing a framework that should help put all Paul's dealings with the Corinthian ecclesia into historical order.

---

* Useful paraphrases are those by J. B. Phillips, and by F. F. Bruce. The latter is produced in a parallel version alongside the Revised Version text, complete with the "fuller" cross references. This provides all a student could need: the text in a form that can aid understanding, and one of the best study versions available.

Suggested Order of Events in the Apostle Paul's Dealings with the Corinthian Ecclesia

1. Paul spent at least 18 months in Corinth during the second missionary journey (Acts 18:11), before moving on to Ephesus.

2. From Ephesus, Paul wrote a letter to the ecclesia in Corinth that has not been preserved (referred to in 1 Corinthians 5:9).

3. Visitors to Ephesus from Corinth told Paul of problems in the city (1 Corinthians 1:11).

4. Brethren from Corinth brought a letter to Paul from the ecclesia.

5. Timothy was sent from Ephesus to Macedonia and Achaia (Corinth).

6. Paul wrote 1 Corinthians, and sent it with Titus.

7. While in Corinth, Titus helped to organize the collection for the poor saints in Jerusalem.

8. Timothy returned to Ephesus with news of a rapidly deteriorating situation in Corinth.

9. Paul made a short and hurried visit to Corinth, and was strongly opposed by adversaries in the ecclesia.

10. After returning to Ephesus, Paul wrote a very severe letter to the ecclesia, probably sending it again with Titus who must have returned to Ephesus.

11. After sending the letter, Paul was anxious about its effects. He left Ephesus for Macedonia, and met Titus, probably at Philippi, who brought encouraging news about the majority in the ecclesia (2 Corinthians 2:12,13; 7:5-16).

12. From Macedonia, Paul wrote the letter we have as 2 Corinthians, and sent it by Titus and two other brethren: one of whom was probably Luke (2 Corinthians 8:16-23).

23

IDENTIFYING THE ADVERSARIES

W E considered in the last chapter the events that occurred between the writing of 1 and 2 Corinthians and the serious deterioration in the relationship between the apostle and the ecclesia at Corinth. Despite the personal visit he made to them "in sorrow" (2 Corinthians 2:1) and the letter he wrote that was very severe in its message, Paul was worried that the breach might be irremediable. He was therefore eager and impatient to receive the news that Titus was bringing to him, as he returned from delivering the "severe letter", and was overjoyed to learn that, despite some continuing strong opposition, the ecclesia generally wished to restore the former good relationship they had enjoyed with him.

Worsening Situation

It will be helpful towards an understanding of the letter to try and discover why the situation in Corinth deteriorated so badly after Paul departed from the city. How did the various conflicting groups arise, the groups that caused Paul such anguish when he wrote 1 Corinthians? And what made the situation so much worse that it demanded the hasty visit and the severe letter before Paul was able to write in 2 Corinthians that the ecclesia had finally started to tackle some of the deep-seated problems?

Once again it will be necessary to try and answer these questions by piecing together small snippets of information out of the epistles. The conclusions that are reached depend to a large degree how much emphasis is placed on the apostle's various comments. On a number of occasions Paul denies that he acts, or has acted, towards the Corinthian brethren and sisters in particular ways. It is reasonable to assume that these are answers to the critics who made these allegations publicly and widely. Some of them are set out below.

Allegations against Paul

1. Paul had arrogated to himself leadership over the ecclesia ("Not that we have dominion over your faith", 1:24).

2. The message Paul preached was of his own invention; it was not the Lord Jesus' gospel ("We do not preach ourselves, but Christ Jesus the Lord, and ourselves your bondservants for Jesus' sake", 4:5).

3. Paul was mentally deranged ("If we are beside ourselves, it is for God; or if we are of sound mind, it is for you", 5:13).

4. Paul had defrauded the ecclesia of money ("We have wronged no one, we have corrupted no one, we have cheated no one", 7:2; "I preached the gospel of God to you free of charge ... in everything I kept myself from being burdensome to you", 11:7-9).

5. Paul was only bold in his letters, not when he was personally present – he soon betrayed his lack of education ("I, Paul – who in presence am lowly among you, but being absent am bold toward you", 10:1; "Even though I am untrained in speech, yet I am not in knowledge", 11:6).

6. His refusal to accept Corinthian support was because his claim to be an apostle was false ("Did I commit sin in humbling myself that you might be exalted, because I preached the gospel of God to you free of charge?", 11:7).

It is apparent from occasional comments in 1 Corinthians that some of these criticisms had existed for some time, and had intensified rather than diminished during Paul's absence from Corinth. The following brief quotations from the first epistle give a flavour of how the apostle saw those who opposed him:

"Now some are puffed up, as though I were not coming to you. But I will come to you shortly, if the Lord wills, and I will know, not the word of those who are puffed up, but the power." (4:18,19)

"My defence to those who examine me is this: Do we have no right to eat and drink?" (9:3,4)

"If anyone thinks himself to be a prophet or spiritual, let him acknowledge that the things which I write to you are the commandments of the Lord. But if anyone is ignorant, let him be ignorant." (14:37,38)

Paul's Description of his Adversaries

This picture of arrogant men, claiming to be spiritual but displaying very fleshly attitudes, is greatly expanded in 2 Corinthians. From Paul's comments it is possible to build up quite an accurate representation of the nature of his opponents:

1. Their teaching was not consistent; often it was negative ("The Son of God, Jesus Christ, who was preached among you by us ... was not Yes and No, but in him was Yes", 1:19).

2. Their teaching corrupted God's Word ("We are not, as so many, peddling the word of God; but as of sincerity, but as from God", 2:17).

3. Their supposed authority lay in the Letters of Recommendation they carried with them ("Do we need, as some others, epistles of commendation to you or letters of commendation from you?", 3:1).

4. They rested on the work done by others, not by themselves ("not boasting ... in other men's labours" (10:15).

5. They claimed to be, or to be associated with, "Super-apostles" ("I am not at all inferior to the most eminent apostles", 11:5).

175

With "Authority" from Jerusalem?

The clue to the identity of these detractors of the apostle Paul lies in the comment about "Letters of Commendation". Brethren who had learned the truth in Corinth, and who were baptized following Paul's visit there would not need any introduction to the ecclesia. These critics must have come from elsewhere to impose themselves on the Corinthian ecclesia. They came with letters that linked them to some supposed hierarchy among the ecclesias, and they were keen to have the pre-eminence. All these factors fit very well with the adversaries Paul often met on his travels. The most scathing and persistent of his enemies were found in the Jewish communities in the cities where he travelled. On his first missionary journey Jews plotted to stone him when he was in Iconium (Acts 14:5), and he was actually stoned when he was in Lystra (14:19). On his second journey, he had to leave Thessalonica and Berea because of the Jews who persecuted him (17:5,13-15); and in Corinth itself the opposition to his teaching grew so strong among the Jews who met in the synagogue that Paul declared, "Your blood be upon your own heads; I am clean. From now on I will go to the Gentiles" (18:6). We can be certain that this statement did little to calm Jewish fears; it would more likely inflame their leaders to even greater opposition.

In 2 Corinthians, Paul describes these adversaries as "false apostles, deceitful workers, transforming themselves into apostles of Christ" (2 Corinthians 11:13). They were most likely members of the Judaising party who had tried unsuccessfully to demand that all Gentile converts should be circumcised. In his impassioned defence of his position, Paul openly challenges their credentials: "Are they Hebrews? So am I. Are they Israelites? So am I. Are they the seed of Abraham? So am I" (11:22).

What a grief of heart this must have been to Paul. His work was being hindered by the very people who had most benefited from God's care throughout the centuries of their existence. The Jews had every advantage, "because to them were committed the oracles of God" (Romans 3:2). The deceitful handling of this precious word was the greatest indignity that was indulged in by Paul's fellow countrymen.

A Direct Challenge

The picture presented by these various comments in both of Paul's New Testament letters to Corinth is of a group of Jewish-born brethren emanating from another ecclesia and claiming strong connections with the apostles in Jerusalem. They may have included some of the group mentioned in Acts 15: "Certain men came down from Judea and taught the brethren, 'Unless you are circumcised according to the custom of Moses, you cannot be saved'" (Acts 15:1). But there is also some evidence that there was one brother in particular, who led the opposition to Paul. At some stage in the dealings between the apostle and the Corinthian ecclesia there was an incident of severe misconduct directed personally against the apostle, either in his presence during the "painful" visit, or possibly when Timothy visited the city on Paul's behalf. Paul's reaction formed the main part of his "severe" letter to the ecclesia.

We learn about this incident from a comment in 2 Corinthians 7: "Although I wrote to you, I did not do it for the sake of him who had done the wrong, nor for the sake of him who suffered wrong, but that our care for you in the sight of God might appear to you" (verse 12). This comment is clearly directed towards an individual, rather than a group, even if the brother had a number of followers. Thankfully, as we considered in the previous chapter, Titus who took the strongly worded letter to Corinth, returned to Paul with the good news that the ecclesia was not alienated from him by the behaviour of this one strong-minded brother. Presumably action had been taken to disarm his worst effects, and Paul was able to look forward to a greatly improved relationship with his dearly loved brethren and sisters in Corinth.

Overview of the Letter

He was keen to cement this new stage in their relationship, and therefore he wrote immediately out of a full and overflowing heart the letter we know as 2 Corinthians. The letter was designed to ensure that the problem would not flare up again. Paul took great care to explain how he laboured on behalf of the ecclesia, and how their needs were paramount at all times, even to the detriment of his own. In the process he answered in detail all the allegations made against him (chapters 1-7). So far as his leading opponents were concerned, and particularly the one who challenged him directly, Paul concluded the letter with a passionate defence of his position and apostolic authority (chapters 10-13).

Between these two parts of the letter is a section advising how the ecclesia should make a collection towards the needs of the brethren and sisters in Judea who were poverty-stricken due to their faith (chapters 8,9). At first sight, this has nothing to do with the main subject matter of the letter; but in fact it is vital. The only way Paul's critics could make any progress was by concentrating attention on the needs of Corinth and ignoring the wider responsibilities of fellowship. When problems arise in ecclesias today, it is often because the focus has turned completely inward, and in such circumstances molehills soon become mountains.

The antidote in cases like this is to be active in fellowship, and this was the great object of the Judean Collection that Paul organised wherever he travelled. Details of the great collection are therefore central to this second epistle (see detailed analysis alongside), and not a strange digression as some commentators see it.

Analysis of 2 Corinthians

Paul Defends His Conduct Towards the Ecclesia
(chapters 1-7)

Salutation (1:1-2)

Mutual affliction and consolation (1:3-14)

Reasons for Paul's changes of plan (1:15–2:4)

Forgiving the Offender (2:5-11)

Disappointment and Joy at Troas (2:12-17)

The Corinthians – a Letter from Christ (3:1-6)

A Fading and an Abiding Glory (3:7-16)

The Message of Christ faithfully delivered (3:17–4:6)

Treasure in Earthen Vessels (4:7-15)

The Sustaining Hope (4:16–5:10)

The Ministry of Reconciliation (5:11–6:10)

Their response to the apostle's labours (6:11–7:4)

The Comfort Titus Brought (7:5-16)

The Collection for the Poor Saints in Judea
(chapters 8, 9)

Generosity Encouraged (8:1-15)

Titus and Companions sent to Corinth (8:16 – 9:5)

Results of Generous Giving (9:6-15)

Passionate Defence Against His Opponents
(chapters 10-13)

Defence of his Authority and Mission (10:1-18)

"Foolish" Boastings (11:1 – 12:21)

Final warnings (13:1-10)

Final greetings (13:11-14)

24

PAUL DEFENDS HIS CONDUCT

KNOWING the contentious background events that caused Paul to write 2 Corinthians makes its opening salutation even more surprising. The apostle did not change his usual practice, despite the ridicule and opposition he had received. Nor did he open his letter with any special comments that his readers could claim were insincere. His words can be compared to the start of his other New Testament letters, and they are virtually the same.

There was, however, one significant difference, and this is also true of 1 Corinthians. Both are addressed specifically to the ecclesia. Paul's letters are normally addressed to "saints and faithful brethren at _____", but these two letters are written to the ecclesia as an entity. The reason is not difficult to deduce. Corinth's problems arose because of the deep division in the ecclesia. Anything that helped unite the brethren and sisters would encourage the resolution of their difficulties.

Spiritual Cooperation

Timothy's name is combined with Paul's in the introductory greetings because of the close relationship they both had with the Corinthian ecclesia. But even more importantly, the relationship between Timothy and Paul – "as a son with his father he served with me in the gospel" (Philippians 2:22) – was a model of spiritual cooperation that Paul wished the Corinthians to adopt. He therefore begins his letter by describing the benefits of the Christian life. He acknowledges that the path to the kingdom is not always easy, that "we must through many tribulations enter the kingdom of God" (Acts 14:22); yet God "comforts us in all our tribulation, that we may be able to comfort those who are in any trouble, with the comfort with which we ourselves are comforted by God" (2 Corinthians 1:4).

There must have been many occasions during the apostle's missionary journeys when this principle was confirmed. We can envisage the travellers at the end of a long hard day, sitting down to discuss the day's events. There may have been serious Jewish opposition or a hostile crowd. Yet the conversion of just one faithful member of that crowd would lift their spirits, and make them rejoice. Like their Lord, they experienced both suffering and joy: "For as the sufferings of Christ abound in us, so our consolation also abounds through Christ" (verse 5). Whether the Corinthians realised it or not, they were beneficiaries of the tribulations suffered by Paul and his companions. The road to Corinth involved countless incidents of difficulty, affliction and opposition. All these were thrust aside because of the need to preach the gospel to every creature. What Paul and his companions brought to Corinth was the word of comfort. When the Corinthians accepted that word, they fellowshipped all the sufferings that were involved in bringing it to them: "And our hope for you is steadfast, because we know that as you are partakers of the sufferings, so also you will partake of the consolation" (verse 7).

Sentenced to Death

At the point of writing his letter, Paul had undergone another period of severe trial. He mentions a specific "trouble which came to us in Asia ... we despaired even of life" (verse 8). What could this trouble have been? We know of the mob of Diana-worshippers in Ephesus who were concerned about the effect of Paul's teaching on their livelihood, but that incident significantly predated the writing of 2 Corinthians. There is, however, a comment in Romans 16:3 about Aquila and Priscilla, who were in Ephesus with Paul when he wrote 2 Corinthians. He writes of them risking their own lives to save his, and this may be the perilous incident he refers to. His own life was obviously in serious danger, for he said: "We had the sentence of death in ourselves" (2 Corinthians 1:9).

Paul realised that his release from this predicament was only through God's grace. Prayers were offered for him in Corinth, and contributed greatly to his being delivered from "so great a death". Here was a practical expression of the principle of cooperation he was speaking about, and he thanked God for the comfort it brought to him. Furthermore, the Corinthians were able to pray for him because they knew that his dealings were always beyond reproach. Any sentence against him must have been unjust, because "we conducted ourselves in the world in simplicity and godly sincerity" (verse 12).

This care and concern shown towards Paul was far from being in one direction only. Many in Corinth acknowledged their great debt to Paul who brought the gospel to them; but Paul also gloried in them: they were the fruit of his labours. Why then should anyone in Corinth doubt his intentions towards them? Much had been made in some quarters about his change of plans, and certain incorrect conclusions were drawn from his failure to visit Corinth. He had to correct any wrong interpretation of his behaviour.

Detailed comments were made on 2 Corinthians 1:15-17 when we tried to piece together what happened between the writing of the two New Testament letters to Corinth (page 165). It is sufficient at this point to note Paul's insistence that his dealings with the ecclesia – as with the authorities in Ephesus – were always with honesty and sincerity. He was not a hypocrite. The Corinthians knew him from his time among them and could confirm that he was upright in all his dealings. He did not vacillate, saying Yes on one occasion, and No on another, for that would be incompatible with the truth he preached. The same is true of the Father, "with whom there is no variation or shadow of turning" (James 1:17).

Great is His Faithfulness

How could Paul preach about the God of Truth and be untrue himself and in his dealings with others? The fulfilment of God's word is based on His faithfulness. He has made "great and precious promises", and a believer accepts faithfully and unquestioningly that these promises will be fulfilled. The assurance to first century believers (who did not have the completed New Testament scriptures) was in the spirit-gifts they received: "God ... has sealed us and given us the Spirit in our hearts as a guarantee" (2 Corinthians 1:21,22).

These comments about the Truth of God's Word, and the requirement that believers should therefore be truthful and upright in their behaviour forms a very fitting introduction to Paul's explanation of the real reason for his change of plans. It all turned on the ecclesia's handling of a serious moral incident. We must remind ourselves of the details.

Paul knew that the ecclesia had initially turned a blind eye to this serious immorality, and he wrote about it in the early letter that has not been preserved in our scriptures (1 Corinthians 5:9). By the time he came to write his first epistle, he felt able to give specific details about the problem: "there is sexual immorality among you, and such sexual immorality as is not even named among the Gentiles – that a man has his father's wife!" (verse 1). His advice was clear: the ecclesia ought to take action: "When you are gathered together, along with my spirit, with the power of our Lord Jesus Christ, deliver such a one to Satan for the destruction of the flesh, that his spirit may be saved in the day of the Lord Jesus" (verses 4,5).

It seems that some in the ecclesia were outraged by Paul's advice. Who was he to tell them what to do? As we considered in the previous chapter, these attitudes to Paul probably intensified when a group of Judaisers came to Corinth. His plan not to visit the city personally, but to send Timothy instead, backfired dramatically. Timothy was psychologically mauled by Paul's opponents, causing the apostle to make his hurried visit, which gave him so much anguish and sorrow (2 Corinthians 2:1).

How much he wished the situation could be different. Why should he "have sorrow over those from whom (he) ought to have joy" (verse 3)? This is the clear objective of his letter. Things could not get any worse between him and his brethren and sisters in Corinth, so he embarked on trying to rebuild their shattered relationship: "For out of much affliction and anguish of heart I wrote to you, with many tears, not that you should be grieved, but that you might know the love which I have so abundantly for you" (verse 4).

Ecclesial Action

The disagreement over the case of immorality in the ecclesia had resulted in the whole process coming to a standstill. From his comments in the second epistle, we learn what happened when the ecclesia received Paul's advice: "punishment ... was inflicted by the majority (Greek, *pleion*)" (verse 6). Most, but not all in the ecclesia agreed that the offender should be "delivered to Satan for the destruction of the flesh" (1 Corinthians 5:5). It would be wrong to conclude that the minority saw no problem in his offence; some of them probably thought that ecclesial action was precipitate, and that more time should be given for repentance. It is possible, however, that there were still some who were "puffed up", and tried to rationalise the offending behaviour. But the outcome of the deliberations of the whole ecclesia was that the offender was denied access to the Lord's table, and with it the benefits of fellowship.

The purpose, as with all cases of withdrawal, was to encourage the brother to appreciate his error and repent. By the time Paul wrote his second epistle, it is apparent that this process had been effective. He was sincerely sorrowful, and Paul wondered if the man might "be swallowed up with too much sorrow" (2 Corinthians 2:7) if the ecclesia refused to welcome him back.

It is easy to see how the case inflamed such sharp tensions within the ecclesia that the easiest course was to leave the brother in the wilderness. But easiest courses are not always the right ones to follow, and in the Corinthian case, Paul urged the ecclesia "to reaffirm your love to him" (verse 8). They need not fear Paul's disapproval of their action, if that was holding them back. And there was the possibility that, in the absence of any mercy being shown towards the brother, he may become disillusioned and indulge in some greater immorality, and so "Satan should take advantage of us" (verse 11). Sin's devices are well-known, and worldly temptations soon attract men who are in that state of mind.

"I had no rest in my spirit"

The contentions in Corinth that arose when this issue was discussed were complicated by the different views in the ecclesia about Paul himself, and the desire of some to have greater prominence. Paul's short and hurried visit to Corinth did not resolve the problem, and he followed his visit by writing the severe letter, sending it with Titus, who had probably also delivered the first epistle. Paul was so disturbed by the serious disagreements in Corinth that he did not feel able to take advantage of an open door to preach in Troas (verse 12), but hurried along the road towards Corinth, the sooner to meet Titus travelling towards him in the opposite direction.

Titus brought the best news of all. The Corinthians responded generously to Paul's letter, and in turn Paul responded by putting the matter behind him. He was now free to concentrate on the work of preaching, which he describes in the terms of a victory parade: "God … always leads us in triumph in Christ, and through us diffuses the fragrance of his knowledge in every place" (verse 14). In this analogy, the Lord Jesus, who won the battle against sin, is the victor; Paul and his associates are his bodyguard and officials. The Roman practice was to burn incense along the route of triumphal processions. In Paul's mind, the fragrance that was diffused was the knowledge of Christ.

These triumphal processions were always bitter-sweet affairs. Soldiers were returning home to a heroes' welcome, to live out the rest of their days as respected men of courage. For them, the incense was "an aroma of life leading to life". But there was also another group in the procession, a group of captured prisoners, and lying before them was derision, torture and death. As they caught the odour of the incense, it was "the aroma of death leading to death" (verse 16).

The gospel also divides into two groups those who hear it; all depends on how the hearer responds. Those who hear and accept it, join the procession as followers of the victorious Saviour who gives them life; while those who reject its message will themselves be rejected and face eternal death, cast out from the glories of the kingdom.

Peddling the Word of God

What caused Paul to introduce this wonderful vision of a triumphal procession? Was he aware that his severe letter had a similar effect in Corinth? Some – most in the ecclesia – responded generously to his rebuke; but there were a few who still harboured evil thoughts towards him. So he concludes his comments by repeating the defence of his integrity: "We are not, as so many, peddling the word of God; but as of sincerity, but as from God, we speak in the sight of God in Christ" (verse 17).

In the process of explaining his own uprightness, Paul strongly implies the hypocrisy of his critics. He talks of *"the many"* (Greek, *hoi polloi*; i.e., the rabble) who adulterated the word of God – a practice he specifically denounces engaging in himself: "we have renounced the hidden things of shame, not walking in craftiness nor handling the word of God deceitfully" (4:2). But in this earlier comment he makes an additional and very telling point. Like a wine dealer who waters down his product in order to increase his profit (see Isaiah 1:22), there were some in Corinth who were trying to make gain from the Word of God. Ironically, it was these very hawkers or pedlars who charged Paul with using his ministry for mercenary purposes. Introduced at this early stage in his epistle is thus a theme to which Paul will return later.

First, however, he wants to talk about his and the Corinthians' relationship to the Lord Jesus Christ, and about the privileges and benefits that flow from this relationship. His keen appreciation of these prevents him from acting deceitfully, either towards Christ, or towards them.

25

THE GLORY THAT EXCELS

PAUL's critics in Corinth were influenced by visitors from elsewhere. When we tried to identify his adversaries (Chapter 23), we concluded that they were probably Judaisers who claimed association with the apostles in Jerusalem. There were certainly some who arrived in Corinth with "letters of commendation", and who were critical that Paul was not able to produce anything similar himself. By brandishing their letters, they challenged Paul's authority in the ecclesia.

Not that there was anything wrong with the principle of letters of commendation. The ecclesia in Ephesus commended Apollos when he travelled to Corinth (Acts 18:27); Paul himself commended Phoebe to the ecclesia at Rome (Romans 16:1), and Timothy to Philippi and Corinth (Philippians 2:19-24; 1 Corinthians 16:10,11). The practice was good, and is followed today when brethren and sisters are welcomed as visitors from their home ecclesias, and when letters are exchanged as individuals transfer from one ecclesia to another.

Paul was not therefore questioning the practice of providing or receiving letters of commendation. When the visitor and his associations are not known, such information is important. But Paul founded the ecclesia in Corinth! There would not be an ecclesia in the city unless the apostle had preached there. If a letter of commendation was needed for him, it existed in the brethren and sisters themselves: "You are our epistle written in our hearts, known and read by all men" (2 Corinthians 3:2).

By describing the brethren and sisters in Corinth as his letter of commendation, Paul expected them also to enquire who wrote the letter. Who commended him to them? So he adds that "clearly you are an epistle *of Christ* ... written not with ink but by the Spirit of the living God, not on tablets of stone but on tablets of flesh, that is, of the heart" (verse 3). Surely there could be no one in Corinth who would doubt a commendation received directly from the Lord Jesus Christ. So why should they be questioning Paul's position among them?

This is the ground of his confidence, and of his authority. Paul does not try to argue his own sufficiency, but says, "our sufficiency is from God" (verse 5). Therefore his comments about the situation in Corinth – the unchecked immorality and the divisive squabbling – were not simply from him; he and his companions were "ministers of the new covenant, not of the letter but of the Spirit; for the letter kills, but the Spirit gives life" (verse 6).

By mentioning "letters of commendation" and the contrast between "the letter" and "the spirit", it is apparent that the apostle's adversaries were trying to persuade the ecclesia to act on the basis of law. The history of the infant New Testament ecclesias shows time and again the problems that can arise when the doctrines of Christ are not treated as guides that encourage godly living, but as restrictive rules used by some members of the ecclesia to exercise power over others.

Letter and Spirit

Paul's condemnation of this is fierce and final. "The letter kills, but the Spirit gives life" (verse 6). This may sound extreme, but it is true. If the Judaisers were allowed to continue unchecked, it would soon lead to the disintegration of the Corinthian ecclesia and the spiritual death of the brethren and sisters. Individually as well, adopting 'law' as a motivating principle rather than 'spirit' or 'grace' denies that: "by grace you have been saved through faith, and that not of yourselves; it is the gift of God" (Ephesians 2:8). "The letter" puts all the emphasis on the individual who has to strive to obey, but who in the end will fail; "the spirit" places the emphasis on the Lord Jesus Christ and his Father, whose grace saves us. In this way, "the letter kills, but the Spirit gives life".

Doubtless, the Judaisers quoted the importance of the Law of Moses, so Paul counters immediately by showing how, when the law was received by Moses, its limited and temporary position was revealed. First of all, he calls it "the ministry of death, written and engraved on stones" (verse 7). This contrasts with the Corinthians themselves, who Paul has already described as: "an epistle of Christ, written … not on tablets of stone, but on tablets of flesh". They were not therefore converted in order to become servants of the law, for that leads to death.

Yet the law when it was given to Israel was accompanied by God's glory. After forty days in the mount in the company of the angel, Moses' face shone as it reflected the divine glory (Exodus 34:29). Even though the law was only temporary, "the children of Israel could not look steadily at the face of Moses" (2 Corinthians 3:7). But no one could say that the problem lay with the law, for: "the law is holy, and the commandment is holy, righteous and good" (Romans 7:12). The problem lies in man, so that Paul was able to say, "the commandment, which was to bring life, I found to bring death" (verse 10).

Fading Glory

The value of the law was, therefore, only temporary; so, in addition to being a "ministry of death", its glory was also fading. This was Moses' own experience. When he descended from Mount Sinai, he had to place a veil over his face: "the children of Israel could not look steadily at the face of Moses because of the glory of his countenance" (2 Corinthians 3:7). Paul tells the Corinthians something about this incident that can only be inferred from the Exodus passage: the brilliance shining from Moses' face gradually faded away, allowing him eventually to dispense with the veil when he spoke to the Israelites.

By contrast, the new covenant – "the ministry of the Spirit" – is "more glorious" (verse 8); it "exceeds much more in glory" (verse 9); it is "the glory that excels" (verse 10). The glory that accompanied the Mosaic covenant is completely overshadowed by the new covenant, of which Paul was a minister. These contrasts can be shown most effectively by tabulating the differences using Paul's own words in his letter:

Old Covenant	New Covenant
on tables of stone	on fleshy tables of the heart
ministry of death	ministry of the Spirit
ministry of condemnation	ministry of righteousness
passing away	to remain

The New Covenant's most essential difference – the difference that made it "more glorious" – was that it did not condemn. It is a covenant that provides forgiveness and not punishment for sins, as declared by Jeremiah in his wonderful prophecy about God's purpose with Israel: "I will make a new covenant with the house of Israel and with the house of Judah ... I will forgive their iniquity, and their sin I will remember no more" (Jeremiah 31:31-34).

The promise of forgiveness is the basis of the Christian hope; so Paul was able to speak to the Corinthians boldly and clearly. He draws a comparison between Moses speaking to Israel and his own relationship with the Corinthians. Moses had to cover his face, and the message was veiled: "their minds were blinded. For until this day the same veil remains unlifted in the reading of the Old Testament" (2 Corinthians 3:14). Israel became obsessed with the law; their minds were blinded by the glory that accompanied the giving of the law, and their hearts were hardened so that they were not led by the law to acknowledge Christ.

When he speaks in this way Paul must have recalled his own history. Before his conversion, he was blinded by the glory of the law; a veil covered his mind so that he could not see the greater glory of the new covenant in Christ; and he had to be temporarily blinded by "the glory that excels" so that the veil could be taken away when he turned to the Lord. Paul understood better than almost anyone else the attitude of mind of the law-centred Jew, who could not rid himself of the shackles of the law even after learning about Christ.

Preaching About Christ

Paul's relationship with the Corinthians was different from Moses' relationship with Israel: "we use great boldness (plainness, AV) of speech" (verse 12), he said. After he arrived in Corinth, Paul "determined not to know anything among you except Jesus Christ and him crucified" (1 Corinthians 2:2). Under Moses, the end of the law – i.e., Christ – was veiled; in Paul's preaching, he was openly declared.

While speaking about the Jews' reaction to the law, Paul explains that the veiling of the truth about Christ will remain, however often they read the scriptures, for "even to this day, when Moses is read, a veil lies on their heart" (2 Corinthians 3:15). Moses' veil was only removed when he "went in before the LORD" (Exodus 34:34); so Israel's veil can only be removed by their turning to the Lord. The repentance of a remnant of the nation was therefore foreseen by Zechariah: "I will pour on the house of David and on the inhabitants of Jerusalem the spirit of grace and supplication; then they will look on me whom they pierced" (Zechariah 12:10). Though a few individual Jews have turned to Christ, this prophecy still awaits its complete fulfilment at the time of Christ's return.

There is therefore a great difference between "the law" and "the Lord". "The letter kills, but the Spirit gives life" (2 Corinthians 3:6); the law is a "ministry of death", but "the Lord is the Spirit; and where the Spirit of the Lord is, there is liberty" (verse 17). The law treated its subjects as slaves, making men and women prisoners by convicting them of sin. In Jesus, Paul told believers in Rome, "you did not receive the spirit of bondage again to fear, but you received the Spirit of adoption by which we cry out, 'Abba, Father'" (Romans 8:15).

Under the old covenant, only Moses appeared unveiled before God. In Christ, "all, with unveiled face" are able to see God's glory (2 Corinthians 3:18). We see this, "as in a mirror", because the Lord Jesus reflects and manifests his Father's glory. As the Apostle John wrote in the prologue to his gospel: "we beheld his glory, the glory as of the only begotten of the Father, full of grace and truth" (John 1:14).

Changed from Glory to Glory

Beholding the glory of God revealed in Christ is not a passive state; it is active, and it is a continuing process. Moses' face shone when he beheld the glory of the Lord, and believers are "transformed" as they look upon and meditate about God's glory in Christ. The object is to be changed into the image that is beheld. This explains why Paul uses the figure of a mirror: we see ourselves and we see Christ; and we seek to be changed in order to become more like him. Rotherham therefore renders this verse: "And we all, with unveiled face, *receiving and reflecting* the glory of the Lord".

Reliance on law is thus shown by Paul to be ignoring the power of God, who "has delivered us from the power of darkness and conveyed us into the kingdom of the Son of His love" (Colossians 1:13). All that he says on this subject of 'the glory that transforms' is based on a careful and detailed exposition of Exodus 34:29-35: a passage that his adversaries would treat with deep respect because it is in the Pentateuch.

This glorious ministry, the "ministry of the spirit" and of "righteousness", was entrusted to Paul. He was also a beneficiary of the new covenant, for he "received mercy" when his sins were forgiven for Christ's sake. For these reasons, it is impossible for him to lose heart, whatever difficulties may arise. But as a minister of Christ, he has to act completely without reproach: his behaviour must always match his profession. He therefore renounced absolutely all underhand practices; what he calls, "the hidden things of shame", linking back to his comments about the veiled heart of Jewry (2 Corinthians 4:2; cp. 3:15). He and his companions do not act "in craftiness" (Greek, *panourgia*), like the subtilty of the serpent that beguiled Eve (see 11:3).

They do not "handle the word of God deceitfully", like the man who waters down good wine so that he can increase his profits.

This is the second time in this letter that the apostle charges his opponents with dishonesty concerning their use of the word of God (see also 2:17). The Judaisers, by demanding obedience to the law of Moses as well as to Christ, were tampering with God's word, and thus stood self-condemned. Paul appealed to the Corinthians to judge the case by the evidence available to them. His conscience was completely clear, and his behaviour among them should commend itself to their consciences. His work was a frank and open declaration of the truth, and he challenged anybody to say otherwise.

The most likely retort of his critics was to say that, despite his protestations, the message he preached was veiled. We know there were some who complained that his teaching contained: "some things hard to understand" (2 Peter 3:16); and there were others who rejected it while still claiming to follow Christ. Paul answered this criticism by saying that if there is any veiling it must be with the hearer and not with the preacher. The Jewish mind was veiled by the apparent glory of the law; and another equally blinding effect was created by "the god of this age" (called by Jesus in John's gospel, "the prince of this world" – John 12:31; 14:30; 16:11). Sin's appeal is so strong that the light of the gospel often does not even shine on men and women in the world.

Developing God's Likeness

Paul shows that the gospel concerns "the glory of Christ", referring back to his comments about "the glory that excels". Man was made "in the image of God" (Genesis 1:27), but failed to manifest His moral qualities. Jesus, as the last Adam, was a new creation, and he developed God's moral likeness, showing forth His glory (Hebrews 1:3; John 1:14). This is the objective of all true disciples, so the gospel Paul preached was Christ's gospel. He was not promoting himself, as his critics slanderously suggested; everything he did in connection with Corinth was as a bondservant (Greek, *doulos*), whose master is Christ.

How could he possibly preach himself when the gospel originated with God? In the beginning, God "commanded light to shine out of darkness" (2 Corinthians 4:6; cp. Genesis 1:3-5); and as with the physical creation, so with the spiritual creation, "The people who walked in darkness have seen a great light; those who dwelt in the land of the shadow of death, upon them a light has shined" (Isaiah 9:2; cited in Matthew 4:15,16; Luke 1:79). Paul himself was enlightened at his conversion so that he in turn could enlighten others. This light of the gospel: "has shone in our hearts to give the light of the knowledge of the glory of God in the face of Jesus Christ" (2 Corinthians 4:6).

26

AN EARTHLY TENT AND A HEAVENLY HOUSE

HOW would the apostle's adversaries respond to his direct challenge to their assumed authority? He spoke about the glorious gospel that he preached in Corinth as he did elsewhere; and he mentioned how the glory of God in the face of Jesus Christ can change men and women, transforming them "from glory to glory, just as by the Spirit of the Lord" (2 Corinthians 3:18). What then of his own position? He was scorned by his critics because of his supposed unworthiness to be an apostle. Had his comments about "the glory that excels" exposed him to personal ridicule?

As if to counter any adverse response, Paul immediately follows his comments about God shining in our hearts, "to give the light of the knowledge of the glory of God in the face of Jesus Christ" (4:6), to explain that this should not cause any individual to be puffed up. It was a reason for deep humility, and not a cause of human pride: "We have this treasure in earthen vessels, that the excellence of the power may be of God and not of us" (verse 7).

Gideon and the Midianites

The suggestion that earthen vessels can contain "the light of the knowledge of the glory of God" is probably based on the example of Gideon and his three hundred God-chosen men. They surrounded the Midianite army surreptitiously, carrying trumpets in one hand and torches shielded by an empty pitcher in the other. At Gideon's command, they blew the trumpets, broke the jars and cried out, causing mayhem in the Midianite camp, and bringing Israel a great victory over their enemies (Judges 7:15-22). The lesson for Israel was the one Paul taught the Corinthians: they needed to learn "that the excellence of the power (is) of God and not of us (i.e., man)".

In this helpful parable, the "earthen vessels" or "empty pitchers" relate to man's mortal nature. "Man is of the earth, earthy" (1 Corinthians 15:47), and he can be enlightened only by learning the truth of the gospel. The Midianites stand for "those who are perishing, whose minds the god of this age has blinded" (2 Corinthians 4:3,4). The underlying message is the same as the one in Paul's first letter to Corinth: "that no flesh should glory in His presence" (1 Corinthians 1:29). Salvation is God's work, and He sometimes uses men and women as instruments to fulfil His purpose.

Paul was very aware from his own experiences how the preaching of the gospel involved personal humiliations and difficulties. In many ways, the messenger was being broken as he sought to publish the message: "We are handicapped on all sides, but we are never frustrated; we are puzzled, but never in despair. We are persecuted, but we never have to stand it alone: we may be knocked down but we are never knocked out!" (2 Corinthians 4:8,9, J. B. Phillips).

There is great encouragement here for today's preachers, who often face difficulties in a world that grows increasingly hostile to the gospel of truth. To follow Paul's example is to allow the message to predominate, so that the messenger becomes almost invisible. He saw himself as a soldier in Christ's army: hard pressed, but not hemmed in; ignorant of the next move yet confident of the ultimate victory; never forsaken by the captain of his salvation despite being pursued by enemies; appearing to be fatally wounded, but able to continue the fight.

"Knocked down but not knocked out!"

This last point was graphically demonstrated during the first missionary journey when Paul was stoned at Lystra. We may even speculate whether the Jews who stirred up the people to attack him on that occasion were involved in the opposition he now faced in Corinth. The attack in Lystra seemed at first to be final: "They stoned Paul and dragged him out of the city, supposing him to be dead" (Acts 14:19).

He may have been knocked down, but he was not knocked out, for, "when the disciples gathered around him, he rose up and went into the city" (verse 20).

It is apparent that Paul saw this, and all his subsequent deliverances from peril, as further proof of the resurrection of the Lord Jesus Christ: "we who live are always delivered to death for Jesus' sake, that the life of Jesus also may be manifested in our mortal flesh" (2 Corinthians 4:11). This dying, which took the form of sufferings endured by the apostles during their journeyings, brought life to others by means of the message they preached. The earthen vessels may be broken and damaged again and again, but the light of the knowledge of the glory of God continued to shine forth.

Paul was also able to take comfort from another Old Testament character. He had "the same spirit of faith" as the Psalmist who responded to his deliverance from death by offering a sacrifice of thanksgiving, and calling on God's name. The writer of Psalm 116, from which Paul quotes, was probably Hezekiah, who was granted an extension to his life of fifteen years following a mortal sickness. "The pains of death surrounded me ... I found trouble and sorrow. Then I called upon the name of the LORD ... I was brought low, and He saved me ... I believed, therefore I spoke" (Psalm 116:3-10; verse 10 quoted in 2 Corinthians 4:13).

Hezekiah believed, and God granted him – as well as an extension of life – a son to succeed him who was not yet born when he fell ill. Paul believed, and God granted him the converts who had not heard the message of gospel truth when he was struck down. The belief of both men was, however, less about their immediate deliverance from death than the certainty of a future resurrection: "He who raised up the Lord Jesus will also raise us up with Jesus, and will present us with you" (verse 14).

Far from separating himself from the Corinthians and setting himself on a pedestal, Paul was showing how he devoted himself to danger, persecution and ridicule wholly on their behalf: "*All things* are for your sakes, that grace, having spread through the many, may cause thanksgiving to abound to the glory of God" (verse 15).

Renewal of the Inward Man

In any other circumstances, all the troubles Paul suffered would cause him to lose heart; but, "Even though our outward man is perishing, yet the inward man is being renewed day by day" (verse 16). The "inward man" (sometimes, "the new man") is a favourite expression of Paul's. He uses it here, and in his letters to the Romans and the Ephesians (Romans 7:22; Ephesians 3:16), to describe the new creation in Christ, who dwells in the hearts of his disciples by faith. This new creation is a process, and the Lord looks for growth and maturity as believers try to apply the principles of the truth in their daily lives. The secret is to look beyond the temporal and transient, to the unseen things that are eternal. Paul did not concentrate on present things, but on things to do with the future in the purpose of God, as he goes on to explain to the Corinthians.

He has earlier described man's mortal human nature as an "earthen vessel". In a subtle change of figure, he now calls it "our earthly house", and "this tent" (2 Corinthians 5:1). Tents are temporary dwellings, often needing repair; and eventually they must be replaced, as a tentmaker like Paul would know well. Our "earthly tent" is destroyed at death, but the promise is that it can be replaced by something infinitely better. The replacement is "from God", and not of man; it is "eternal" and not temporary; it is "in the heavens" and not earthly.

An Eternal House in the Heavens

The idea that our future immortality is presently "in the heavens" appears also in other New Testament passages. To the Colossians, Paul wrote, "When Christ who is our life appears, then you also will appear with him in glory" (Colossians 3:4). Those faithful disciples who are to be immortalised were also revealed in vision to the Apostle John: "I, John, saw the holy city, New Jerusalem, coming down out of heaven from God, prepared as a bride adorned for her husband" (Revelation 21:2).

Until that wonderful day arrives, when "mortality will be swallowed up of life ... we groan, earnestly desiring to be clothed with our habitation which is from heaven" (2 Corinthians 5:4,2). Our present life, even though it can be burdensome, is a preparation for that time. God gave a pledge of the future in the spirit-gifts granted to the apostles; and the pledge was repeated for the benefit of others in the inspired message they preached. Because God's word is His promise, and because He is faithful, it is a guarantee of immortality to come.

Paul describes two situations that will pertain when Jesus returns, based on his analogy of the tent-dweller, waiting for a permanent home with the Lord. The first of these concerns believers "who are alive and remain until the coming of the Lord" (1 Thessalonians 4:15). He describes this as being "at home in the body ... absent from the Lord" (2 Corinthians 5:6). The other situation involves those believers who die before the Lord's coming. He describes their state as "absent from the body ... present with the Lord" (verse 8). Of the two states, Paul believes the second is preferable; but he acknowledges that the choice is not man's but God's. In these circumstances, there is only one thing for faithful believers to do: "Therefore we make it our aim, whether present or absent, to be well pleasing to him" (verse 9).

This is necessary because both those who are still alive when Jesus comes, and those whom he raises from sleep, "must all appear before the judgment seat of Christ, that each one may receive the things done in the body, according to what he has done, whether good or bad" (verse 10).

There is much muddled thinking about the judgement seat, and the translators have not helped the situation by using an additional word – "done" – that is not in the original text. The common misunderstanding is clearly shown by the translation in the NIV: "We must all appear before the judgment seat of Christ, that each one may receive what is due to him *for the things done while in the body*, whether good or bad." However reasonable this may appear, for the allocation of reward will certainly relate to the life that has been lived, it is not what the apostle was saying about the body.

He has been talking about "being clothed" or "being naked", and about tent-dwellers waiting for a permanent house. His comments about the judgement continue this theme, as we would expect. He explains that the result of the Lord's judgement will be experienced "in the body". The body will either be changed or destroyed – "clothed upon" with immortality, or "unclothed" and left to perish. The whole passage is a vindication of bodily resurrection and a future earthly kingdom.

The Judge of all the Earth

He calls the judgement, "the terror of the Lord", or more accurately, "the fear of the Lord" (RV), meaning that our lives should reflect the knowledge that they come under the scrutiny of the Judge of all the earth. Just as men and women will be called to "appear" (Greek, *phaneroo*) before their Judge when he returns, so the apostle is "well known (*phaneroo*) unto God" at all times, and "well known (*phaneroo*) in your consciences" (verse 11). Nothing can be hidden from God, who knows the thoughts and intents of the heart, and Paul has not hidden any of his dealings with the Corinthians. His teachings about the gospel should have impacted on their consciences – on the inner man of the heart.

Ever conscious of his detractors in Corinth, Paul reaffirms that he does not intend providing any separate testimony to his apostleship (cp. 3:1). There is sufficient evidence of his absolute sincerity for them to glory on his behalf, and to answer those who are more concerned with the outward man that is perishing, than with the inner man that is being renewed day by day (5:12, cp. 4:16).

Paul's zeal and enthusiasm was such that it was possible for his enemies to claim that he was deranged. "Paul, you are beside yourself!", said the Roman governor Festus, "Much learning is driving you mad!" (Acts 26:24). Some Athenians who heard his robust declaration about the resurrection of Christ "mocked, while others said, 'We will hear you again on this matter'" (17:32). Whatever caused some to think he was mad – the things he taught, or the visions he claimed to have seen – all were "to God"; he was an ambassador for Christ.

A Restrictive Teaching

While some people were attributing his behaviour to madness, others were complaining that he was too sober. His teachings restricted their freedom of behaviour. But if he was "sober", encouraging believers to be self-controlled, it was totally "for your cause" (2 Corinthians 5:13, AV). The constraining force in everything he did – in his apparent excesses, as well as when he seemed most sober – was his recognition of what was achieved by the love of Christ. He saw the sacrifice of Christ as the greatest evidence for unity amongst brethren and sisters: "if one died for all, then all died; and he died for all, that those who live should live no longer for themselves, but for him who died for them and rose again" (verses 14,15).

Men and women enter into Christ through baptism. They share in his death and resurrection. They should live only for him, and no longer for themselves. All the external things which often form the basis of judgement of an individual are therefore no longer important. Paul admits that he once judged the Lord himself in that way. He must have seen him during his ministry, possibly at one of the feasts, and his assessment was completely wrong. He had to learn that the important things are unseen; he no longer knows Christ "after the flesh", i.e., after the outward appearance, but as the Son of God: the firstborn of the New Creation.

This leads Paul to explain what the new creation achieves and how it was implemented. For all believers, "old things have passed away; behold, all things have become new" (verse 17). This does not occur through any human toil, for "all things are of God", and His work is a work of reconciliation achieved by the forgiveness of sins for Jesus' sake. This forms the basis of the gospel message preached by Paul and the other apostles. They prayed "on Christ's behalf, be ye reconciled to God" (verse 20).

With this talk of reconciliation, Paul is ready to make a direct and personal appeal to all those in Corinth. But before he does so, he summarises the basis of the believer's standing in Christ in a remarkable verse that has unfortunately often been misrepresented: "He made him who knew no sin to be sin for us, that we might become the righteousness of God in him" (verse 21).

He was Made Sin

Some have had problems with the suggestion that the Lord was "made sin". They point to his sinlessness and his complete obedience, as if the two statements are mutually incompatible. First of all, it is important to note the context. Paul has spoken of the outward man and the inward man, of our earthly tent and our house from heaven. Jesus was "made sin" in the sense that he shared with us "the outward man" and the "earthly tent" of mortality. But in Christ, the "inward man" predominated, so that after his death "the grave could not hold him" and he was "clothed upon by the house which is from heaven". It was the Father's response to his righteousness, and the earnest or guarantee of what is in store for those who love his appearing.

This understanding of the verse is not unique to Christadelphians, as the following extract from Professor J.J. Lias' commentary on 2 Corinthians (in the *Cambridge Bible for Schools* series) shows:

> "God appointed him to be the representative of sin and sinners, treated him as sin and sinners are treated. He took on himself to be the representative of humanity in its aspect of sinfulness and to bear the burden of sin in all its completeness. Hence he won the right to represent humanity in all its respects, and hence we are entitled to be regarded as God's righteousness (which he was) not in ourselves, but in him as our representative in all things."

On the cross the basis of reconciliation was established. It is now for all who associate themselves with Christ's death and resurrection to become reconcilers themselves. The hardest part of the Gospel message is not believing it to be true, but making it true in our individual lives. Would the Corinthians continue to receive this great grace of God in vain?

27

WE IMPLORE YOU ... BE RECONCILED

SPEAKING about the reconciling work of the Lord Jesus Christ led Paul naturally to appeal for reconciliation with his brethren and sisters in Corinth. God's work in Christ cannot be considered in isolation from what it was always intended to produce in the lives of believers. We glory in the fact that our sins are forgiven "for Jesus' sake", but are told: "Judge not, and you shall not be judged. Condemn not, and you shall not be condemned. Forgive, and you will be forgiven" (Luke 6:37). In this sense, we are "workers together with God", and should not "receive the grace of God in vain" (2 Corinthians 6:1).

Pressing home the point, Paul quotes from Isaiah's words about God's work in Christ: "In an acceptable time I have heard you, and in the day of salvation I have helped you" (Isaiah 49:8). Though these words originally referred to the Lord Jesus, the apostle now applies them to the members of the body of Christ: "Behold, now is the accepted time; behold, now is the day of salvation" (2 Corinthians 6:2). An "accepted time" refers to the exercise of God's pleasure or favour; and for Paul's adversaries in Corinth there was an uncomfortable force to his argument. God daily extends His offer of salvation to men and women. He does so freely of His good will. The honest response to the word of salvation is to show the same generosity of spirit in return, treating our brethren and sisters as God has treated us, and as we would wish to treat our Lord if he was present amongst us.

This was always Paul's intention. He tried always to be consistent in his dealings, so that the truth of the gospel was never brought into disrepute: "we give no offense in anything, that our ministry may not be blamed" (verse 3). There was every excuse for inconsistency, as the experiences of the apostles were incredibly varied. But as Paul describes his life as an itinerant preacher of the gospel, he produces one of the most lyrical sections in all his letters (verses 4-10). This masterly review of his life as a "minister of God" showed his complete integrity, and his transparency in all aspects of his work. Various analyses of this passage have been attempted; one of the most convincing divides his comments into three sections: the hardships he suffered "in much patience"; the inward efforts by which he was armed to meet those hardships; and the contrasting attitudes he experienced both from others, and in his own personal circumstances.

"In much patience" (verses 4,5)	The Armour of God (verses 5-7)	Contrasting Attitudes (verses 8-10)	
Tribulations	Purity	Honour	Dishonour
Needs	Knowledge	Evil Report	Good Report
Distresses	Longsuffering	Deceivers	True
Stripes	Kindness	Unknown	Well-known
Imprisonments	Holy Spirit	Dying	Living
Tumults	Sincere Love	Chastened	Not Killed
Labours	Word of Truth	Sorrowful	Rejoicing
Sleeplessness	Power of God	Poor	Enriching
Fastings	Righteousness	Having nothing	Possessing everything

The first two of these sections appear again in other of his writings: he lists later in 2 Corinthians some of the hardships he endured as an apostle (chapter 11); and there is the section about "the whole armour of God" in Ephesians 6. These two sections led him to describe how his work was viewed. There were some in Corinth who did not hold him in "honour"; they were "deceivers", and circulated an "evil report" about him. He made a direct challenge to this attitude, holding nothing back in his appeal:

"O Corinthians! We have spoken openly to you, our heart is wide open" (2 Corinthians 6:11). In contrast to their dealings with him, Paul had always been absolutely frank and transparent. Any awkwardness arose from their failure to accept his complete integrity: "Any stiffness between us must be on your side, for we assure you there is none on ours" (verse 12, J. B. Phillips). Addressing them as a father to his children, he asked them to be as open in their dealings with him as he was towards them.

The Problem of Mis-mating

This appeal for openness on the Corinthians' part, based on the fact that their assessment of Paul was seriously in error, continues in the next chapter. Paul had been completely open in his dealings with them (6:11), now he challenges them to: "Open your hearts to us. We have wronged no one, we have corrupted no one, we have cheated no one" (7:2). Between these two passages lies a section (6:14 – 7:1) that some regard as a later interpolation because they find it difficult to trace the connection of thought. But it is no easier to explain why the passage was introduced here if it is not part of the original letter. It is most probable that Paul sees the Corinthians' treatment of him as characteristic of the worldliness of Corinth: it was a provincial and commercial centre, and wholly consumed by idolatrous practices. The influence of surrounding society is always present in ecclesial life: brethren and sisters cannot escape from their surroundings, but they must make every possible effort to walk by a different rule. This is now Paul's appeal to the brethren and sisters in Corinth:

"Do not be unequally yoked together with unbelievers. For what fellowship has righteousness with lawlessness?" (6:14). Paul draws out a principle that existed in the Law, "You shall not plow with an ox and a donkey together" (Deuteronomy 22:10); and the word he uses to describe unequal yoking (Greek, *heterozygeo*) is found in the Septuagint of Leviticus 19:19 where Israelites were told not to mate different kinds of animal. The issue is thus wider than just a prohibition against marrying out of the faith, Paul spoke of all kinds of partnership that would compromise the standing of a believer because he or she would become intimately associated with the pagan practices that were so prevalent in Corinth.

He emphasised the problem of mis-mating by drawing the contrasts as sharply as possible: light and darkness; Christ and Belial; believer and unbeliever; the temple of God and idols. In this list, the brethren and sisters formed the Temple of God: "As God has said: 'I will dwell in them and walk among them. I will be their God, and they shall be my people'" (2 Corinthians 6:16). This composite quotation from Exodus 6:7, Leviticus 26:11,12 and Jeremiah 31:33 confirms the apostle's message. He wrote in an earlier chapter that the Corinthians were his epistle: "written not with ink but by the Spirit of the living God, not on tablets of stone but on tablets of flesh, that is, of the heart" (2 Corinthians 3:3), and this was a clear echo of Jeremiah's well-known words about the need for a new covenant that would be written by God on the human heart (Jeremiah 31:31-34). This can only happen when men and women invite Him into their lives, knowing that they cannot serve both God and Mammon:

"Therefore 'Come out from among them and be separate, says the Lord. Do not touch what is unclean'" (2 Corinthians 6:17). The urgency of this appeal is allied to the fact that these words were first addressed by God through the prophet Isaiah to the Babylonian exiles who were encouraged to leave behind the rampant paganism of that heathen society and return to Judea. Another short quotation, this time from Ezekiel, was also first used in the same context. God promised those who were bold enough to leave Babylon: "I will receive you" (verse 17; cp. Ezekiel 20:34, LXX). A similar appeal was now being made through Paul. His next statement is based on God's promise to David, but with subtle changes to make it applicable to the Corinthians: "I will be a Father to you (plural), and you shall be my *sons* (plural) and *daughters*, says the Lord Almighty" (2 Corinthians 6:18, cp. 2 Samuel 7:8,14).

Cleanse your Minds

Paul, however, unlike the Old Testament prophets was not advocating the physical removal of believers from Corinth, but rather a separation of mind and purpose from that of the surrounding society. This is apparent from his final comment in this section: "let us cleanse ourselves from all filthiness of the flesh and spirit, perfecting holiness in the fear of God" (2 Corinthians 7:1).

In confidence, therefore, he can renew his appeal to the Corinthians to receive him open-heartedly as they did at the beginning. He dismisses all their charges of underhand dealing, not in order to rebuke them but merely by way of explanation. He is so emotionally bound up with the ecclesia, that he is able to say, "you are in our hearts, to die *together* and to live *together*" (verse 3). These emotional extremes actually happened while Paul was waiting for news from Corinth. Apart from his own brief and hurried visit when he first learned of the serious breach in his relationship with the ecclesia, he had sent Timothy and Titus at different times to represent his case to the brethren and sisters. He now speaks of the agony he felt as he waited for Titus to return and report on the situation: "our bodies had no rest, but we were troubled on every side. Outside were conflicts, inside were fears" (verse 5).

Beneficial Effects of the Severe Letter

The apostle returns to the account of his travels from the point where he broke off in 2:13, when he travelled from Ephesus to Macedonia hoping to meet Titus as he returned from Corinth. Paul was so upset by the problems in Corinth that he was not able to take advantage of the open door for preaching that he encountered in Troas, and crossed over into Europe because activity helped to calm his spirit. Many have found before and since that strained spiritual relationships are a barrier to effective preaching. This is one of the reasons why our Heavenly Father deplores conflict between brethren.

Paul was "downcast" as he arrived in Philippi, but soon was "exceedingly joyful in all our tribulation" (verse 4). The difference was all due to the meeting with Titus, "and not only by his coming, but also by the consolation with which he was comforted in you, when he told us of your earnest desire, your mourning, your zeal for me, so that I rejoiced even more" (verse 7).

The difference had been achieved in large measure by Paul's severe letter. He regretted sending it almost as soon as it left his hands; but the Corinthians' attitude had changed towards him, and he was now able to see the beneficial effects it had caused, and rejoice. The letter touched their hearts; they were sincerely sorry for their past behaviour, leading them to repent: "For godly sorrow produces repentance leading to salvation, not to be regretted; but the sorrow of the world produces death" (verse 10). The emphasis here is on "*godly* sorrow"; the attitude of mind that acknowledges the true cause of the problem and tries to institute a change of heart, not merely regret for what has happened. The latter has no re-generating power, and leads only to death; godly sorrow, by contrast, will lead to life.

And all this was accomplished by the letter that was nearly never sent! "Look how seriously it made you think, how eager it made you to prove your innocence, how indignant it made you and, in some cases, how afraid! Look how it made you long for my presence, how it stirred up your keenness for the faith, how ready it made you to punish the offender! Yes, that letter cleared the air for you as nothing else would have done" (verse 11, J B Phillips).

Paul's main object in writing his letter was the recovery of the whole Corinthian ecclesia. It was not primarily directed against his leading opponent, nor did he write it to defend the one who was dreadfully treated. It is generally taken that this is a reference to Paul himself, and to the unjustified criticisms that were levelled against him in Corinth. But it is possible that his almost incandescent reaction was caused by the brutal treatment experienced in Corinth by his first emissary, Timothy. We know how worried Paul was as soon as Timothy left (1 Corinthians 16:10,11), and we can imagine how he would feel if Timothy received the treatment Paul's critics intended to bring upon him. It is one thing to endure persecution personally, but quite different to stand on the sidelines when the treatment intended for you is being meted out on another.

Titus' Visit to Corinth

Titus, therefore, and not Timothy was sent to Corinth with the task of discovering the response to Paul's visit, and bearing his "severe" letter, written with the intention of reprimanding those who had not acted in brotherly ways, and clearing the air so that they could make a fresh start. Before sending Titus to Corinth, Paul reminded him of the brethren and sisters there who so gladly embraced the truth during his first visit. It was revealed to the apostle that the Lord had much people in that worldly city, so Paul's confidence was well-founded. Titus returned with a full account of his visit, explaining how fearful the brethren and sisters were that relations had been damaged irretrievably. As a result, Titus felt very close to them: "his affections are greater for you as he remembers the obedience of you all" (verse 15).

There was now an opportunity for the Corinthians to show that the difficulties were really behind them, and Paul's appeal includes a challenge they would find hard to resist. This challenge concerns the collection for the poor believers in Judea, and extends over the next two chapters in 2 Corinthians (chapters 8 & 9) to which we must now turn.

28

THE MACEDONIAN CHALLENGE

HOW could the Corinthians prove that Paul's confidence in them was not misplaced? Was there a practical way of responding to the grace of God, to show they did not receive it in vain (cp. 2 Corinthians 6:1)? The example of the ecclesias in Macedonia provided a model for them to follow. The Roman province of Macedonia included all the areas of Greece north of the Isthmus of Corinth, where the ecclesias of Philippi, Berea and Thessalonica were situated. Being a Christian believer in those cities was not easy. Paul himself was imprisoned in Philippi, and persecuted in Thessalonica, and he speaks now of the "great trial of affliction" suffered by the members of these ecclesias. The general inhabitants of Macedonia also suffered: civil wars were fought on this territory before Augustus became sole emperor and brought stability across his realm; and the Romans exploited the natural mineral resources in the area. The Greeks thus bore a burden of "*deep* poverty". The word means that they were at rock bottom, or as J. B. Phillips puts it, "down to their last penny" (8:2).

Expansive Language

Despite these drawbacks, the grace of God was bestowed on the Macedonian brethren and sisters just as much as on those in Corinth, and they responded abundantly. A characteristic of the apostle's language in this section of 2 Corinthians is his use of superlatives: their joy was abundant, their poverty deep, and their liberality rich. The picture is drawn in expansive terms because it is not possible to measure God's abundant grace; and the brethren and sisters in Macedonia responded magnificently.

210

With every excuse to be inward looking, they showed a practical expression of their concern for other believers who were also experiencing difficulties. Paul himself had always been eager to remember the poor (Galatians 2:10), and he encouraged the same attitude in the ecclesias wherever he travelled. In this context, "the poor" were specifically the brethren and sisters in Judea. Their reduced circumstances arose from a combination of factors: the serious famine in AD 45 when Claudius was emperor (prophesied in Acts 11:28); rapidly increasing numbers (Acts 2:47); the general absence of any wealthy converts (1 Corinthians 1:26); persecution by leading Jews, including the confiscation of goods (Acts 8:1; 9:1,2; Hebrews 10:34; James 5:4); expulsion from the Synagogue, and thus from the care and welfare it was able to provide; and the belief of some that the Lord's return was so near, they saw no need to work (cp. 2 Thessalonians 3:10).

Judean Poverty

All these contributed to their difficulties; and there was also another factor that does not seem to have applied outside Judea, perhaps not even outside Jerusalem. In the earliest days the disciples "had all things in common, and sold their possessions and goods, and divided them among all, as anyone had need" (Acts 2:44,45). They shared their goods, but there is no evidence that they also organised their labour to replenish the common fund. In the end, the shared pot was empty, leaving them worse off than they were at the beginning.

Knowing that the New Testament ecclesia started in Jerusalem, the Macedonian ecclesias felt a great debt of loyalty to their brethren and sisters in Judea. Though they were poor themselves, they saw that as no excuse, and responded with grace to the report of poverty in Judea. "Grace" is a widely misunderstood concept, but this section in 2 Corinthians is very helpful in making it clearer. The offer of salvation is God's grace to mankind, something He is prepared to bestow freely. Man's response to the divine offer is also described as grace (Greek, *charis*), in this case meaning thankfulness (as in the RV margin of Hebrews

12:28). There is also a third meaning, and this is the main thrust of 2 Corinthians 8 & 9. An appreciation of God's grace cannot stop with mere feelings of thankfulness. His grace is exemplary, demanding that those who benefit from it act graciously towards others as He has to them. In particular this requires being aware of others' needs and, where it lies within one's powers, extending assistance without thought of recompense. In addition, therefore, to translating *charis* as "grace" (8:6,7), it also appears as "gift" (verses 4,19), and "liberality" (1 Corinthians 16:3, AV).

The brethren and sisters in Macedonia provided the best possible example of this practical gratitude, but it was an example intended to shame the Corinthians into action. The Macedonian ecclesias were generous beyond their ability; and because they had a willing spirit they pressed the apostle, absolutely insisting that they be allowed to share the responsibility of helping the brethren and sisters in Judea. To give generously in these circumstances was a practical expression of the fellowship that existed between the ecclesias in Macedonia and Judea. Like "grace", "fellowship" (Greek, *koinonia*) becomes a word closely connected with the collection for the poor saints in Jerusalem, sometimes translated as "sharing" (9:13, or "distribution" AV), and "contribution" (Romans 15:26). Fellowship is very personal, and the Macedonians completely understood what they were doing, for before giving anything they possessed, they gave *themselves*.

Dedication

This is the principle of dedication, where the things that are dedicated represent the person. Without personal involvement, dedication is valueless. When Jesus commented on the failure of many of his contemporaries, he focused on this point: "you say, 'If a man says to his father or mother, "Whatever profit you might have received from me is Corban" – ' (that is, a gift to God), then you no longer let him do anything for his father or his mother" (Mark 7:11,12). Gifts must involve the giver. The brethren and sisters in Macedonia therefore "first gave themselves to the Lord, and then to us by the will of God" (2 Corinthians 8:5).

Their generosity would have been meaningless as an act of fellowship if they were separated from Christ, or from representatives of other ecclesias, like the Apostle Paul and his companions.

Would the Corinthians understand the Macedonian example? Would they understand their willingness to help, despite their abject poverty? Would they appreciate the importance of having a willing spirit, and of giving themselves before giving anything they owned? The willing spirit had been there at one time, for they responded to Paul's message in 1 Corinthians 16:2, "let each one of you lay something aside, storing up as he may prosper, that there be no collections when I come". But what had started well did not continue once relations with the apostle became strained. This is a desperately sad aspect of any tension between brethren – it saps the energy from all worthwhile pursuits and diverts attention from important things to matters that ultimately are trivial and unimportant.

Live up to Your Boasting

One of Titus' tasks when Paul sent him to Corinth was to encourage the ecclesia to return to this work: "we urged Titus, that as he had begun, so he would also complete this grace in you as well" (2 Corinthians 8:6). A full year had passed, and matters were no farther advanced. In their communications with Paul the Corinthians had claimed to "abound in everything – in faith, in speech, in knowledge, in all diligence, and in your love for us". Here was the test: let them "abound (Greek, *perisseuo*) in this grace also" (verse 7). Here is a third word closely connected with the subject of the Poor Fund, and it is one of the superlative, expansive words that express the character of the Macedonians' gift, and the challenge to brethren and sisters in Corinth.

Before any objection could be raised, Paul made it clear that he was not *commanding* them to take up collections – he had no authority to issue commands – but he was advising them to fulfil their early promises. He emphasised this advice by reminding them of "the grace of our Lord Jesus Christ". They could not claim poverty as an excuse, for "though he (Jesus) was rich, yet for your sakes he became poor, that you through his poverty might become rich" (verse 9). This is a theme Paul also uses in his letter to the Philippian ecclesia (Philippians 2:4-8), one of the ecclesias in Macedonia whose conduct was intended to stir the Corinthians' consciences. The Lord's faithfulness did not waver: he put his hand to the plough, and never looked back (cp. Luke 9:62). The same faithful commitment is expected of his followers. They could not do any more than they were able to do: "no one is asked to give what he has not got" (2 Corinthians 8:12, J. B. Phillips).

This was not a new concept, though many would have ignored it. The Law of Moses encouraged giving in response to God's goodness. When the Jews were called to present themselves before God three times each year, "they shall not appear before the LORD empty-handed" (Deuteronomy 16:16). Exactly what they should take with them was not specified, but *every man shall give as he is able*, according to the blessing of the LORD your God which he has given you" (verse 17). The apostle's advice followed closely this Old Testament example.

Israel in the Wilderness

The apostle was well placed to make this appeal, for he was involved in an earlier endeavour to assist the ecclesias in Judea. The response in Antioch to news of their poverty-stricken brethren and sisters was that "the disciples, each according to his ability, determined to send relief to the brethren dwelling in Judea. This they also did, and sent it to the elders by the hands of Barnabas and Saul" (Acts 11:29,30). As on that occasion, which was a genuine attempt to have "all things common" but without the problems of completely communal living, Paul was not advocating "that others should be eased and you burdened; but ... that there may be equality" (2 Corinthians 8:13,14). This was foreseen, he said, in Israel's history during the wilderness wandering. God's provision of manna to meet their physical needs was "a certain quota every day", so that "he who gathered much had nothing left over, and he who gathered little had no lack" (verse 15; Exodus 16:14,18). The record does not reveal exactly how this was achieved, but it established a pattern whereby those with the ability to offer assistance should meet the real and pressing needs in the common-wealth of Israel. The provision of necessities requires the application of brotherly care.

Paul suggested to Titus that he should encourage the Corinthians to take up the Macedonian challenge, but Titus was already thinking along the same lines; he had "the same earnest care" for the brethren and sisters in Corinth. He "accepted the exhortation" from Paul; but they needed to be aware that his visit would have happened in any case: "being more diligent, he went to you of his own accord" (2 Corinthians 8:17). But he would not be travelling alone: "we have sent with him the brother whose praise is in the gospel throughout all the churches, and not only that, but who was also chosen by the churches to travel with us with this gift" (verses 18,19).

There is a reference here to the wide-ranging nature of the collection. Paul encouraged all the ecclesias to get involved, and by the time he wrote his second epistle to Corinth there was a large group of ecclesias contributing funds that could be transported to Jerusalem. Although the initial encouragement was the apostle's, the task was willingly embraced by the different ecclesias, so that a team of ecclesial representatives was ready to accompany the joint fund and Paul himself to Jerusalem. Those who were involved are mentioned by name in Acts 20:4, "Sopater of Berea … also Aristarchus and Secundus of the Thessalonians, and Gaius of Derbe, and Timothy, and Tychicus and Trophimus of Asia." One significant omission from this list is Titus or any other Corinthian represen-tative, yet it is almost unthinkable that no contributions were sent from Achaia.

Who was The Brother?

In fact, Titus is not only absent from this list of ecclesial representatives in Acts, he is never mentioned at all in Luke's account of the early ecclesias. This has caused the suggestion to be made that Luke – who masks his own involvement in the work, so that we can only tell when he was present by subtle changes in pronouns – also deliberately refrained from mentioning Titus, possibly because they were closely related. Looking back at the list of ecclesias in Acts 20:4, it is also apparent that Philippi is not represented. Luke had very close associations with Philippi, staying there when Paul moved on to Thessalonica after establishing the ecclesia during his second missionary journey (Acts 17:1, note "they"). Luke was certainly present with the group that accompanied the Fund, for he speaks of the brethren waiting "for *us* in Troas" (20:5).

The list of ecclesias and representatives should probably therefore read as follows:

Berea	Sopater
Thessalonica	Aristarchus & Secundus
Derbe	Gaius
Lystra?	Timothy
Asian ecclesias	Tychicus & Trophimus
Philippi	Luke?
Corinth	Titus?

We can therefore look again at Paul's words in 2 Corinthians 8:18,19: "we have sent with him the brother whose praise is in the gospel throughout all the churches, and not only that, but who was also chosen by the churches to travel with us with this gift". The suggestion is that the brother chosen by the ecclesias to travel with Paul and the Fund was Luke, and that he was not only "*the* brother" who was well known to many ecclesias for his work in the gospel, but "*his* brother", i.e., Titus' brother. Luke's presence with Titus (if indeed it was he) provided also two honest witnesses to confirm Paul's honesty: "Did I take advantage of you by any of those whom I sent to you? I urged Titus, and sent our brother with him" (12:17,18).

Another Brother

There was probably also another brother who travelled with Titus and Luke to Corinth: "we have sent with them our brother whom we have often proved diligent in many things, but now much more diligent, because of the great confidence which we have in you" (8:22). The identification of this brother is much more difficult. The only clues in the text are that Paul had "often proved (him to be) diligent in many things" – he had used him under similar circumstances on a number of previous occasions. There is a name that can be suggested, and one that appears in the list in Acts 20. Tychicus was known to be "a beloved brother and faithful minister in the Lord" (Ephesians 6:21). Whenever he is mentioned, he is being "sent" by the apostle for one purpose or another (Ephesians 6:22; Colossians 4:7; 2 Timothy 4:12; Titus 3:12), and it is possible that he was sent to Corinth by Paul to help with the work (2 Corinthians 8:22).

Despite the credentials of these three brethren – Titus, who was already well known in Corinth; a second brother (Luke?), praised by all ecclesias; and a third (Tychicus?) who had often been proved diligent in many things – Paul guessed that his critics would still ask questions. This was one reason for sending these brethren and not going himself. There had been allegations that the Fund was really for Paul's personal benefit, and not to help the poor brethren and sisters in Judea. He therefore wanted to avoid completely, "that anyone should blame us in this lavish gift which is administered by us" (verse 20). It was necessary to act honourably, "not only in the sight of the Lord, but also in the sight of men" (verse 21). The answer to any enquiries about Titus was that "he is my partner and fellow worker". The other brethren are "messengers (Greek, *apostolos*) of the churches" – ecclesial apostles, and thus representative of "the glory of Christ" of whom all ecclesias are servants (verse 23).

Paul concludes the chapter by repeating his appeal: "show to them (the three brethren), and before the churches the proof of your love and of our boasting on your behalf".

29

INCREASE THE FRUITS OF YOUR RIGHTEOUSNESS

AFTER appealing to the brethren and sisters in Corinth to respond to the challenge created by the generosity of the Macedonian ecclesias, the apostle continued to press upon them the value of making a liberal contribution to the Jerusalem Poor Fund. In the first place, it was really not necessary for him to remind them of the need, for they had previously raised the subject with him in a letter (cp. 1 Corinthians 16:1-4). Paradoxically, Paul used the news of their readiness to help as an encouragement to the ecclesias in Macedonia to contribute to the collection. He therefore reminded them: "your zeal has stirred up the majority" (2 Corinthians 9:2).

To save everyone from embarrassment, Paul sent three brethren with the specific task of ensuring that the promise made by the Corinthians "a year ago" was fulfilled. He was not, therefore, writing to tell them what to do, but to ensure they were ready when the time came. He could picture the humiliating scene if he arrived with brethren from Macedonia – brethren to whom he had boasted about Corinth's generous contribution – only to discover that the collection they had begun was languishing. The humiliation would be Paul's because of his previous boasting, but deep shame would also attach to the Corinthian ecclesia. The three brethren's specific task was to arrange for the collection to be complete by the time Paul and his companions arrived in Corinth. At the time of writing his letter, Paul was visiting the ecclesias in Macedonia. It would not be long before he left to go to Greece, and therefore to Corinth, as Luke recorded faithfully in Acts 20:1-3 – "Paul ... departed to go to Macedonia. Now when he had gone over that region and encouraged them with many words, he came to Greece and stayed three months".

Cheerful Giving

If the collection was complete before Paul arrived, it would be seen as an act of great generosity, and not as something given grudgingly. J. B. Phillips renders the verse: "I should like it to be a spontaneous gift, and not money squeezed out of you by what I have said" (2 Corinthians 9:5). He reminded them of the scriptural principle that, "whatever a man sows, that he will also reap" (Galatians 6:7). This relationship between sowing and reaping applies both to kind – "men do not gather figs from thorns, nor do they gather grapes from a bramble bush" (Luke 6:44) – and to quantity: "He who sows sparingly will also reap sparingly, and he who sows bountifully will also reap bountifully" (2 Corinthians 9:6).

There is an important lesson here, and it has wide application. What we get out of any endeavour is related to what we are prepared to put in. If we are restricted, or hold back from full involvement, or even if we give – but without enthusiasm, there will not be a complete benefit. To give "grudgingly" or out "of sorrow" (verse 7, RV margin) reflects an individual's attitude, and it ought not therefore to be surprising that "God loves a *cheerful* giver" (cp. Proverbs 22:8, LXX). The emphasis here, in contrast to verse 6, is on the motive for giving and not on the amount that is given. A similar consideration led the Lord himself to explain to his disciples that the widow woman with her two mites put more into the temple treasury than all the others, who cast in "of their abundance" (Luke 21:4).

This takes Paul right back to where he started on the subject of the Poor Fund at the beginning of 2 Corinthians 8. There were compelling practical reasons for supporting the Fund, but even more important was the spiritual imperative. God's grace was manifested by the ecclesias in Macedonia: despite the poverty that afflicted them, their generous giving was a response to the gift of salvation they had received. Now, he tells the Corinthians, "God is able to make all grace abound toward you, that you, always having all sufficiency in all things, may have an abundance for every good work" (2 Corinthians 9:8). The implication of this was surely not lost on the brethren and sisters in Corinth; they should be giving because of what they had received from God. As God's gift to them was beyond human reckoning, there should be no restraint in their response.

Counted as Righteousness

The Psalmist wrote about the extent of God's beneficence: "He has dispersed abroad, He has given to the poor; His righteousness endures forever" (verse 9, quoting Psalm 112:9), and Paul draws on this to emphasise the responsibility that devolves on all true believers. God provides seed for sowing and food for eating. He looks after mankind generously in natural things, and from this stems an important spiritual lesson – He will also bless unselfish generosity undertaken in His name, and count it as righteousness. This principle was enshrined in the Law of Moses: for those who showed mercy to the poor, "it shall be righteousness to you before the LORD your God" (Deuteronomy 24:13). The teaching is also picked up in the gospels, when the Lord Jesus tells his disciples to "Take heed that you do not do your charitable deeds (righteousness, RV) before men, to be seen by them. Otherwise you have no reward from your Father in heaven" (Matthew 6:1).

The Paradox of Giving

The simple message is that those who give most receive most – what has been described as "the paradox of giving". This paradox is taught in the book of Proverbs: "One man gives freely, yet gains even more; another withholds unduly, but comes to poverty. A generous man will prosper; he who refreshes others will himself be refreshed" (Proverbs 11:24,25, NIV). Paul can therefore write to the Corinthians and say: "you are enriched in everything for all liberality, which causes thanksgiving through us to God" (2 Corinthians 9:11). He was confirming the Master's teaching in the sermon on the Mount: "do good, and lend, hoping for nothing in return; and your reward will be great, and you will be sons of the Most High ... Give, and it will be given to you" (Luke 6:35,38). The word Paul uses for "liberality", Greek *haplotes*, picks up this idea. It literally means 'singleness', in the sense of selfless devotion, and occurs in a similar context in his letter to the ecclesia at Rome: "having then gifts differing according to the grace that is given to us, let us use them ... he who gives, with liberality" (Romans 12:6,8).

The great message of giving is that the benefit is not only to the one who receives, and nor does it stop with him; first the giver himself is rewarded, and like a pebble thrown into a pond, the effects of his generosity spread and spread: "the administration of this service not only supplies the needs of the saints, but also is abounding through many thanksgivings to God" (2 Corinthians 9:12). Describing the collection as a "service" (Greek, *leitourgia*, liturgy, cp. Luke 1:23) explains that the apostle saw the responsibility to assist fellow believers as equivalent to the work of Levites and Priests under the old covenant. In both cases, the gifts offered were directed primarily to God Himself.

The practical act of giving by the Corinthians would be proof, if it were needed, of their integrity and faith. No one could doubt their sincerity and obedience to the truth, and the bonds of fellowship would be strengthened considerably as a consequence. How could the gift be received, and not those who gave it? All this, the apostle said, flowed from the initiative of "God's unspeakable gift" – the Lord Jesus Christ himself, who was sent to reconcile to God men and women from all different backgrounds.

A Practical Expression of Love

Why should it be necessary for the Corinthians to provide proof of their belief in the gospel? Was there any individual or group who doubted their faithfulness, or who refused to accept them? The history of apostolic preaching in Macedonia and Achaia is dominated by the problems caused by groups of Jewish opponents to gospel truth. In Thessalonica, Berea and in Corinth itself, disagreement soon turned into conflict, often requiring Paul to leave hastily in order to preserve his life. There were also problems, not yet solved, with Jewish believers who were suspicious of pagan Gentiles believing the gospel. The worldly background in Corinth was particularly ungodly, and the circumstances of daily life in the city would be anathema to anyone brought up under the Law of Moses.

Paul was planning his journey to Jerusalem, where questions had always been raised about the faithfulness of Gentile converts. How better to convince the critics of the fellowship into which both Jews and Gentiles were now entered than to present in the form of the Great Collection, a practical expression of love and care for the brethren and sisters in Judea? As if to remind him of the difficulties that lay ahead, the Jews in Corinth plotted to capture and arrest Paul, possibly with the intention of bringing him once more before the Roman proconsul (Acts 20:3, cp. 18:12).

There can be no doubt that, in Paul's mind, one objective of the collection was to unite Jewish and Gentile believers in a common purpose, because he also wrote to believers in Rome at this time, explaining the great benefit that would ensue: "I am going to Jerusalem to minister to the saints. For it pleased those from Macedonia and Achaia to make a certain contribution for the poor among the saints who are in Jerusalem. It pleased them indeed, and they are their debtors. For if the Gentiles have been partakers of their spiritual things, their duty is also to minister to them in material things" (Romans 15:25-27).

It is also clear from his next comments that there was some doubt whether the collection would be accepted by the Jewish brethren who were most opposed to the gospel being preached to Gentiles: "I beg you, brethren ... that you strive together with me in prayers to God for me, that I may be delivered from those in Judea who do not believe, and that my service for Jerusalem may be acceptable to the saints" (verses 30,31).

Quiet Solitude and Reflection

This problem preyed on his mind to such an extent that he became almost totally preoccupied with it. The large party of brethren who had been charged by their various ecclesias to accompany the collection to Judea spent a week in Troas with Paul and with the local ecclesia (Acts 20:6).

From Troas, they set out to travel by a coastal vessel around the province of Asia. The first part of their journey required them to go round the treacherous Cape Lectum. Paul decided not to go with them in the ship, but to cross the peninsular on foot – a distance of about 20 miles by Roman road – to meet them at the port of Assos. This provided a period of quiet solitude and reflection. We know that Paul, like his Lord before him, had "steadfastly set his face to go to Jerusalem" (Luke 9:51; Acts 19:21). He told the elders of the Ephesian ecclesia that he was going "bound in the spirit to Jerusalem, not knowing the things that will happen to me there" (Acts 20:22).

These concerns only increased as the journey progressed. There were disciples at Tyre who "told Paul through the Spirit not to go up to Jerusalem" (21:4); when he came to Caesarea, Agabus the prophet bound Paul with his own belt, and predicted: "So shall the Jews at Jerusalem bind the man who owns this belt, and deliver him into the hands of the Gentiles" (verse 11). Agabus had previously prophesied the onset of the great famine that ravaged the Roman Empire "in the days of Claudius Caesar" (11:28), providing the occasion for Paul to go with Barnabas to Jerusalem (as representatives of the Antioch ecclesia), and for the first time to "send relief to the brethren dwelling in Judea" (verses 29,30).

The lonely walk from Troas to Assos was thus an opportunity to consider all that lay ahead, and to prepare himself for whatever ordeal lay in store. The example of the Lord Jesus' determination would doubtless encourage him in his endeavour, and it is possible to see many parallels between Jesus' and Paul's journeys to Jerusalem. Some of these are shown in the table overleaf.

In Time for Pentecost

Paul was eager to reach Jerusalem in time to celebrate Pentecost (20:16). He did not deviate from this course, even to visit his beloved Ephesus, and called the elders of the

Paul	Jesus
"I go bound in the spirit to Jerusalem" (Acts 20:22)	"He steadfastly set his face to go to Jerusalem" (Luke 9:51)
"When we had departed from them" (21:1)	"He was withdrawn from them" (22:41)
"He knelt down and prayed" (20:36; 21:5)	"He knelt down and prayed" (22:41)
Philip's daughters prophesied— about affliction? (21:9)	"Women also mourned and lamented him" (23:27)
"We pleaded with him not to go up to Jerusalem" (21:12)	"Lord; this shall not happen to You!" (Matthew:16:22)
"The will of the Lord be done" (21:14)	"Not my will, but Yours, be done" (Luke 22:42)

ecclesia to meet him at Miletus. He made such a quick journey that, by the time he reached Caesarea, he had time in hand, and spent "many days" in Philip the evangelist's house (21:10). Philip was one of the seven who were chosen to ensure the fair distribution of assistance between Jewish and Gentile believers (Acts 6:1-6), and there was opportunity for Paul to discuss with him the Fund he and his companions were transporting to Jerusalem.

But why was it so important for him to reach Jerusalem in time for Pentecost? Under the Law, it was the practice during the feast to provide "two wave loaves ... baked with leaven" (Leviticus 23:17). True believers would see the significance of these as representing the Jewish and Gentile parts of the one loaf in Christ. There could be no more appropriate time for Paul and the other brethren to present the gift collected from among the Gentiles to succour their Jewish brethren.

Only one task was left; to ensure that all was in order and fully accounted for. The Revised Version says: "we took up our baggage" (Acts 21:15); J. B. Phillips has: "we made our preparations". This must have been done with great care, each brother ensuring that his ecclesia's contribution was complete. As we have seen, the collection was from the ecclesias, and Paul distanced his own involvement so that he would be free from any malicious suggestion that he misused the help that he encouraged the ecclesias to give. Brethren today who are involved with funds collected within the brotherhood need to exercise the same care: they are stewards and not masters, and are accountable firstly to those who have made donations, and ultimately to the Master himself.

Did the Collection achieve all that Paul hoped for it? Were the brethren and sisters in Judea eased, and did relations between Jews and Gentiles suddenly improve? It would be wonderful if there was evidence in the scriptures to show there was great success. Unfortunately this evidence does not exist. We do not know if the brethren and sisters in Jerusalem were helped, for once the Fund was handed over, James and the other elder brethren in Jerusalem immediately began to explain that criticism of the apostle's work among the Gentiles was still being strongly voiced (Acts 21:17-21). Agabus' prophecy was soon fulfilled: Paul was arrested, bound and imprisoned (verse 34).

But all this still lay in the future when he wrote to the Corinthians. It was sufficient at this time to encourage them to work hard to cement good relations with their Jewish brethren, without whom they would never have received the good news of the grace of God.

30

IN DEFENCE OF HIS APOSTLESHIP

T HERE seems to be an abrupt change of subject at the start of 2 Corinthians 10. The apostle has spent two chapters dealing with the Jerusalem Poor Fund, answering criticisms that the collections were for his personal benefit. He resisted these charges by emphasising the mutual dependency of ecclesias, and how the work was being handled by accredited representatives – he was not touching any of the money himself.

It is possible that his critics would use this argument and take it a stage further. Paul had distanced himself from the collection for the saints and spoken about the importance of ecclesial representatives, why then did he feel able to speak to the Corinthian ecclesia as if he was in a position of some authority? He was merely a representative of the Syrian Antioch ecclesia, and had no right to comment on affairs in Corinth. There is a very modern ring to this criticism, in an age where there is much sensitivity about human rights and little respect for authority whatever its form. This extended argument explains the apparent abrupt change, where Paul defends his apostleship.

Personal Attacks

Those who criticised Paul described him as being weak and two-faced: "who in presence am lowly among you, but being absent am bold toward you" (2 Corinthians 10:1). A little later he quotes some other things they were saying: "his letters are weighty and powerful, but his bodily presence is weak, and his speech contemptible" (verse 10). There is no substance to these charges; they follow a common pattern, where someone who works according to different principles is attacked personally, without any discussion about the issues giving rise to the disagreement. This is an *ad hominem* argument, where charges are directed against the person and not at the real issue. As he has dealt elsewhere with the issues that exist between him and the Corinthians, Paul sets out courageously to answer these personal attacks. He does not try to deflect this criticism onto his companions, or even allow them to be included in the criticism, but acknowledges that he alone is the butt of the critics' comments, "I, Paul, myself am pleading with you by the meekness and gentleness of Christ ..."

If they think he pretends to be bold when he is away from Corinth, they should consider what he would do if he showed the boldness when he was next present with them that they said he displayed when he was absent. He could, if necessary, come with a rod. But that would be a natural, human response, and Paul could never forget that he was an ambassador for Christ. He was human, he walked "in the flesh" in common with the Corinthians and all other men and women, yet he tried not to "war according to the flesh" (verse 3). That would be the easy line to follow, and it happens repeatedly in dealings between man and man, nation and nation.

True believers are more powerful than the mightiest human army, thanks to the help God provides in Christ; they can pull down strongholds. Paul sees human systems of thought, arranged to rely on man's strength and not God's, as citadels that must be attacked and overcome. The "carnal weapons" being used in Corinth were expressions of human cleverness – techniques designed to impose one man's will over another's; methods of organisation or powerful propaganda. Paul had met all sorts of opposition before, and he spent his time as an apostle, "casting down arguments and every high thing that exalts itself against the knowledge of God". Just as a conquering army takes captives, so the faithful believer brings "every thought into captivity to the obedience of Christ" (verse 5). He understands that to be "in Christ" is to acknowledge Christ's rule in all things. If we expect to work under the Lord's direction when he returns to put down all human rule, authority and power, we should be subject to his direction in our lives now.

As human kings have their military generals who carry out their commands and who act with their authority, so the Lord Jesus had his apostles. Paul was giving the Corinthians opportunity to show their obedience to Christ, but if they were stubbornly disobedient he had authority from the Lord to punish them (verse 6).

Paul's Authority

The problem was that the Corinthians could only view Paul's apostleship in human terms; they were not really thinking as members of the body of Christ. They looked on the "outward appearance", while God, as Samuel was told, "looks on the heart" (verse 7, cp. 1 Samuel 16:7). The true test of a person belonging to Christ depends on his inward association with the Lord, and this will be shown outwardly by the presence of Christian virtues. Prominent among these is the desire to encourage and edify fellow-believers. Paul was suspicious of those in Corinth who were always complaining, criticising and grumbling. His authority as an apostle of Christ was given to him with the object of "edification, and not for your destruction". If members of the ecclesia were terrified by what he wrote in his letters to them, they must beware his presence when he visits them. The true edification of the ecclesia will involve the exposing of those who deliberately withstood Christ's authority vested in Paul.

These adversaries were completely self-satisfied; they commended themselves! In an ironical passage, Paul said that he dare not compare himself with such elevated personages! The problem was that, as they preened and complimented each other, they were only indulging in self-comparison. If they had stopped to compare themselves against the Lord Jesus they would not dare to offer any commendation on their own behalf.

Their criticism centred on the assertion that Paul had no jurisdiction over Corinth, so he restricts himself "to the limits of the sphere which God appointed us" (2 Corinthians

10:13). This sphere, he told them, "especially includes you" in Corinth. Despite what they said, his authority as an apostle did extend to them. Had they forgotten that it was Paul who first took the gospel to the city? In that sense, he was a father to them, and they were his children. He was not like false teachers who trespass on the work of others, but he hoped that, with present troubles behind them, they would help him in the further work to which he was committed. They could help to enlarge the sphere of his preaching, which was not really his, but the Lord's. He reminded them of a verse in Jeremiah that he used in the first epistle to show the problem of cliques and schisms in the ecclesia: "Thus says the LORD: 'Let not the wise man glory in his wisdom, let not the mighty man glory in his might, nor let the rich man glory in his riches; but let him who glories glory in this, that he understands and knows me, that I am the LORD, exercising lovingkindness, judgment, and righteousness in the earth'" (Jeremiah 9:23,24, cp. 1 Corinthians 1:26-29; 2 Corinthians 10:17).

If any were looking for approval, they should not look for human approval. God lays down the duties of every believer; God brings the increase of anyone's work; yet the glory is never man's but always God's. They should seek His commendation, and never the commendation of their fellow-men: "for not he who commends himself is approved, but whom the Lord commends" (verse 18).

"As the serpent deceived Eve ..."

As an apostle, Paul realised he had no grounds for self-praise. The only justification for his defence against false attacks was his care for the critics, and for all in Corinth, so that they would not be at the mercy of unscrupulous men who might draw them away from Christ. Above all else he has a deep love for the Corinthians, like a father for his children. Just as God is jealous over His people, so Paul had a "godly jealousy" for the brethren and sisters in Corinth. He had acted among them as "the friend of the bridegroom", espousing them to Christ "as a chaste virgin" (11:2).

In many places in scripture the man-woman relationship described in Genesis 2 is used as an example of the relationship of groups of individuals to God and His purpose. The prophet Isaiah explained to Israel: "your Maker is your husband, The LORD of hosts is His name" (Isaiah 54:5), and through Hosea, God said: "I will betroth you to me forever; yes, I will betroth you to me in righteousness and justice, in lovingkindness and mercy" (Hosea 2:19). Believers in Christ are betrothed to him now, and await his return. Our probation is a time of preparation, "as a bride adorned for her husband" (Revelation 21:2).

The example was fitting for the Corinthians. Through Paul's work they had become part of the second Eve, who has her beguilers seeking to seduce her away from the things of God, "as the serpent deceived Eve by his craftiness" (2 Corinthians 11:3). They were in danger of being corrupted by falsehoods – a complex web of deceit and lies that contrasted completely with "the simplicity that is in Christ". The Greek word *haplotes* has the meaning of "singleness" and lack of hypocrisy, rather than something easy to understand.

The deception at work in Corinth came from those who had not presented a faithful account of the Lord Jesus and his teaching. Their message was therefore about "another Jesus whom we have not preached". This teaching had come from visitors to Corinth who tried to separate the brethren and sisters from their dependence on Paul's teaching. He warns strongly about the implications of following them. As it is likely that these so-called "Super-apostles" (verse 5, NIV) would lead them back into the strictures of the Law (see verse 22), Paul said ironically 'put up with it, if you will, and reap the consequences'.

However eminent these "Super-apostles" were, Paul was prepared to measure himself favourably against them. He might not be a practised orator (though the training at the feet of Gamaliel probably prepared him for this aspect of his work much better than he was willing to admit); but his knowledge had been used effectively in Corinth to call men and women – including his critics – to Christ.

IN DEFENCE OF HIS APOSTLESHIP

A Tent Maker

The major difference between Paul and the false apostles (verse 13) was that he took up his tentmaking trade in the city, much to the embarrassment of some in the ecclesia who presumably thought that he and they were demeaned by him undertaking this trade (Acts 18:1-4). They viewed it as sinful! Could it really be a sin, he said, when it provided the means for them to receive the gospel of Christ without charge? The fact was that brethren and sisters from a completely different area continued to support Paul when he was in Corinth. Effectively, this made him a robber of those ecclesias, "taking wages (from them) to minister to you" (verse 8). Paul was helped by the ecclesia at Philippi, both when he was in Thessalonica and when he was in Corinth (Philippians 4:15,16; Acts 18:5), and at a time when the Philippian ecclesia was going through "a great trial of affliction" (2 Corinthians 8:2). He could reasonably expect them to look after him while he was in Philippi, but they went way beyond the call of duty. He does not propose altering his ways merely to save the Corinthians' embarrassment, and nor will he remain silent about it: "As the truth of Christ is in me, no one shall stop me from this boasting (i.e., on behalf of the brethren and sisters in Macedonia) in the regions of Achaia" (11:10, see 8:1,2).

He also rebuts any suggestion that his love for the Corinthians is less than for those in Macedonia because of this arrangement. The reason he cannot accept help from Corinth is that this will be used against him by his adversaries. If they could criticise him for not accepting help, they would be even more scornful if he now received their aid. Here is the measure of their supposed apostleship: they practice deceit, but with an outward show of righteousness. It is a device of sin: "Satan himself transforms himself into an angel of light" (11:14).

Paul has been defending his apostleship and his relationship to the Lord Jesus Christ. He describes those who oppose him as the apostles of Sin: "Therefore it is no great thing if his ministers also transform themselves into ministers of righteousness, whose end will be according to their works" (11:15). What they show outwardly only masks an inner corruptness, and this is manifested in their works, by which they will be judged.

Because the outward appearance is so important to them, Paul foolishly boasts about the reports that could be made of his work, as judged by such men. They attributed his finer conduct to weakness, and described their own ways as strong. Let them measure themselves against a list of Paul's achievements!

Hardships and Persecutions

No Jew had a better pedigree than Paul (verse 22), and his work proclaimed him to be a true minister of Christ. He embarks on a remarkable catalogue of events, many only hinted in the account in Acts, showing the hardships of the apostolic life. We are given a picture of a hazardous existence, at the mercy of the elements on land and sea, and daily at risk of attack from opportunist thieves or vagabonds, and from those who should know better: his own countrymen who benefited from the mercy of God. These hardships were not previously mentioned; Paul took them to be integral parts of the work he undertook. He only mentions them now because he has been criticised for "living off the gospel". It is an implicit challenge to his critics to 'put up, or shut up'.

There is a danger that we, like the false apostles in Corinth, will be awe-struck by this description of distresses, and seek to test today's disciples by the same rule. Hardships and even persecutions can strangely be made to sound glamorous and exciting, and those who suffer them can be accorded a special degree of honour and respect. But with a masterly change of subject, Paul explained that the most fundamental part of his work was not those physical trials and tribulations, which he will never mention again, but what was with him daily: "my deep concern for all the churches" (verse 28). These were the aspects of his life that could not be seen, and here lay the true test of apostleship. If he heard of someone's weakness of faith, he felt weak himself; or if a brother or sister stumbled into sin, Paul stumbled with them, longing to help in their restoration.

Here, and not in the outward signs of his ministry, was the weakness which caused him to boast. Here he can glory in God's strength, and not his own.

Looking back at the years since his conversion, he could see that a moment of his greatest personal indignity declared God's strength most eloquently. The proud Pharisee heretic hunter was led by the hand into Damascus because of his blindness, and later had to leave the city ignominiously, let down over the wall in a basket to escape the governor's guards. But trusting in God's power gave him liberty to travel and preach in many lands, including Achaia and the city of Corinth. It was a sign of things to come, where human dignity is often shamed by God's providence. It was a lesson the Corinthians needed to learn.

31

BOASTING IN WEAKNESS

RIGHT from the beginning of his discipleship, when he had to leave Damascus like refuse let down over the wall of the city, Paul suffered every indignity for the sake of Christ. But mixed with these daily sufferings were occasions of enormous privilege, as he received revelations of God's purpose that lifted him into heavenly realms. First, there was the vision on the Damascus road, and it may have been his memory of the escape from the city that caused him to move on "to visions and revelations of the Lord" (2 Corinthians 12:1). During the second missionary journey he saw the man of Macedonia calling him over into Europe for the first time (Acts 16:9,10), and shortly afterwards he was encouraged by a vision of the Lord who told him that he had "much people" in Corinth (18:9-11). When he wrote to the Galatians, he explained that he received the gospel "by the revelation of Jesus Christ" (Galatians 1:12).

In particular there was an occasion fourteen years previously that was especially outstanding. The exactness of this reference suggests that it is possible to identify the occasion. It is generally accepted that 2 Corinthians was written in AD 56 or 57, so the "revelation" occurred in AD 42 or 43, and was probably the one Paul mentioned in the defence that he made to the crowd at Jerusalem from the stairs of the barracks: a vision that occurred on the occasion of Paul's second visit (as a believer in Christ) to Jerusalem:

"Now it happened, when I returned to Jerusalem and was praying in the temple, that I was in a trance and saw him (i.e., Jesus) saying to me, 'Make haste and get out of Jerusalem quickly, for they will not receive your testimony concerning me.' So I said, 'Lord, they know that in every synagogue I imprisoned and beat those who believe on you. And when the blood of your martyr Stephen was shed, I also was standing by consenting to his death, and guarding the clothes of those who were killing him.' Then He said to me, 'Depart, for I will send you far from here to the Gentiles.'"   (Acts 22:17-21)

According to Paul, this was the great confirmation of his mission to preach the gospel to the Gentiles, partially fulfilled in his work at Corinth, and by which many of his detractors learned the message of salvation. If they questioned his authority, they needed to explain – or more accurately, explain away – this revelation. Paul could not say with certainty if he was transported bodily, or if it was all a vision, so graphic were the things he saw; but he "was caught up to the third heaven (i.e., paradise, verse 4) ... and heard inexpressible words which it is not lawful for a man to utter" (2 Corinthians 12:2,4).

Heavens and Earth

Scripture often uses the figure of "heaven" when referring to governing powers. In Isaiah 1:2,10, for example, the prophet addresses the rulers and people of unfaithful Jerusalem, calling them the "heavens" (the rulers) and the "earth" (the people). Later in his prophecy, Isaiah explains that God will "create new heavens and a new earth" (65:17). Both these passages refer to God's dealings with Israel, and applying Paul's three heavens to Israel's history leads to the first "heaven" being the Mosaic order. Moses was therefore the first to address Israel using the terms "heavens" and "earth" (Deuteronomy 32:1). During Israel's scattering and the "times of the Gentiles", there were no Jewish "heavens", and the disciples asked Jesus shortly before his ascension when he would "restore the kingdom to Israel" (Acts 1:6). The kingdom will be restored for the benefit of the mortal population during the Millennium. This is the second "heaven" – the "*new* heavens and new earth" that Isaiah and Peter spoke about, "in which righteousness dwells" (2 Peter 3:13).

The third "heaven" is thus a reference to the period beyond the Millennium, about which very little is revealed in the scriptures. A description of this period would need to use "inexpressible words, which it is not lawful for a man to utter", for a similar comment occurs in the book of Revelation, where John is told to "seal up the things which the seven thunders have uttered, and *do not write them*" (Revelation 10:4). How fitting that this future time should be described as "paradise", the blessed state promised by Jesus to the repentant thief (Luke 23:43). Paradise contains the tree of life and its healing leaves (Revelation 2:7; 22:2), as well as other "inexpressible" things.

Here was a revelation indeed. If Paul's vision of paradise was associated with the confirmation of his commission to preach to the Gentiles, it was highly appropriate to include details of the restoration of the kingdom to Israel, and of the end to which that kingdom will lead – a world at peace, and in complete harmony with its Creator. Anyone granted such a vision had the best possible grounds for boasting. Yet Paul refused to boast "of such a one", preferring instead to explain how God is glorified when His work is undertaken by weak and infirm human beings. God's true servants have no grounds for human pride; all that is stripped away by their humbling circumstances.

A Thorn in the Flesh

Great trial tends to accompany great privileges; and the prophets who were privileged to be the channels of God's message were generally men afflicted. Paul too had his "thorn in the flesh", which prevented him being "exalted above measure" (2 Corinthians 12:7). Whatever the weakness was, Paul also called it "a messenger of Satan", because it was an adversary to his desires, strongly opposing his wishes on many occasions. Many explanations have been suggested as to the exact nature of Paul's "thorn in the flesh". Was it a recurring moral temptation; some bodily ailment; periodic doubts; a personal opponent or opponents; or a defect in his character?

Whatever it was, Paul acknowledged that it "was given to" him, presumably by God, to limit his grounds for pride. Something that was specially introduced into his life by God to curb pride would appear to rule out moral temptations, for God does not "tempt anyone" (James 1:13). A similar objection can be raised to the idea that Paul was beset by frequent doubts, or had a particular defect in his character, for the Father knew him long before he was given his commission to preach to the Gentiles.

The field is therefore narrowed considerably, to either a particularly debilitating physical handicap, or to a special opponent who dogged his steps. Most commentators favour the first of these. J. B. Phillips, for example, does not talk of "a thorn in the flesh", but of a "physical handicap ... to harass me and effectually stop any conceit." Similarly, F. F. Bruce calls it "a bodily ailment, a sharp rankling pain ... to keep me under and prevent me from becoming too proud". Specific suggestions as to the nature of this physical malady focus on the possible effects on his eyesight of the blinding vision on the Damascus road, or the possibility that he caught malaria on one of his travels. If the problem was physical, it must be something that could be accurately described as a sharp stake in the flesh, crippling him unexpectedly.

The other alternative is a particularly forceful opponent, such as the Judaisers who hampered his work and sapped his energy. They subjected him to stoning and beating, so it would be appropriate to describe their actions as a "thorn in the flesh". This is an attractive suggestion, but it seems less likely that Paul would refer to his human opponents in this way in a section of his letter designed to answer their specific criticisms of his work. This would simply provide them even greater encouragement to "buffet" him and reduce his future effectiveness.

The trouble was so great, that Paul begged God to remove it from him. He pleaded on three separate occasions, following the pattern set by Jesus in the garden of Gethsemane (Matthew 26:44). The angel who appeared beside the Lord strengthened him (Luke 22:43), and Paul was reminded that God's grace was sufficient for him: His "strength is made perfect in weakness" (2 Corinthians 12:9). Throughout his letters to Corinth, Paul was at pains to preach this important truth. In the first Letter he established the principle "that no flesh should glory in his

(God's) presence" (1 Corinthians 1:29). Now he expresses it like this: "Most gladly I will rather boast in my infirmities, that the power of Christ may rest upon me ... when I am weak, then I am strong" (2 Corinthians 12:9,10).

Help in Time of Need

Jesus prayed earnestly to "him who was able to save him from death, and was heard because of his godly fear" (Hebrews 5:7). He still had to 'drink the dreadful cup of pain', but he was strengthened to endure the trial. Paul prayed for the thorn in his flesh to be removed; and he too received an answer. The thorn must remain, but he would receive strength to bear it. This enabled him to say that, whereas he refused to boast about the revelations and visions he received, he would boast and even "take pleasure in infirmities"! In this he was totally different from his opponents. If they had been granted visions of paradise, nothing would have stopped their boasting; they would be insufferably proud, hiding even the smallest hint of personal weakness.

How dare his critics suggest that they were more eminent apostles than he? They had not received heavenly revelations, nor had they suffered reproach for the name of Christ. They had witnessed in Paul all "the signs of an apostle ... signs and wonders and mighty deeds" (2 Corinthians 12:12), and risked being guilty of blaspheming against the holy spirit if they failed to acknowledge that Paul's commission came from the Lord himself (cp. Matthew 12:31,32). They actually suggested that Corinth was belittled in comparison with other ecclesias, and Paul was moved to complain with gentle irony: "What makes you feel so inferior to other churches? Is it because I have not allowed you to support me financially? My humblest apologies for this great wrong!" (2 Corinthians 12:13, J. B. Phillips).

A Promised Visit

The letter was sent to prepare the ecclesia for Paul's forthcoming visit – his third to the city. Once again he did not expect, and nor would he ask for any support (cp. 11:9).

He did not seek their money. In the natural order of things, children do not provide for their parents, "but the parents for the children" (verse 14). Paul saw himself as their father, for spiritually he brought them to the birth (see 1 Corinthians 4:15). He therefore intended to spend himself fully on their behalf. Indeed, he had always expended his complete energies; giving his life for theirs. But by an awful paradox, "the more abundantly I love you, the less I am loved" (2 Corinthians 12:15).

An example of his opponents' failure to respond to Paul's love for them was the complaint that he had obtained their support by deception: "granting that I myself did not burden you, I was crafty, you say, and got the better of you by guile" (verse 16, RSV). He refused to answer this charge on his own behalf, but appealed to the upright behaviour of all the companions he had sent to Corinth. Was there a breath of complaint about any of them? Of course not. When Titus went, accompanied by another brother (probably his own brother, Luke the physician, see page 217), there were no complaints about his dealings with the Corinthians; yet Paul and Titus walked "in the same spirit ... in the same steps" (verse 18). Just as the behaviour of Titus and other emissaries from Paul was exemplary, so was his; there were no grounds whatsoever for complaint.

Anticipating the response to this, Paul explains that his mentioning of his co-workers is no excuse. All he did on the Corinthians' behalf was with the sole aim of building them up and encouraging them in the faith. Even his answering of their charges was not undertaken in order to clear his name, but to help them realise the corrosive effects of false criticism. To charge someone wrongly with error demeans the critic much more than it does the one who is falsely accused. Things may start in a small way: a murmur here, and a complaint there. But like an uncontrolled fire, it can soon be a raging inferno. Paul said, "I fear ... lest there be contentions, jealousies, outbursts of wrath, selfish ambitions, backbitings, whisperings, conceits, tumults" (verse 20). It would require firm handling to prevent the

Corinthian attitude of criticism from affecting the whole ecclesia.

Living in a Pagan City

Brethren and sisters in Corinth had previously left behind the corrupt ways of their immoral city, yet there was every possibility that worldly attitudes had not been completely forsaken; and attitudes quickly determine conduct. If, when Paul arrived in the city, he found no evidence of the fruit of the spirit, he would be in mourning, "for many who have sinned before and have not repented of the uncleanness, fornication, and lewdness which they have practised" (verse 21).

This was a sharp condemnation of those who criticised Paul. They boasted of themselves that they were "super-apostles", but Paul has shown how, by their unfounded and undeserved opposition they were no longer true followers of the Lord they professed to serve. Instead, they had returned to (possibly they had never properly left) the immorality and idolatry of the surrounding Corinthian society.

What would Paul find when he visited the city?

32

AIM FOR PERFECTION

A FTER cancelling his original plans to visit Corinth, and waiting for Titus to return with a report about conditions in the ecclesia (2 Corinthians 1:15,16), Paul made it clear on a number of occasions that he would quickly follow his second epistle with a personal appearance in the city: "the third time I am ready to come to you" (12:14); "this will be the third time I am coming to you" (13:1). He prepared them for his coming by explaining that his attitude towards them when he visited would depend upon their response to his letter: "I beg you that when I am present I may not be bold with that confidence by which I intend to be bold against some, who think of us as if we walked according to the flesh" (10:2); and he was very unsure that his letter would achieve what he intended: "I fear lest, when I come, I shall not find you such as I wish" (12:20).

If his letter was likely to fail in its objective, what other plans did Paul have to remedy the unacceptable situation? There is little doubt that he had no intention of overlooking the serious problems that caused him such concern, or of allowing them to continue unchecked if he was able to rectify them. The scriptural support for his impending visit was to be found in Deuteronomy 19, where the law of evidence was noted: "by the mouth of two or three witnesses every word shall be established" (2 Corinthians 13:1, quoting Deuteronomy 19:15).

There is some doubt about the application of this verse. Was Paul saying that his three visits – the first long one when many conversions and baptisms occurred; the second short one when he tried to correct the serious situation; and the impending third visit – would provide the evidence of the unbrotherly behaviour in the ecclesia? Or was he explaining that, when he arrived, he intended to commence a full and detailed examination of the conditions in the ecclesia; an examination that would be handled on the basis set down in the law, where only evidence supported by two or three witnesses would be allowed? Any charges the Corinthians may want to bring against Paul would also be subject to the same rigorous examination; they would need the support of two or three witnesses. It was a direct challenge to all who opposed him.

"I will not spare"

This second view is more probable. Paul uses a very severe tone. The opening verses of chapter 13 have short staccato sentences, and no longer contain the appeals he makes in previous sections. If the brethren in Corinth do not respond favourably to his earlier comments, there will be no other option than the use of his apostolic authority: "if I come again I will not spare" (2 Corinthians 13:2); "I write these things being absent, lest being present I should use sharpness, according to the authority which the Lord has given me" (verse 10). On his previous visit, Paul issued a sharp warning to all who had sinned. His warning was given with the objective of bringing them face to face with their sins, so that they would mend their ways. He threatened action, but did not carry out the threat during his second visit: "I warned those who sinned before and all the others, and I warn them now while absent, as I did when present on my second visit, that if I come again I will not spare them" (verse 2, RSV).

Paul was going to Corinth as the Lord's apostle and with his authority. The critics charged Paul with weakness, but surely they had no doubt of Christ's strength: "who is not weak towards you, but mighty in you" (verse 3). Even when he is being stern and severe, Paul has to make a further appeal, reminding the Corinthians that the Lord was being formed in them. He too was once weak through mortality, but was raised to life and power. Brethren and sisters, as part of the Christ-body, although presently weak and mortal creatures, share in the Lord's resurrection life now in the power of their new life in him, and have the wonderful prospect of sharing in everlasting life when he returns.

Test Yourselves!

Was the Lord really at work in the Corinthian brethren and sisters? Individuals could only answer this on the basis of honest self-examination, and Paul challenged them: "test yourselves"! (verse 5, RSV). They were very willing to test *him*, and to find fault, now he wants them to look with equal rigour at themselves. Did their behaviour match their profession of faith? Could Christ be seen in them? They needed to undergo a process of proving. Paul had honestly responded to all their allegations, and wished them to apply the same rigorous tests in their own lives. Would they stand the test, or would they be disqualified (Greek, *adokimos*)? Paul uses the same word he used about himself in 1 Corinthians 9:27, where he explained how he always had to keep control of his body, smothering the temptations that could lead to sin, lest "when I have preached to others, I myself should become disqualified (a castaway, AV)".

Despite the possibility that sin might bring about his downfall at any time, Paul was able to say to the Corinthians that they would see when he was with them that he was not disqualified, for he would be accompanied by the evidence of apostolic power. He was not asking them to revise their judgement of him just so that he could receive their personal approval, but so that their actions would be honourable. This was what Paul could not understand about their behaviour. They claimed to be in the Truth, but they did not allow truth to affect every aspect of their lives. Paul could only speak for himself, and about his own approach: "we can do nothing against the truth, but for the truth" (2 Corinthians 13:8).

Here was the essential difference between Paul and his critics, and it underlies all that has gone before in the letter. Paul challenged them to look at his whole life, and not to single out selected parts from which to form unsound judgements. The whole of his life was open to examination, and was a token of his commitment and faith. He knew there were no episodes that he hoped would never be discovered; there were no secret dealings that he wanted to remain buried, or financial transactions that he trusted would never see the light of day. Truth ran though every aspect of his life, even bringing him near to death time and again.

The Lord's Authority

The Corinthians saw this as a sign of weakness, and would probably have preferred an apostle who was more worldly-wise, with better public relations skills. These things were of no account to Paul: "we are glad when we are weak and you are strong" (verse 9). He was not at all concerned with vindicating his own position, so long as he could be assured of their soundness in spiritual things. Even his personal position could be sacrificed on their behalf: "what we pray for is your improvement" (verse 9, RSV). This was both the purpose of his original preaching, and now the objective of his letter: "I write these things being absent, lest being present I should use sharpness, according to the authority which the Lord has given me" (verse 10).

Paul has previously threatened to use his authority to take severe action against the offenders in Corinth, and obviously hoped that his uncompromising words would have their effect so that he need not carry out the threat. He was always conscious that the authority he received from the Lord was "for edification and not for destruction". He has used the phrase before in this section of the epistle (verse 10, cp. 10:8), yet Paul obviously does not take it to be a reason for overlooking serious difficulties, or a principle that prevents him from advising the tearing down of parts that are threatening the destruction of the ecclesia and the truth. It was his guiding principle, but it would not stand in the way if severe action was merited in order to achieve its fulfilment.

A Template of Honesty

Faced with the extremely serious problems that existed in Corinth, Paul used every method available to him to encourage the brethren and sisters there to remedy the situation themselves. He described the true situation in graphic terms, analysing exactly where the problems lay. He answered the charges against him specifically and in detail, and not with generalised, ambiguous or dismissive statements. He spoke openly about his work, explaining the pressures that were with him constantly, and also the measures he took to ensure that his actions could not be misinterpreted, other than by those with warped minds. He knew that, as the apostle of Christ, he was accountable to the Lord for everything he did. His life was lived under a spotlight, and his dealings needed to be completely transparent and open. Never did he allow the ends to justify the means. All that he wrote sought to draw his brethren and sisters to think and act more spiritually and less carnally; his love and concern for each brother and sister are apparent in everything he writes. The letters to the ecclesia – particularly the second epistle – are masterpieces, providing templates for brethren and sisters of all ages to follow.

He now makes his final appeal: "Mend your ways (Greek, *katartizo*; 'Aim for perfection', NIV), heed my appeal, agree with one another, live in peace, and the God of love and peace will be with you" (verse 11, RSV). Paul dearly wanted the turmoil in Corinth to cease, for there is nothing worse than friction and tension in ecclesial life. He, the ecclesia and his critics needed to be "perfectly joined together" (1 Corinthians 1:10, same word). This required that they work hard to become "of one mind", and not separating into the factions that were the source of all the ecclesia's problems. As believers of the gospel, they should aim to "live in peace". Preparing for the coming of the Prince of Peace requires that his manifesto of peace should be adopted now; by manifesting love and peace in their dealings in the ecclesia, they would show the presence of "the God of love and peace" in their midst.

A Holy Kiss

This peaceful harmony would only be achieved if it was attempted wholeheartedly; nothing was more calculated to destroy it than feigned practices. Paul therefore challenges the members of the ecclesia – all of them – to "greet one another with a holy kiss" (verse 12). He wrote similarly to the ecclesia at Rome, explaining that greetings between individual brethren and sisters reflected the greetings that should also flow warmly between ecclesias: "Greet one another with a holy kiss. The churches of Christ greet you" (Romans 16:16). The first epistle to Corinth (1 Corinthians 16:20), and the first epistle to Thessalonica (1 Thessalonians 5:26) also concluded with the same advice; Corinth could not complain that it was being singled out for special attention. Peter too, in his first epistle, makes the same point, yet uses a slightly different phrase: "Greet one another with a kiss of love" (1 Peter 5:14).

In New Testament times the kiss was the accepted form of greeting, just as the handshake is today in many Western cultures. Jesus, for example, was critical of the Pharisee who gave him no kiss when he entered his house (Luke 7:45). But this misses the real point. It is very unlikely, even when the situation in Corinth was at its worst, that brethren and sisters were not going through the motions of greeting each other. The problem was that they were pretending to show brotherly affection; they were kissing, but it was not a *holy* kiss.

In this respect, the apostle's words apply to every age and every culture. Our greetings, whatever form they take, should be sincere, holy and in love. If they are ever feigned, this indicates the existence of a problem that needs to be tackled, and tackled quickly, before it leads to a situation like the one that characterised first century Corinth.

Final Blessing

The epistle concludes, following the apostle's usual pattern, with a blessing. What distinguishes the blessing in 2 Corinthians from those in every other epistle of Paul's is that it is the only one where God, Jesus and Holy Spirit are invoked together. It is therefore claimed by Trinitarians to be evidence from a very early date (within thirty years of the crucifixion) supporting the doctrine of the Trinity. It is very poor evidence indeed, for the doctrine of the Trinity is not about the existence of the Lord Jesus Christ, of God or of the Holy Spirit; it is a doctrine claiming that all three are

God, and that they are co-equal and co-eternal. None of these aspects is mentioned in Paul's blessing at the end of the epistle.

His more usual blessing at the conclusion of his letters is simply, "the grace of our Lord Jesus Christ be with you" (for example, Romans 16:20). In 2 Corinthians this is expanded: "the grace of the Lord Jesus Christ, and the love of God, and the communion of the Holy Spirit be with you all". In the context of 2 Corinthians, the emphasis is on grace, love and fellowship: qualities of the gospel that were not being practised by some brethren and sisters. Earlier in the letter, he challenged the members of the ecclesia to show the same grace in giving as Jesus showed when he suffered for their sakes (8:9). Now they were being asked to show the same love to each other as God showed by providing the Lord to be our Saviour. And finally, an attitude of grace and love provides the right basis for true fellowship – fellowship that comes from a shared spirit, acknowledging God's work of salvation in Christ.

One little word makes all the difference to this wonderful final verse, and it epitomises the appeal Paul makes throughout both epistles to Corinth. He prays that Jesus' grace, God's love, and the Spirit's fellowship "be with you *all*"! He wants the ecclesia to be united, to be "perfectly joined together", and knows that this can only be accomplished through God's blessing, for "no flesh should glory in his presence" (1 Corinthians 1:29). No one can charge Paul with favouritism, or having his own clique or faction in Corinth. He is concerned for all, and wants each member of the ecclesia to play his and her assigned part.

Events after Sending the Letter

Humanly speaking, it would be good to know the outcome of these important epistles; but the only available information is circumstantial. The second epistle was followed, as Paul indicated, by his third visit to Corinth. He travelled from Macedonia into Greece, staying there – presumably in Corinth – for three months (Acts 20:3). Luke does not mention anything about the ecclesia, either good or bad. While Paul was there, he wrote the epistle to the Romans, and it is difficult to think that he would be able to write such a masterly account of the gospel if he was being constantly troubled by the difficult conditions mentioned in his letters to Corinth.

Yet difficulties did arise, causing him to alter his plans once again. During his final preparations to transport the great Collection to Judea, "the Jews plotted against him as he was about to sail to Syria, (and) he decided to return through Macedonia" (Acts 20:3). There is no indication that this plotting started in the Corinthian ecclesia, and it is much more likely that the Jews who dogged his steps throughout all his travels in Macedonia and Achaia made one more concerted effort to remove him from the scene.

This hurried change in his plans probably led to an inauspicious departure from the city; and there is no evidence in the scriptures that he ever returned. On his journey to Jerusalem, "the Holy Spirit testifies in every city, saying that chains and tribulations await me" (20:23). He left behind him an ecclesia that was better prepared to face trials and difficulties, and there can be little doubt that they arose sooner or later, but the scripture record leaves us only the snapshot of Paul's dealings with their early formative problems. In their experiences there is a microcosm of all the difficulties faced by believers in every age. As we await the return of the Prince of Peace, great encouragement can be found in learning from their example; seeking to unite around gospel truths and sound Bible-based practices; and dealing with difficulties by applying the great principles taught by the apostle in his dealings with our brethren and sisters in first century Corinth.